Composer AND *Critic*

Composer AND Critic

TWO HUNDRED YEARS

OF MUSICAL CRITICISM

BY

Max Graf

The Norton Library
W · W · NORTON & COMPANY · INC ·
NEW YORK

W. W. Norton & Company, Inc. is the publisher of current
or forthcoming books on music by Putnam Aldrich, William Austin,
Anthony Baines, Philip Bate, Sol Berkowitz, Friedrich Blume, How-
ard Boatwright, Nadia Boulanger, Paul Brainerd, Nathan Broder,
Manfred Bukofzer, John Castellini, John Clough, Doda Conrad,
Aaron Copland, Hans David, Paul Des Marais, Otto Erich Deutsch,
Frederick Dorian, Alfred Einstein, Gabriel Fontrier, Harold Gleason,
Richard Franko Goldman, Noah Greenberg, Donald Jay Grout,
James Haar, F. L. Harrison, Daniel Heartz, Richard Hoppin, John
Horton, Edgar Hunt, A. J. B. Hutchings, Charles Ives, Roger
Kamien, Hermann Keller, Leo Kraft, Stanley Krebs, Paul Henry
Lang, Lyndesay G. Langwill, Jens Peter Larsen, Jan LaRue, Maurice
Lieberman, Irving Lowens, Joseph Machlis, Carol McClintock,
Alfred Mann, W. T. Marrocco, Arthur Mendel, William J. Mitchell,
Douglas Moore, Joel Newman, John F. Ohl, Carl Parrish, Vincent
Persichetti, Marc Pincherle, Walter Piston, Gustave Reese, Alexander
Ringer, Curt Sachs, Denis Stevens, Robert Stevenson, Oliver Strunk,
Francis Toye, Bruno Walter, J. T. Westrup, Emanuel Winternitz,
Walter Wiora, and Percy Young.

SBN 393 00497 X

Contents

Acknowledgments

I AM INDEBTED to Mr. Olin Downes for valuable
advice on the sections on musical criticism in the
United States and to Dr. Jan Loewenbach for material concerning the history of musical criticism
in Bohemia. I hold in grateful remembrance the
pains taken by my publisher, Mr. W. W. Norton,
and by Miss Paula Thibault and Mr. Willard
Trask in preparing the manuscript for the press.

Foreword

MUSICAL criticism is two hundred years old. Yet the history of musical criticism has not been written. The art that, ever since the middle of the eighteenth century, has accompanied composer and performer on his road to fame or oblivion — now in the guise of a stern judge, now as a mentor, now as a jester — has been surveyed historically only in great dictionaries of music, such as Riemann's, Mendel's, or Grove's, or in manuals of musical history like Adler's. These surveys are all short. None of them gives any adequate idea of the wealth of literary figures of which musical criticism can justly boast or of the role played by music critics in the development of esthetic ideas and of taste in general.

As I chanced to be at one and the same time a music critic and a historian of music, the idea of writing a history of musical criticism occupied my mind for many years. I wanted to know the history of my profession — its origin and development — just as men in general are interested in their family history and in the lives of the ancestors whose traits they perceive curiously mixed together in themselves. As I sat at my desk to write my criticisms on the great events of our musical development from the times of Brahms and Bruckner to the times of Stravinsky and Schœnberg, I felt that I was a member of a vast family of writers, and I heard the ghostly voices of my literary grandfathers in the room where their grandson was carrying on their work. Everyone who writes sometimes has the feeling that his pen is wiser than himself and that it moves over the paper with its own life and its own energy. I wanted to understand this mysterious life of my pen historically.

The method I employed was the "History of Ideas" Method, which, as a young student, I helped to apply to art criticism with my friend Max Dvořák, who was later to become famous as a professor of the history of the arts and whose books on "the history of the arts as the history of ideas" rank among the masterpieces of modern art history. We tried to understand the history of the arts as a part of the general development of ideas through the changes of history. The arts and their evolution presented themselves to us as a reflected image of the basic concepts of great epochs. In many discussions with Professor Masaryk — later the famous philosopher-president of Czechoslovakia, at that time a member of the Austrian Parliament and a scholar and writer who fought valiantly against the prejudices of his people — we defended our viewpoint against his, for this quiet thinker held the "realistic" view that economic processes were the moving forces of intellectual life. Since then, many years have passed, but I still hold to the concepts of those vigorous days, and the reader of my book will see that I analyze the development of musical criticism against a background of the struggles and battles of the seminal ideas of the great epochs of modern history. The spirit of musical criticism is only a part of the whole spiritual activity of history. The modern critical spirit was one of the keen weapons that helped to destroy the society, the economy, and the state of the Dark Ages. Or again, it was a beam of the great sun that rose to usher in the new age of reason and enlightenment. Even bad criticism is the spoiled child of a noble ancestry.

Since this book is the first to deal with the history of musical criticism and to connect that history with the cultural and intellectual developments of the past two centuries, no one is more keenly aware than myself of how much it leaves to be done by others. I am particularly conscious that the survey of modern musical criticism in Europe and the United States, with which the book closes, is in no sense exhaustive. It was not, however, my intention in this chapter to make a complete survey; I merely wished to show how different conditions in different countries have influenced critical methods, approaches, and manners. That I have dealt with no living American critic and given considerable space to two living English ones may seem illogical.

But there are two good reasons for it: First, musical criticism in America reached its classic heights a generation before it did in England; second, the work of Newman and Shaw is already embalmed in books, that of Olin Downes, Virgil Thomson, Oscar Thompson, and other American contemporaries still awaits that consummation, and the historian must wait too. With the Russian critics, I was obliged to stop with the founders, because the work of later generations has, with few exceptions, not been translated into any world language.

The writer of this book is but too well aware that he is not omniscient, though there are plenty of critics who think that they are. I shall be satisfied if this book, with all its defects — and defects give a personality part of its particular flavor — is read with pleasure and interest and if it assists toward an understanding of the work of musical criticism and of the music critic's complex role. I have made no attempt to hide the dark underworld of musical criticism — the part played by vanity, stupidity, and even worse faults, which are found in every field of human activity and which are especially conspicuous in men who undertake to point out their neighbor's faults. The dark places make the bright ones still lighter by contrast, and there has been much light in the work of criticism, the light of great writers, keen thinkers, brave fighters. I like to turn on all that light.

I dedicate this book to my colleagues in musical criticism. Our work was common work even when we fought against each other. Musical criticism came into the modern world a fighter, and only as a fighter will it remain a living force. Without the fighting spirit, musical criticism would be like a smiling face without teeth.

MAX GRAF

THE AUTHOR PRESENTS
HIS CREDENTIALS

I. VIENNA AROUND 1900

FROM 1890 to 1938 I was a music critic in Vienna. During those years I wrote my reviews of musical events — criticisms good and bad, judicious and shortsighted, benevolent and malicious; full-fledged essays and condensed notes, for daily papers and for magazines. The earliest criticisms that I wrote as a young and enthusiastic musician were occasioned by the first performance of Anton Bruckner's Eighth Symphony, the first performance of Johannes Brahms's quintet for strings and clarinet, and Hugo Wolf's *Spanish Songbook*. Today these compositions belong to the history of music. But at the time when I first tried my critical pen, they were the news of the day.

Strolling on the beautiful streets of Vienna, one encountered musical history in the making at every corner. There was modern history and there was old history, life and memories, both woven on the same loom by the same moving shuttle. One could meet Johannes Brahms any day on the Ringstrasse, a heavy, broad-shouldered, middle-class man, with the long beard of a professor. He would be walking slowly from his near-by apartment, with a somewhat rocking gait like an old Newfoundland dog, and was always ready to snap at friends and adversaries alike. Hans Richter, the famous Wagner conductor, would pass by — a great man, imposing as an old oak tree, with the big blue eyes of a German god. Among the malicious or flirtatious members of Vienna society, one might meet a strange man, who doffed his artist's hat with a flourish from his close-cropped old peasant head. He was dressed in a broad jacket made of thick rustic cloth, and in wide, wrinkled trousers that looked like the legs of an elephant. This was Anton Bruckner, the strange

saint, who was a subject of merriment to all Vienna. Carl Goldmark, too, the famous composer of the *Queen of Sheba*, would
come strolling by. He looked like a mushroom — a small man,
almost disappearing under his broad felt hat. Only one of the
great composers did not walk, but was driven in his smart carriage along the Ringstrasse. He was dressed elegantly, but in
somewhat old-fashioned taste. An artist's hat shaded the pale
face, with its dyed whiskers and the burning black eyes of an
Oriental. When he passed, the strollers would laugh happily
and exclaim "Look! Johann Strauss." When they met a small
old man who looked like a hawk, with his big nose, his white
beard, and his bent back, they would all doff their hats. It was
Eduard Hanslick, the famous music critic.

All these great musicians were part of Vienna herself. They
had yet to take their place in the impressive chapters of the history of music. Their biographies had not yet been written by
scholars; students had not yet studied the first-performance dates
of their works, nor examined them for traces of Beethoven's influence. They were living beings like ourselves. They wrote on
ruled music paper bought in the same stationer's shop that we
frequented. They lived in our midst. In the concert hall Anton
Bruckner and Hugo Wolf were our neighbors in the standing
room. Brahms, of course, sat in the directors' box, grave and
dignified; but after the concert we might see him in a restaurant,
sitting with friends, the glass of Pilsen beer with foaming head
in front of him. He liked drinking, as we did, and it was not
yet ambrosia he drank, but good fresh beer, which he grum-
blingly sent back when it was not cold enough. Opposite the
table where Brahms sat with reddened face, were Anton Bruckner and his friends. Bruckner would be carving his pork and
piling up the great dumplings that rose from hills of steaming
cabbage — the Sunday dish of peasants in Upper Austria. From
time to time he would cast a distrustful and furtive glance at
Brahms's table, and Brahms would glance back just as distrust-
fully at Bruckner's table and snarl some malicious comment.

Great men were but men, with love and hatred, kindness and

malevolence, like any others, and no legend had yet spun its threads around them. Hugo Wolf, like any music critic, still wrote fanatical criticisms in a venal paper, which nourished the vanity of men and women about town at a fixed tariff. Vienna swarmed with the great figures of musical history, then ordinary mortals, eating and drinking, strolling and gossiping, loving and joking like the rest of mankind.

Now and again a new work by one of the great composers was performed for the first time. Brahms used to come to the platform behind the singers or other artists, somewhat bashfully. He accompanied new songs, or played the piano part in a new chamber-music composition, with heavy hands and weighty bass. He did not disdain to bow to the audience. In his last year he used to acknowledge the applause of the audience from a box. Here he made his appearance only a short time before his death, at a performance of his Fourth Symphony. He was already thin, his face yellow. It grew chilly in the great hall when we saw him. It was as if we had heard the wings of death.

Bruckner was seldom given the opportunity of bowing at a performance of one of his symphonies. But at the first performance of his Eighth Symphony the public did call the old composer to the platform. The work had been dedicated by old Bruckner to the Emperor Franz Josef, who was still older than the composer. The audience was touched by so much old age, and applauded.

Hugo Wolf never had occasion to bow to the cheering public. He was an outcast, living in the wilderness, since he had dared to attack Hanslick, the emperor of music critics in Vienna. Carl Goldmark was regularly present at performances of his compositions, works in which all the glowing fire of the Orient had been kindled. He would bow with a peculiar mixture of modesty and self-consciousness, and the audience was always respectful.

Music history was still being made in the beautiful opera house of Vienna, too. The heated battle over Richard Wagner, which had shaken all the cities of Germany, had not cooled off here. We had the feeling of being in the tent of great warriors and generals after a victorious battle. In the center of the glorious orchestra, Hans Richter rested heavily on his comfortable cane chair, and conducted with swinging, buoyant movements of his heavy arm. Later Claude Debussy wrote that Hans Richter conducted as the Lord himself would conduct after taking lessons from Richter. On the stage were the great singers who had been the collaborators and friends of Richard Wagner: Hermann Winckelmann, the first Parsifal in Bayreuth; Amalia Materna, the first Brünnhilde of the festivals; Theodor Reichmann, the first Amfortas. An indescribable feeling that we were contemporaries of one of the greatest composers of all times filled our young souls when we heard the works of Wagner performed by artists who had taken their every gesture and accent from the creator himself. The spirit of Richard Wagner was still alive in the Vienna opera house. He had sat in one of the boxes at the first performance of *Lohengrin* he ever heard and had bowed to the public, which broke away, for once, from Hanslick's domination, and applauded enthusiastically. We took an oath to continue fighting for Wagner, for his work, and for his ideas. It was a sacred oath and we kept it.

The music of Wagner had conquered the city on the banks of the Danube, whose dirty gray waters only a romanticist like Johann Strauss ever saw as blue. In those days the city was just beginning to be transformed from an old fortress-town, with ramparts and moat, into a modern capital. The new festive Ringstrasse surrounded the city, shining with palaces and gardens, like a necklace of pearls and sapphires around the neck of a beautiful woman. Life was easy, sensual, and merry. Elegant men and women walked on the streets, drove in carriages to the green chestnut trees of the Prater, or rode horseback along the Ringstrasse. The city seemed to have been created for music, as other cities seem to have been created for business, for the things of the intellect, or for religion. Music was in the air, in the rustling of the leaves in the forests near Vienna, in the fragrance of the gardens, in the smiles of girls, in the joy of living, and in the gayety.

The past, too, surrounded us in Vienna. In many streets stood old houses in which the classical composers had lived and worked. In a crooked, shadowy street, right under the steeple of St. Stephen's cathedral, was the old house in which Mozart had written the melodies of *The Marriage of Figaro*. Only a few steps away was the house where he had sat at the servants' table of the Archbishop of Salzburg, with the cook, the confectioner, and the valet. In the suburbs stood Haydn's low house, where soldiers of Napoleon's army had watched by the old man's dead body. There were still some thirty houses in which Beethoven's deaf ears had heard great music — the *Eroica* and *Pastoral*, the Ninth Symphony, the *Missa Solemnis*, *Fidelio*, and the piano sonatas, in the phrases of which the human heart beats and bleeds. From the old Viennese house in which Schubert was born, from those in which he studied, wrote his first great songs, taught children writing and arithmetic, drank with his friends, and eventually died, one could read his whole life, as from the pages of an illustrated book.

Some houses of composers have been torn down since then. The large monastic building in which Beethoven expired while thunder crashed no longer exists. The great old complex of houses, named the "Freihaus," on the banks of the Wien (where we used to play Indians, hiding in the willow bushes) has given way to a modern quarter. In the days of our youth it still stood. It had three courtyards, in the middle one of which Mozart wrote his *Magic Flute* in a summerhouse. In the third court was the theater where people laughed for the first time at Papageno's jokes, while Mozart conducted and laughed happily with them.

When we wandered with a girl in the outskirts of Vienna on fresh summer evenings, it was along the rustling brook of Beethoven's *Pastoral* that we sauntered; it was the chirping of the quail and the call of the cuckoo, preserved in that music like flies in amber, that we heard. We drank our sour wine in little inns where Schubert had once sat, drinking with his friends and playing waltzes on the untuned piano; or in the garden of the restaurant where he once wrote the melody of *Hark, Hark, the Lark* on the back page of the bill of fare. Musical history was bound up with the life of Vienna and with our lives.

Old and new music were more alive in that city of music than anywhere else. We young people were taken into this musical life as new members of an old community. Nothing seemed more important there than music. It was the meaning and the ultimate object of our life.

II. BRUCKNER'S PERSONAL INFLUENCE

When I entered the Renaissance Hall of the University of Vienna to study the history of music, I met musical genius for the first time, in the person of Anton Bruckner.

I have to confess that the reason I attended my first lecture was not that I knew him to be a great composer. At that time I had not yet heard his music and knew nothing about him. One day a fellow student induced me to visit the class, promising me "a lot of fun." As no young student would decline such an invitation, I joined him; I wanted to laugh, to have the fun he promised.

Bruckner's lectures on counterpoint were under the auspices of the Faculty of Philosophy of the University. He had then just returned from Berlin, where his *Te Deum* had been exceptionally well received, in spite of the abysmal lack of understanding of his art elsewhere. We greeted him enthusiastically in the customary student fashion, stamping our feet until clouds of dust rose from the floor. The critics in Berlin had called him a second Beethoven. He related this with considerable distaste, and crossed himself, with a fervent "That, one dares not say." He spoke in the Upper Austrian peasant dialect, different, of course, from the dialect of the Vienna of the Emperor Franz Josef, which was like the aroma of subtle spices. Bruckner's was the speech of his home, of his parents; it belonged to him and to his soil, like the flowers in the windows of the peasant huts, like the trout in the mountain brooks, like the wine in the inns of Upper Austria. The "fun" I had expected was only partly realized, for suddenly something happened that I shall never forget. From a near-by church the Angelus sounded; and when that little bell rang, Anton Bruckner interrupted his lecture, knelt down, and began to pray: "*Ave Maria* . . ."

I have watched the devout at their prayers in the churches of many cities, but I have never seen anyone pray as Bruckner did. He seemed to be transfigured, illuminated from within. His old peasant face, with the countless wrinkles covering it like furrows in a field, became the face of a priest. Like many peasants in the Alpine provinces of Austria (which were settled by Italians in Roman times), Bruckner had a Roman profile, and when he prayed, or when he played fragments of a new symphony at the piano (that was a prayer, too) his face took on a magnificence that was reminiscent of the busts of old Roman emperors. But his expression may best be compared with that of the Apostles in the paintings of Giotto. He looked like an aged saint; his countenance was transformed, as that of St. Francis must have been when he knelt and prayed before the Manger.

I saw that face before me when I heard him playing the organ in the old Gothic Court Chapel — playing tenderly, with chromatic harmonies on soft registers, or setting forth powerful fugues. I saw it again when I listened to his First Symphony. And I have seen it each time I have heard his symphonies well played.

When Bruckner left the lecturer's table and sat at the old piano which stood beside it, to play one of his symphonies, one could understand the religious background of his music. In its highest climaxes the themes are transformed into hymns. Sometimes the music sounds like a flourish of trumpets, such as Bruckner had heard at the services at St. Florian's Monastery. Sometimes it sounds like the organ — and what are the abrupt pauses of his symphonic music if not the Elevation of the Host in the Mass, when the priest lifts up the chalice, the bell is rung thrice, and the worshiper kneels and bows his head. The concept of God descending from Heaven is the final vision in Anton

Bruckner's symphonies and the meaning of the climaxes, sounding the voice of eternity in celestial splendor of sound, soul, and song.

Mysticism also prevailed in his lectures on harmony and counterpoint. The laws of tones and their association were for him infinite laws. The fundamental steps of the bass had in his mind a cosmic importance. Thus we understand the greatness, the occasional rigidity, and the solemnity of Bruckner's harmonies. He pondered over chords and chord associations as a medieval architect must have contemplated the mysteries of arches, rose windows, and buttresses. They were the path to the Kingdom of God.

And this musician who lived in God and whose music is a cathedral itself — with high pillars, bold arches, rich windows, and a glowing altar at which a lonely worshiper kneels and prays — was laughed at by the music critics of Vienna, and rejected by her gay, elegant, witty, and superficial society. When one of Bruckner's "liturgic" symphonies was to be played in a Philharmonic Concert in Vienna, half of the elegant audience left the hall before his composition began, Eduard Hanslick being the first of the fleeing crowd; the other half followed after the close of the first or second movement. By the end of the fourth movement there was no one left but some two hundred enthusiastic young standees, who cheered and bravoed until they were hoarse, while Bruckner stepped onto the platform and bowed, humble and childlike, with his hand over his heart, and threw kisses to Hans Richter, the conductor, and to the smiling orchestra. The fashionable audiences of the Philharmonic would decide the next day that their conduct had been justified, when they read in the great newspapers that Bruckner composed "like a drunkard," or that he was a composer who had become "confused by Wagner's music."

As I sat at Bruckner's lectures, stood at the concerts or in the opera house, listened to the glowing orchestral descriptions of Hector Berlioz or Franz Liszt, delighted in the magnificence and greatness of Richard Wagner's works, was moved by the shining solemnity of Bruckner's symphonies and by the lyric expression of Hugo Wolf's songs, I came to a resolution. I resolved to play my part in Vienna's musical life as a critic. I wanted to make my contribution to the better understanding of the great masters of my time, whom I believed to be the equals of the great masters of the past. They were giving color, light, warmth, romantic adventure, bold vision to our age. The creative imagination of such great composers added importance, meaning, and beauty to our life.

I wanted to fight against the sensual conservatism of Vienna, which tried to bar the great musicians of our day, abusing Wagner and Liszt, deriding Bruckner, silencing Hugo Wolf. Conservative music criticism — there was no other in the great Viennese dailies of that period — tried to place all modern music under interdict. Johannes Brahms was being used as a battering ram to tear down the music of his contemporaries. The great composer was misrepresented as a new classic. The public of Vienna evidently understood the modern romanticism of Brahms better than the critics did, for they hissed at the dusky moods of the Fourth Symphony, where yellow autumn leaves seem to fall from the boughs, and death leads his *danse macabre* in the variations of the last movement. To the public of Vienna at that moment, Brahms was a modern composer like Bruckner.

There was plenty of work needed to bring fresh air into the old musical city, where critics and musical society were one in imprudence and superficiality, in delight in easy pleasure, witty frivolity, and clever small talk. I was young, enthusiastic, excited, full of energy. So I fitted my first arrow to the bow and began shooting.

III. GENERAL POSITION OF THE MUSIC CRITIC

It was a little and insignificant weekly that first published three articles of mine under the promising title "Musico-critical raids." The editor, who did not enjoy much fame in the world of journalism, was happy to have found for his shooting gallery a young David who hit the bull's-eye with his first three shots.

The first article attacked Eduard Hanslick with ridicule, making a scarecrow of the celebrated music critic. The second made fun of Max Kalbeck, the friend and later the biographer of Brahms. He had published a pamphlet against Bayreuth, although he was (as I often said jokingly to him) a born Wagnerian — tall, blond, blue-eyed, the typical German, and very like Siegmund on the operatic stage. The article against Kalbeck consisted only of quotations from his writings, in a comic medley. The third article was an analysis of the great French critic, Sainte-Beuve, whom I opposed to my Viennese colleagues as the model of a wise and objective critic. The articles against Hanslick and Kalbeck ran through the streets of Vienna like foxes with burning brushes.

I had succeeded in breaking into the entrenched camp of musical criticism in Vienna, and my great colleagues accepted me as one of their profession, a young writer, who, like young wine, had still to ferment further in order to become palatable. Eduard Hanslick, personally a charming and witty old gentleman, who liked the good things of life, good food, beautiful women, clever puns, amusing anecdotes, offered me a pinch of snuff when he met me in a concert hall; and Max Kalbeck, a steadfast drinker, invited me to drink a glass of Munich beer with him — which became a number of glasses before the evening was over.

After a short time I was sitting as a music critic in the office of one of the greatest newspapers of Vienna and writing my reviews day by day, always with the aggressive courage of youth, enthusiastic and eager to clear the way for great musicians. Brahms had died, after a long and painful illness, in the old house close to the cupola of the Charles Church, where he had written many of his greatest compositions. He had been buried in the Central Cemetery of Vienna, beside Beethoven, Schubert, and other celebrated composers. Anton Bruckner's coffin had been brought to St. Florian's Monastery in Upper Austria, and set up in the crypt right under the great organ, where Bruckner, as a young musician, had poured forth the festive, gorgeous, beaming sounds of his musical prayers. Hugo Wolf's imagination, enamored with the splendor of the South, had been extinguished and had fallen into dark night, and he was in a lunatic asylum.

But overnight there came others. Gustav Mahler, the new director of the opera house, now walked along the Ringstrasse. He was still a young musician, but he stirred the musical life of Vienna to its depths. When the lights in the opera house slowly dimmed, and the small, slender man, with the face of a medieval ascetic, ran to the desk, waves of strain and suspense flowed through the house from the orchestra to the farthest corner of the gallery. His eyes shot lightning; behind his thick glasses they looked like darting vipers' tongues; the baton was piercing, threatening, wincing, palpitating. There was no longer the majestic quiet of Hans Richter, but the nervousness of a new epoch, shaping the works of Wagner, Mozart, Gluck, and Weber in accordance with the feeling of a new generation.

Mahler's own symphonies also excited the mind: they are huge symphonic mystery plays, starting from earth and climbing to heaven, where choruses of angels and the light of the Almighty hail the newcomer, while in the depths Death plays on a strident violin and hell screams. At the same time Richard Strauss, with his thin stork's legs and his fiery red mane, was storming the concert halls, either conducting his own compositions or accompanying his songs on the piano with fine and delicate hands.

Descriptive music displayed its most masterly devices. New colors gleamed. Polyphony changed into a complex of bright stains. One evening Claude Debussy conducted his own music. He was a rather slow and heavy man, with dark hair and the pointed beard of a French painter. There were pieces diaphanous like sea molluscs, glimmering like satin and silk, phosphorescent like glowworms in the jungle. Others came: Max Reger, who looked like a German student, who drank from morning to night, and who wrote colossal fugues with three subjects — a nervous and incoherent Bach, who produced music as incessantly

as he smoked thick cigars.   Hans Pfitzner, looking like the little
humpbacked tailor from the German fairy tale, and writing fantastic romantic music.   Mascagni, a young Roman epicurean,
with his black tuft of hair and his dark face.   Leoncavallo, who
reminded one of a well-fed butcher.   Later came Puccini, fine and
gentle, taciturn and pensive; and Massenet, with his charming
love songs, a stroller from the Paris boulevards.

After the deaths of Brahms, Bruckner, Goldmark, and Johann
Strauss, it was a new world in which we lived.   Again there was
hissing in the concert halls at the new music that expressed the
struggles and the longings of the changing world.   When Richard Strauss's *Thus Spake Zarathustra* was first played in Vienna,
and the cockcrow of the trumpet announced the new day, the
audience burst out laughing; and after the first performance of
A Hero's Life, the battle of the symphony was carried into the
concert hall itself.   There was hissing at Mahler and Reger, at
Pfitzner and Debussy.   The world was filled with the noise of
battles: modern poetry, painting, and music were all attacked.
Ibsen, Strindberg, Zola, Tolstoy were opposed, like Manet,
Monet, Pissarro.   Public and critics alike tried to stay the march
of modern art.   Certainly there were and always have been fine
and courageous champions of modern art in all the countries of
Europe; but the majority — and especially the leading critics,
the great old mandarins of criticism, like Francisque Sarcey in
Paris — were opponents of the modern movement, encouraging
and supporting all the prejudices, all the personal aversions, and
all the indolence of the public.

There was no change in the following years.   Eventually
Gustav Mahler, Richard Strauss, Claude Debussy prevailed upon
the public and the conservative critics alike, and broke through
all barriers; but already a new generation was arising, which
again refused to cater to the prejudices of the public.   Exasper-
ated opposition tried its best to silence Arnold Schœnberg. There
was hissing at the sextet, *Transfigured Night*, in which the magical sounds of a moonlit night of love and human warmth are
unfolded.   The string quartets, in which he seems to breathe

"the air of other planets," were received with scorn. I can still see Gustav Mahler jumping at a gentleman who whistled on his house key after the final chord of one of Schœnberg's quartets. (House keys, in an old musical city like Vienna, are musical instruments, piercing and shrill like piccolos.) "Stop whistling!" Mahler shouted. But the enthusiastic whistler replied unperturbed, "What for? I whistle at your symphonies too!" We were living on battlefields of music. At one of Schœnberg's concerts not only was there hissing after the performance of Alban Berg's first composition, but one of the hissers received a healthy box on the ear, administered by an enthusiast in the name of modern art. As in Paris, the first performance of Stravinsky's *Rites of Spring* unloosed a hell of shouting, hissing, and laughing.

In every case the majority of music critics invoked the ghosts of classical masters to banish the evil demons of modern music. I do not question the good faith of the conservatives. They wrote what they believed — at least most of them did. If I have my doubts, there is more behind them than personal resentment. I know that all men sometimes think badly or stupidly or rashly. I myself have certainly not been an exception. But more important is the general question with which I have been concerned for many years. There must have been something fundamentally wrong in the position of musical criticism from the middle of the nineteenth century on. Since then, every great or important composer has been opposed by a large proportion of the critics. No doubt, had music critics, from the time of Wagner on, been able to hold back musical evolution by means of their articles, the majority would have done so without hesitating. There would have been no Wagner, no Liszt, no Bruckner, no Wolf, no Richard Strauss, no Mahler, no Debussy, no Stravinsky, and no Schœnberg, if the conservative critics had had their way. One of the most influential commentators on music and the theater in Vienna, Ludwig Speidel, used to say: "Criticism is the sharp-tongued handmaid of artistic creation," in accordance with Matthew Arnold's dictum that "the critical power is of lower rank than the creative." This may be true —

although I, for one, would not engage sharp-tongued maidens, but such as do their work quietly and modestly. At any rate, criticism can be only the handmaid, never the mistress. The first and the only important dweller in the house of art is the creative artist.

The structure of an artistic society in which the critic is not the interpreter of the artist to the public, but the spokesman of the public against the artist, is faulty. This was the conclusion I reached after many years of musical criticism. Personally, I could be content. I was successful, and as I grew older I became a mandarin myself. Musicians doffed their hats and whispered to me (when no other critic was close by) that I was the only one who understood. The worse they sang, the more tenderly opera singers caressed my hand. At parties hostesses presented me to their guests with pride. I experienced what every well-known critic has experienced. But, despite all the honors conferred upon me in deference to my age, I could not be content with the state of my profession, a profession I loved as a man loves a woman who deceives him.

Nobody was satisfied with musical criticism and music critics. Society was skeptical and gibing, abusive and suspicious. Even the fine literary work of the great critics — from Eduard Hanslick in Vienna to Paul Marsop in Munich, Paul Becker in Frankfurt, Dr. Einstein and Weissman in Berlin, Ernst Decsey in Graz and Vienna, Ernest Newman in London, Henderson, Huneker, and Gilman in New York, Camille Bellaigue, Henri Prunières, and Florent Schmitt in Paris — was certainly never valued by the public as it should have been.

Nor was the relationship between musicians and critics any more true hearted than between critics and public. Clever musicians did their best to turn this relationship to good ends. They called critics their friends and assured them of their highest esteem. In reality they wanted to be sure to be praised as much as possible. "Praise me, praise me as excessively as you can; I have a positive need of incense," wrote Hans von Bülow to Draeseke, and he expressed openly what other artists try to deny by assuring the critic that they want only to hear the truth and nothing but the truth. In one of his letters (1897) Mahler wrote to his young friend Bruno Walter: "Keep on good terms with the critics ! . . . Visit the gentlemen now and then ! Consider that you cannot behave with the 'dignity of man' in a kennel, but that you have only to take care that the watchdogs leave you alone." Mahler himself, although a very independent character, laid stress on being on good terms with the critics and used himself to visit them in their "kennels." I too have had some of the leading musicians of our time as friends, Gustav Mahler for a while, Felix Weingartner for many years, and Richard Strauss. But I always found friendly relations with these men to be so ticklish, difficult, complicated, and unstable that they could be destroyed by a few frank words of criticism, like a blimp by a burning match thrown carelessly away.

There was only one way to clarify the doubts that oppressed me as I looked on the accomplishments and the mistakes of musical criticism, on its importance and its sins. I had to go to the old teacher of human greatness and human weakness — to History. Only history could answer the question: Are the mistakes of musical criticism inherent in the system itself, or are they mere accidents, clinging to it like mud to the wheel of a moving car? Only history could teach me clearly to see the position of criticism in the musical life of our time, and its proper function within musical society. Musical criticism is the child of history, and only history, the greatest critic of human accomplishments, could tell whether it is a legitimate child or a changeling. To history I went for the answer.

Chapter One

THE AGE OF REASON

MUSICAL criticism is one of the forces that have molded the modern world, a tributary to the mighty stream of criticism that began to flow through Europe in the middle of the eighteenth century. Since then, criticism has participated in every phase of the formation of modern ideas. It has grown in strength along with the rising tide of the scientific, philosophical, and social ideas of the "Age of Reason." Developing into new forms and expressions, into new techniques and abilities, it paralleled the rise of the middle class, which had been fighting since the middle of the eighteenth century for social and political rights, for wealth, prosperity, and spiritual independence, as well as for economic and industrial progress.

Men believed in human reason as in a new religion. Man's greatness seemed to be based on his ability to subject all institutions to his critical thinking. Nothing was too great or too holy to be summoned before the tribunal of human reason. "Have the courage to use your own reason," Kant challenged in his article "What Is Enlightenment?," written four years before the outbreak of the French Revolution. He termed every effort to suppress free reasoning, "a crime against human nature." It is, he maintained, a sin against the holy laws of mankind to renounce enlightenment, either for oneself or for one's descendants. This belief in the power of independent human reason gave flaming enthusiasm to the speeches and writings of the great figures of the Age of Reason, who seem to hold their heads higher when speaking of mankind. Criticism analyzed the structure of state and society. It approached religion without fear and studied the Bible as a human document. Reason constructed the world from the smallest atoms; it counted and calculated, studying the structure of the universe as a machine is studied. Everywhere man saw numbers and geometry, mechanical processes, the vibration and movement of small particles; and in this strong light of reason, the whole universe was suffused with a glowing clarity, as a crystal bowl shines in the rays of the sun.

Mathematics and physics were the keys that seemed to open all doors of human knowledge. Both were used by scholars of the Age of Reason as religious ideas were used in the Middle Ages. As the medieval scholastics had applied the ideas of the Christian faith to earth and heaven, nature and man, angels and God, so the spirit of the Enlightenment based its interpretation of nature and the state, society and politics, corporeal and spiritual facts, on a mechanical and physical point of view. Science was founded on experience and experiment. Scholars mistrusted general ideas. There was a flurry of scientific activity, of observation and analysis, all over Europe, in the small cities as well as in the great capitals.

The great *Encyclopédie*, founded by D'Alembert and Diderot, published in twenty-eight volumes from 1751 to 1777, was the most ambitious project of the period. It aimed to acquaint the cultivated world with the results of modern science. Everywhere scholars met, corresponded, and exchanged the results of their research, and all these men were possessed of an unshakeable belief that human reason could solve all the problems of the universe. Criticism of religion was one of the chief tasks confronting the modern thinkers of the eighteenth century. The doctrine — already partially expounded in the sixteenth century — that a universal religion is rooted in the soul of all men, now traveled from England and Scotland to Germany and France, and everywhere promoted rational consideration of religious problems as well as criticism of the historical documents of Christianity.

Not only religion but also the Baroque state was to be trans-

formed and rebuilt by reason. This state was feudal in character, preserved from the Middle Ages; and in it the power of
the prince had risen to its greatest height. The court of France
had been the model for all Europe. Here the Sun King had
walked with his courtiers in the magnificent gardens of Versailles, where sandstone deities, elaborate fountains, and formal
rows of box all helped to provide the proper setting for so great
a prince. Versailles was copied in Berlin and Vienna, in Hanover and Stuttgart, in St. Petersburg and Dresden. Petty German princes sold their subjects as soldiers to get money for
castles and festivals, opera performances and fireworks, like
those at Versailles. Immense sums were squandered, by princes
and aristocrats alike, in their efforts to play the role of Sun King
in their own courts.

This mighty society of princes and potentates, celebrating its
feasts in sumptuous palaces, and wasting its money in masked
balls and *carrousels*, in ballets and sleigh-rides, these princes
dressed in motley silk, this aristocracy of bewigged gentlemen
with white stockings and buckled shoes, of panniered ladies
with towering coiffures and lavishly exhibited bosoms, believed the state to be their servant. Existence had no other
meaning than the pleasure of a class. The life of the peasants, workers, and bourgeois was entirely separate from that of
the aristocracy, which inherited great wealth, but left only bank-
ruptcy and debts to its heirs. The organization of the state became senseless, as court society turned into a society of drones,
and the middle classes steadily rose in power. Feudal society,
with Emperor and Pope as its center, while nobles, townsmen,
and peasants revolved around them like the planets around the
sun, lost its meaning as the religious struggles of the sixteenth
and seventeenth centuries destroyed and disrupted its tight organization.

As the new ideas of a democratic society began to assert themselves, rational thinking began to penetrate all levels of life. No
institution was exempt. Each had to justify itself by human
reason. And since reason formulated the laws of all existing

things, no law could derive from religious or other prejudices. The state, like religion, had to vindicate itself, for nothing could escape the searching examination of human reason. Criticism was the most important tool of all these inquiries. It was, in fact, the chief instrument of enlightenment.

Among the Greeks the original meaning of the word had been division or analysis. In the eighteenth century, criticism had come to mean the separation of truth from appearance, reality from phenomenon, and essence from surface.

Art, like all the other activities of the human mind, had to submit to critical examination. And thus modern art criticism and musical criticism were born.

Chapter Two

THE NEW ESTHETICS

BEHIND all the intellectual movements from which modern criticism stems, stands the great and noble figure of René Descartes. We can picture this frail, kindly man, silent and deep in thought, riding among the officers of the Imperial Army. We can imagine him going on a pilgrimage to Italy and praying at the church in Loreto. Perhaps we see him sitting in a spotless Dutch room with his books of mathematics or philosophy, or discussing religious questions with Queen Christina of Sweden in her palace at Stockholm.

However we may imagine him, Descartes begins the history of modern thought. To open one of his books is to enter a spiritual atmosphere entirely different from that of the Middle Ages. Here is nothing mystical, nothing deriving from religious conceptions. All is clear, logical, and human, for the personality of the thinker does not vanish into mystical clouds or belittle itself in comparison with heavenly powers. Self-reliance is Descartes's creed. In every page of his work the reader meets the wise yet modest utterance of a man who believes that nature has made all men equal, and that differences of opinion do not arise from the fact that one man has more intelligence than another, but only from the different modes of thinking natural to different men.

He touches us when he describes the doubts and mistakes that accompanied him in his struggle after the truth. He convinces us when he examines the foundations on which the complicated structures of Aristotelian science had been built, and everywhere finds flaws in their construction. He is the modern Faust, who has studied philosophy, medicine, law, and theology, only to conclude that man can never really know anything. And yet he is not a titanic Faust, like Goethe's superthinker, but a modest, simple fellow, affecting in his humanity.

Searching in his own soul, Descartes finally found the solution for the riddles that had oppressed him for so many years. In his time all knowledge had become doubtful and insecure. There was no sure foundation, even in theology, since the revealed truth that is the basis of theology transcends human understanding. One conception only was rocklike in its strength: the thinking of man. For one cannot separate the process of thinking from the thinker, and surely the thinker exists. There can be no doubt of that. Even if the thinker merely thinks haphazardly, merely dreams, one fact cannot be altered: the fact that he is thinking. It is I who have the experience of perceiving, and even if none of the things I perceive is true, my experience of perception would still exist. *Cogito ergo sum:* I think, therefore I exist.

Descartes exalted human reason to the rank accorded to divine wisdom by the theologians of the Middle Ages. Even God was conceived only as the clearest and greatest of man's ideas. Hence man was no longer a feeble, groping creature, hoping for the mercy of God, but a being made strong by his power of thought. Man has only to think clearly, and heaven and nature reveal their secrets to him. The clarity of the French spirit, so evident in every phase of French life, derives from Descartes. He formed the French spirit as a sculptor molds clay or carves marble. It is to Descartes that France owes her tendency to mathematical clearness, it is to him that she is indebted for her logical force and the transparent brilliancy of her thought which, in the eighteenth century, flooded the whole of Europe with its splendor, and spread its light to the shores of the new world.

II. ESTHETIC THEORY; BOILEAU

Descartes's belief in the importance and validity of clear thinking, in addition to its influence on the critical theory of the seventeenth and eighteenth centuries, transformed the esthetic ideas of the period. Clarity, reasonableness, and naturalness became the highest principles of art as well as of thought.

The art of the seventeenth century had been exuberantly extravagant, for all Baroque art aspired to the colossal, to the theatrically pompous, and the luxuriously gorgeous. During these years, the purity of line so characteristic of the early Renaissance had begun to yield to the heavily ornamented styles that have given the period its name. Forms had begun to break up, the grand pattern lost in the profusion of detail, and great architectural rhythms smothered in a plethora of grace notes. In painting, too, in place of the architectonic grandeur of the Quattrocento and early Cinquecento, we find increased use of chiaroscuro, of motion, and intense personal feeling. Witness the martyrs of Guercino and Domenichino, the luxury and splendor of Rubens, and the mystical light of Rembrandt. Everywhere one notices the same restless, passionate, pathetic feeling, which in its struggle to reach the infinite dissolves all fixed border lines. This same tendency toward the extravagant is apparent in all other walks of seventeenth-century life. Grandiose titles, ceremonious wigs, courtly pomp, mannerism and bombast — all express the same idea. To this idea, which gave to Baroque art its theatrical character, the estheticians of the nascent Age of Reason opposed a sense of proportion and lucidity.

Passion was no longer the dominant note in painting and sculpture, and the excited imagination was condemned. No longer were glowing color and intense feeling to flow from the painter's brush as they had from that of Rubens. No, art was once again to be simple, clear, and human. The pure light of reason was henceforth to guide man's creative force.

When Voltaire characterized Shakespeare's plays as "the art of an intoxicated savage," or when Scheibe criticized the music of Bach as "intricate and bombastic," they were expressing such judgments as might be expected from men imbued with the critical spirit of the eighteenth century, who denied all romanticism, all extravagance, and all incalculable flights of fancy to the realm of art.

The French esthetician who adapted the ideas of Descartes to the criticism of art was Boileau. The dictator of artistic taste in France for many decades, his influence was no less important in England and in Germany. He fully deserved his title of "Legislator of Parnassus," for he prescribed the laws that were obediently observed by the artists of the Age of Reason. Boileau, like Descartes, held that nothing is beautiful but the true, and in that phrase we find the key to all his critical theory.

Boileau was the scion of a Parisian family whose members seem to have been gay, witty, and satirical. Even as a young man he had begun to attract attention, and the lawyer Mathieu Marais said of him, "It is a pleasure to listen to this man. He is reason embodied." And well he might be, for he grew up in the old city, in the rue de Jérusalem, where the people behind the counters and in the bars had a reputation for minting common sense into wit.

When his first satires were written and were beginning to be quoted in the salons and coffeehouses, he was only twenty-four years old. The young poet had had the temerity to attack writers favored by those who had access to the anterooms of the palace at Versailles and strolled through its park: among them was Philippe Quinault, librettist for Lully, whose *Armide* Gluck was later to set.

An admirer of Molière, Boileau loved the natural charm of his plays and the sanity of his laughter. Such an admiration and esteem are not difficult to understand, for the two men were essentially alike, both typical of the Parisian middle class. A year before Boileau had written his first satires, Molière had made his mark with a play, *Les Précieuses ridicules* ("The Ridiculous Bluestockings"), which satirized the artificial pomposity and the Baroque bombast that France had been importing from Spain and Italy. Boileau was marching in the same direction. In his *Dialogue des héros de roman* ("Dialogue concerning the Heroes of Novels"), he attacked the puffed-up language and high-flown sentiments of the contemporary novel. Even the favorite court writers of the day, La Calprenède and Mlle de Scudéry, did not escape his attention.

The year 1674 saw published the work that was to become the code of French poetry, *L'Art poétique* ("*The Art of Poetry*"). The first three books of the work develop Boileau's ideas in fluent, charming verse. Foremost is common sense, while almost equally important are clarity and naturalness. Order and regularity are the highest values, which Boileau proclaims as fundamental law. It almost seems as though he wants to transform the realm of poetry into a French park, with graveled walks walled by pruned trees, like the gardens of Versailles where he used to walk with Racine.

This passion for precision and clarity returns like a leitmotiv in the satires written by Boileau after the publication of *L'Art poétique*. One after another they pour forth, mocking, clear, elegant, and courageous. Not for nothing did Sainte-Beuve call him "the most vivacious of all serious minds," for Boileau's sensibility fused completely with his reasonableness and his critical talent. In the refined and sophisticated assemblage at Versailles he represented the spirit of the middle class with perfect ease and simplicity. The bust by Girardon shows him vigorous and proud as he must have looked, with a smiling face under his majestic wig, and a mocking laugh touching the frank mouth under the upturned nose.

When he died in 1711, Boileau had established an unshakeable French national taste in the arts. But he was more than the schoolmaster of France, he was the schoolmaster of his century. His esthetic theory ruled French art as absolutely as Louis XIV ruled France, but unlike the King's rule, Boileau's theory was accepted in the other countries of Europe — accepted as the best and most modern doctrine of artistic beauty. These new canons of clearness and reasonableness, of logic and lucidity, were especially well received in England and Germany, where they seemed to herald a new artistic era, which was to cast off the old, outworn laws that had so long oppressed the artistic spirit.

III. THE GERMAN ESTHETICIANS

As Descartes had worked to prepare the philosophic ground for rational ideas in France, so Leibnitz had worked in Germany.

He had the same confidence in reason. If lucidity and logic lead to knowledge (so ran Leibnitz's thought) it is possible to transform thinking into a kind of mathematics; and, as mathematicians use signs for algebraic calculations, so philosophers will use symbols in their efforts to reach the truth.

Neither the infinitely small nor the infinitely great had secrets from the bright vision of Leibnitz. He constructed his world from monads. These monads are incredibly small, and yet are animated by soul. Each represents the whole universe from its own point of view, and, as they adhere, they form the steps to God, the highest and greatest monad, from which all the others radiate. The clearer the conceptions of any given monad, the more perfect it is. Those which compose material things have only an indistinct and muddy view of the universe, while the monad which is God understands all things clearly and distinctly. Evil, from this viewpoint, is privative: not positive at all, but only a lack of clearness. Hence, to Leibnitz, clarity and reason were gleaming torches, illuminating the darkness of the universe.

These doctrines were preached from the lecturing desks of the universities at Leipzig and Halle by Professor Christian Wolff, the most ardent champion of reason in Germany during the first half of the eighteenth century. It was Wolff who made philosophical thinking popular there, and philosophical thinking, to Wolff, meant clear and distinct thinking. Even pleasure and pain he held to be but functions of thinking: pleasure is awareness of perfection, pain awareness of imperfection. In this way Wolff approached the threshold of esthetics. It remained for Alexander Baumgarten, his most important pupil, to cross over into what was then a new field. In fact Baumgarten created the term, when, in 1750 and 1758, he published the two volumes of his *Aesthetica*, in which he analyzed beauty as the sensual, confused perception of perfection.

Chapter Three

THE FIRST MAGAZINES

I. ENGLAND

EVER since the Restoration the influence of France had been slowly increasing in England. The works of Racine, Molière, La Fontaine, and Bossuet were popular there, while Englishmen who went to France in exile (like Hobbes, for example) came back admiring the French spirit. Nor was the traffic entirely in one direction, for one of the leaders of French thought, Charles de Saint-Évremond, came to London and stayed there until he died. For years he was the lion of the salon which a beautiful niece of Cardinal Mazarin's had set up there in 1670 for love-making, gambling, and witty conversation. Here, in the midst of attractive women and elegant aristocrats, he had dazzled his audience with his ideas on the Baroque opera, which he called "a stupidity loaded with music, dancing, and mechanical contraptions."

This French influence met and joined forces with native English thinking. The founding of the Royal Society in 1660 had given impetus to the scientific spirit throughout England. This impetus was important not only in the realm of science but also in that of literary style, for one part of the Society's program was, in the words of its historian, Bishop Sprat, "a close, naked, natural way of speaking." Sprat's own style, and Newton's, and Ray's prove the importance of this dictum. Their simplicity, lucidity, and clearness must be contrasted with the eccentricity, the fantastic flights, and the overloaded imagery of the Baroque taste to be fully appreciated. Modern English developed in Pepys' and Evelyn's diaries, in Lord Chesterfield's letters, in Dryden's prefaces, in the spicy comedies of the Restoration, and finally, in the great eighteenth-century novels. Even philosophical writing became more graceful and fluent: one can notice the French influence molding the language of Locke, Berkeley, and Hume. Writing became easier, good-humored, and tasteful; sentences inclined to brevity, and the short, sharp strokes of logic and simplicity took the place of Baroque ornamentation and feeling. Dryden began a new style of writing, which in the eighteenth century flowered into a beautiful, classical English prose.

Boileau's criticism was continued by Dryden and by Pope, who imitated the French code of art in his *Essay on Criticism*. But modern criticism may be said to have dawned in England in 1709, when Richard Steele published the first issue of *The Tatler*. This magazine, finding its way into coffeehouses, clubs, tearooms, and assemblies, popularized the new ideas of the Age of Reason.

In England, as in France and Germany, a new middle-class society was rising. Under the reign of Queen Anne, the new ideas of the Age of Reason met with corresponding social changes that helped give them currency. The well-to-do middle classes were hungry for pleasure. They wanted to read during their leisure time. For this middle class, impatient of sophisticated bombast and learned pomposity, Swift wrote *Gulliver's Travels*, Defoe *Robinson Crusoe*, Richardson *Pamela* and *Clarissa*, and Sterne *Tristram Shandy*.

Steele regaled this same public with good sense, humorous morality, and realistic views on life, with reasonable argument and easy talk. And occasionally Addison contributed essays to his friend's periodical — essays that translated French ease and elegance into the texture of English prose. Both were men of the new age, and from the pens of both flowed the new and exciting ideas of the times.

In 1711, *The Spectator* succeeded *The Tatler*. On March 1 of that year, the first issue of the new magazine was published, and Sir Roger de Coverley, Sir Andrew Freeport, Captain Sentry, and the other members of the Spectator's Club began discussing the problems of the day, thoughtfully and with pleasant humor. In March and April of 1711, Addison published his famous attacks on the Italian Baroque opera, thus entering the lists against Baroque music, and paralleling the criticism which was to become so widespread in France.

II. GERMANY AND SWITZERLAND

It was not long before this journalism, with its new simplicity and new theories of criticism, crossed the North Sea into the great German port of Hamburg. The ships that loaded at the London docks and discharged their cargoes at Hamburg brought the new issues of *The Tatler*, *The Spectator*, *The Guardian*, and the other English journals to the great port on the Elbe.

Hamburg, like all seaports, was open to new ideas as well as to trade from foreign countries. Vessels from all parts of the world came there. One might see ships fresh from the Orient, with cargoes of spices and carpets, berthed alongside Dutch ships loaded with wool, or Russian ships loaded with furs, or English ships loaded with cotton fabrics woven in the Midlands. The merchants, shipbuilders, and shipowners of Hamburg were rich, proud, and dignified men who looked with pride on the forest of masts and spars in their port and on the mountains of barrels and boxes piled up on their wharves. Diplomats and ambassadors from many countries formed an international society in the city. Only the clergy was reactionary, and on Sundays the naves of the churches echoed with the thunders directed from the pulpit against new ideas, and particularly against the opera.

The first public opera house in Hamburg was opened in 1678, perhaps as an answer to the opera in Venice, as a way of showing that the northern port was in no way inferior to its Italian rival. The preachers fulminated against the new institution, and called upon God to consume the building and its frequenters with a rain of burning sulphur. Seeing their prayers unanswered, they published pamphlets warning the public against the deadly sin of listening to operatic arias; but in spite of all their efforts, the opera house was successful. In fact, it was even pointed out to visitors as one of the show places of the city.

In 1682 the Great Elector of Brandenburg set the seal of official approval on the opera house by witnessing a performance of Nicolaus Strungk's *Alceste*. The young Handel came to Hamburg in 1703 to take a seat in the orchestra as violinist and harpsichordist. Johann Sebastian Bach, at that time a student in Saint Michael's School in near-by Lüneburg, visited Hamburg more than once to hear the famous old organist Reinken. Indeed, the citizens of Hamburg had a right to feel proud of the musical life in their city.

Literature was no less important in Hamburg than music. The city seemed to be open to all currents flowing from England. Brockes, a poet descended from an old Hamburg family, translated Thomson's *Seasons*, and wrote his *Irdisches Vergnügen in Gott* ("*Earthly Pleasure in God*") after the model of Pope. Inspired by Milton's *Paradise Lost*, Klopstock, the first of the great modern German poets, wrote the sublime verses of his *Messias* ("*The Messiah*").

This literary ferment had been preceded by the influence of the English magazines. Two years after the publication of the first issue of *The Spectator*, the musician Johann Mattheson published the magazine *Der Vernünftler* ("*The Reasoning Man*"). The first issue appeared on May 31, 1713. Its motto — "What men do and practise gives us material for writing" — was carried out in its contents, for it contained short stories with a moral tendency, discussions, letters, and criticisms of social institutions, manners, and luxuries, all after the model of the English journals. The articles frequently referred to Milton and to contemporary literature. The goal of the magazine was the refinement of the middle classes. Mattheson, Handel's most intimate friend in Hamburg, was not connected with England in a merely superficial sense, for he spoke English like a native, and served as secretary to the English ambassador in Hamburg.

In 1724 another magazine, *Der Patriot* ("*The Patriot*") was founded by a patriotic group under the leadership of Brockes. Its circulation was over four thousand copies, and it even had some success in England. This society of patriots was typical of the times; its rise was paralleled in England, where groups of this kind were the precursors of the Freemasons. These societies were groups of liberal men imbued with the ideas of progress, reason, and humanity. In Germany they were the leaders of the intellectual life of the middle class.

The most distinguished of these societies between 1715 and 1718 in Hamburg was the Deutschübende Gesellschaft ("German-practicing Society"). This group, together with the Patriotische Gesellschaft ("Patriotic Society"), exercised great influence on the German language, purging it of the French and Latin diction that had crept in during the Baroque period. The light of reason lit up the dark corners of the German language, where the dust of many decades of artificial solemnity and grandiloquence had piled up.

Over five hundred magazines were published in Germany and Switzerland between 1714 and 1800. Zurich and Leipzig followed the example set by Hamburg. Johann Jakob Bodmer and his friends published a weekly journal, *Die Diskurse der Maler* (*"Discussions between Painters"*) in Zurich from 1721 to 1723; in Leipzig, a center of German thought, Johann Christoph Gottsched published two magazines during the 1720's: *Vernünftige Tadlerinnen* (*"Reasonable Faultfinders"*) and *Der Biedermann* (*"The Honest Man"*). In addition to these periodicals, Gottsched translated *The Spectator* and *The Guardian*. Thus these English magazines appeared in German editions, and played their part in spreading English and French ideas throughout Germany. The criticisms of French and English thinkers, the forces of enlightenment, the gospel of reason, and the ideas of modern science thus became popular with middle-class society, which was preparing to organize a new state according to the dictates of reason.

Nine years after the publication of *Der Vernünftler*, Mattheson

published the first issue of his new magazine, *Critica musica*.[1]
It was in the columns of this magazine that the chief esthetic
ideas of the Age of Reason entered the field of music; Mattheson was accustomed to fill his pages with translations from
French musical articles and to annotate them as well.

In this way the new critical ideas entered musical life, and
Mattheson, one of the leading musical personalities of the first
half of the eighteenth century, begins the procession of music
critics. The "Boileau of music," as Romain Rolland calls him,
Mattheson was receptive to all the progressive ideas of the most
enlightened minds of Europe. He was working for the future,
just as some critics were later to work in the past. The brisk
sea wind that had swelled the sails of the ships heading for the
port of Hamburg were presently to waft Mattheson's ideas to
new shores.

[1] The complete title of this journal runs, with the German portion translated into English: *Critica musica*, a wholly correct Inquiry and Examination of many partly Prejudiced,
partly Silly, Opinions, Arguments, and Objections that are to be found in Old and New,
Printed and Unprinted Musical Writings.

Chapter Four

THE FIRST MUSIC CRITICS

HAMBURG

I. GENERAL CHARACTER OF THE EIGHTEENTH-CENTURY MUSIC CRITIC

THE MUSIC critics of the eighteenth century represent the typical attitude of the men of the Age of Reason. They were experts, men who had a right to influence musical life. Great theoreticians and authoritative composers, familiar with the devices and techniques of actual composition, mused over the technical problems of music. They were the elite of musical society. All of them — Mattheson; Lorenz Mizler, of Leipzig; Johann Adolph Scheibe, of Hamburg and Leipzig; Friedrich Wilhelm Marpurg, of Berlin; Johann Adam Hiller, of Leipzig — were either composers or theoreticians.

At the end of the seventeenth and at the beginning of the eighteenth century the standard of culture had risen among German musicians. Johann Kuhnau, who is commonly credited with writing the first piano sonatas in Germany, had studied law, and his dissertation, *De Juribus circa Musicos Ecclesiasticos* (*"On the Laws concerning Church Musicians"*) had been printed in 1688. Christoph Graupner, one of the most important of Bach's contemporaries, had studied jurisprudence at the university in Leipzig. The famous conductor and teacher of thorough bass, Johann David Heinichen, had been a lawyer in Weissenfels; Friedrich Fasch, another successful contemporary of Bach, had also studied jurisprudence at the university in Leipzig.

Composers such as Christoph Bernhard and Matthias Weckmann were among the most cultured men of their time. They

were both familiar with Latin, Greek, and Italian, and Weckmann was recommended by his teacher to add Hebrew to the
list. Mattheson spoke several languages. Telemann mourned
the death of his wife in a long French poem.

The "pure musician" living in his ivory tower was an antiquated type in the first decades of the eighteenth century. No
reproach could annoy a musician more than the accusation that
he was without culture. When Scheibe attacked Bach, he reproached him with his ignorance of science. How, Scheibe
wondered, could a musician write flawless compositions if he
did not study science in order to analyze the forces of nature and
reason. Telemann gave the matter ironic consideration in a
little poem:

> Music requires a man to give himself entirely to it,
> But the world does not wholly agree with this.
> It demands that one learn and attempt other things
> (As if the head of a note could hold many topics!)
> Therefore it will be necessary to yield to the world.
> What the crowd wants finally becomes law.
> But it is also pleasant to know something of many things,
> And even if it doesn't bring in anything, it doesn't
> Eat one's bread either.

And a pamphlet with the somewhat rhetorical title, *Ob ein
Komponist necessario musse studiert haben* (*"Whether a Composer
Must Necessarily Have Studied"*), answers the implied question
as scientifically as possible with a categorical *yes*.

The glorification of human reason which is the chief characteristic of the eighteenth century assumes an admiration for
science and for scientific culture. Hence the enlightened musician was the cultured musician, not a mere artisan without
knowledge of the spiritual achievements of his age. Men like
Mattheson and Telemann were, as their books prove, laden with
erudition; and when they walked gravely through the streets of
Hamburg, with their black cloaks swelled out by the sea breeze,
the passers-by respected them as they respected the earnest sen-
ators and the fanatic preachers of the city.

II. JOHANN MATTHESON (1681–1764)

Mattheson was born four years before Bach: in 1681. While he was still young the Baroque style was in full flower, with Lully, Scarlatti, Corelli, and Steffani occupying prominent places in the musical world. When Mattheson died in 1764, Haydn was thirty-two years old and had already written his first string quartets and symphonies, in which the pre-classic style had begun to yield to the modern symphonic idiom. Mozart, a child of eight, had already attracted the attention of the world. Thus Mattheson lived between two musical epochs. And he was in no small measure responsible for the development away from the pathos of the Baroque period toward the sober feeling of the age of Rousseau.

As a theoretician and a critic, he was a man of modern ideas. He fought for freer forms and more dramatic expression in church music, for melody and expressive harmonization — in short, for naturalness. Mattheson was especially proud (though "without vanity," he says) to have been "the first to insist energetically and expressly on the importance of melody." He taught that "every piece one writes must be *cantabile*," and insisted that "good, reasonable music that touches the heart and moves and elevates the soul of intelligent men with beautiful thoughts and melodies" must prevail. He boasts that there had not been a musical writer before him who did not make the melody — which ought to be the most accomplished and beautiful part of music — jump about like a cock on live coals.

In 1713 Mattheson engaged in a violent battle with a worthy representative of the older school of contrapuntal music. His opponent, the organist of Wolfenbüttel, was named Bokemeyer. Bokemeyer looked upon canon and counterpoint with religious awe, while Mattheson considered them only forms of intellectual exercise that did not deeply touch the heart. Reinhard Keiser, Heinichen, and Telemann were finally asked to arbitrate the quarrel — which, like all professional quarrels, was carried on with passionate fanaticism. The three musicians decided in favor of Mattheson, whereupon Bokemeyer declared himself beaten and thanked his rival for having converted him to melody, "the one and only source of pure music." The newly converted sinner then wrote a pamphlet on melody and sent it to Mattheson for correction.

Like the French estheticians of the day, Mattheson regarded Nature as the model of art; from which it followed that the musical language of passion must model itself on natural accents and expression. Hence composers ought to express greatness of soul, love, jealousy, and so forth, in such a way that the audience could "grasp the meaning of a musical speech" as well as if it had been a spoken speech. Mattheson regarded the music of Keiser, the chief composer of the Hamburg opera, as the model of natural expression; and wrote of his work: "It takes much art and skill to compose a speech as well as Keiser used to, having regard for feeling as well as for the formal phrases."

Mattheson was a relentless enemy of dry artificiality and pedantic scholasticism. His law was the ear. "Leave your clumsy art at home," he wrote, "lest the ear suffer in any way. What Nature teaches you is good — play it, sing it. What Nature teaches you is bad — avoid or destroy it." Nature, reason, and clarity were the standards by which Mattheson judged all music.

It was in the spring of 1703 that the eighteen-year-old Handel arrived in Hamburg with music blossoming in his head. He became a friend of Mattheson, who preached the gospel of melody to him. In his *Ehren-Pforte* ("*Gate of Honor*"), Mattheson wrote that Handel at this time composed "exceedingly long arias and almost endless cantatas without the proper skill or taste." And, as a matter of fact, there was certainly a superabundance of Baroque feeling in the music of the young Handel, for his cantatas, like all those of the period, were loaded with ornate melody and coloratura trimmings. Handel's colleague, Telemann, testifies how eager his friend was to improve his melodic style.

Indeed, Handel's style needed work before it reached the great simplicity of melody, dignity, and perfect beauty of his mature efforts. Like Beethoven later, Handel did not find the melodic greatness and sublime simplicity that characterize his music, without infinite labor.

It is more than possible that Mattheson's own career as an opera singer influenced his theories. He began in 1690, at the age of nine, and did not take leave of the stage until 1705, after appearing in Handel's *Nero*. His sense of melody must surely have developed as he stood before his audience and tried to impress them with the intensity of his feeling and the sensuous beauty of sound. In his critical work, perhaps as a result of his practical experience, he demands that the composer think always of the singer's acting, and suggests that the gestures and expression of the singers may provide an inspiration for musical invention. Expressive acting was second only to effective singing, for he characterizes pantomime as "silent music."

To Mattheson the theater was something alive: the school of expression and of musical passion. He wanted to replace the contrapuntal style, which had dominated the church music of his time, by the "theatrical style." The task, he thought, of the religious composer was to "arouse virtuous passions." He expanded his ideas in his *Der musicalische Patriot* ("*Musical Patriot*") of 1728, in which he defined the word theatrical as "the artistic imitation of Nature." "All that impresses mankind is theatrical . . . music is theatrical . . . the whole world is a giant theater." It is with such doctrines that Mattheson influenced the church music of his times. His efforts bore fruit in the religious cantata in "theatrical" style, fitted with the recitative and the *da capo* aria of the opera, which Bach favored. Telemann, Hasse, and Graun also composed oratorios in operatic style, and Handel's oratorios are in reality operas for an imaginary theater on whose stage people act, suffer, and celebrate victories.

In his *Critica musica*, Mattheson expanded, popularized, and intensified his fight against the contrapuntal style, at the same time strengthening his propaganda for melodious and expressive music, for reasonable clarity, and for naturalness. In the second issue of his magazine, he had republished the Abbé Raguenet's pamphlet on the difference between Italian and French taste in music and opera, which had been the opening gun in the French battle against the Italian Baroque opera. Mattheson added notes to his translation. Soon afterward he published, once more with his own notes, another French pamphlet, a defense of French music. Thus French critical ideas entered Germany.

One article in the *Critica musica* criticizes Handel's *Passion according to St. John*, attacking without mercy some youthful tastelessness in the work of the young composer. And in the same issue Mattheson takes Bach to task for the repetition of the words at the beginning of the cantata *Ich hatte viel Bekümmerniss* (*"I was in deep affliction"*). He finds Bach's declamation faulty — as indeed it is, for Bach's melody is never so closely adapted to the text as the vigor of French rationalism demanded. Instead, the melody drifts fancifully and luxuriantly down the stream of religious feeling. In another article Mattheson attacks those "devices . . . which are called canons among musicians." Every issue contains, in addition to esthetic and controversial matter, historical or critical news of musicians and music.

Mattheson stands at the threshold of new developments in music, lighting the way with his theories and criticisms. Among his books, which were written after he had left the operatic stage and had become canon and music director of the Hamburg cathedral, are: *Der vollkommene Capellmeister* (*"The Accomplished Capellmeister"*) (1739), the *Generalbass Schule* (*"Method of Thorough Bass"*) (1719), and the *Ehren-Pforte* (1740), a collection of notes on composers. The *Vollkommene Capellmeister* was long regarded as a standard text on theory and esthetics. The period in which Mattheson published this work is one of the great classical epochs of criticism, during which the foundations of modern critical theory were laid. And these foundations have proved so enduring that they resemble the mighty blocks

of stone our ancestors laid down for the ramparts of antique
fortresses.   In addition to Mattheson's *Vollkommene Capellmeister*, we must note Rameau's *Traité d'harmonie* ("*Treatise on
Harmony*") (1722), and Fux's *Gradus ad Parnassum* ("*Steps to
Parnassus*") (1725).   These three books provide the foundation
for all musical development from Bach to the end of the nineteenth century.

III.   GEORG PHILIPP TELEMANN (1681–1767)

Mattheson's ideas are echoed in the works of Georg Philipp
Telemann.   Like his master, Telemann was an enthusiastic fol-
lower of French ideas, and a herald of the new style.   When
the old theoretician Wolfgang Printz lamented the extravagance
of the melodists, Telemann replied, "And I?   I laugh at compositions that are not melodious."   Continuing this line of
thought, Telemann rhymed:

> Singing is the foundation of music in everything.
> He who composes must everywhere sing.

In a similar vein he advised young students of music not to go to
"the old fellows who believe in counterpoint rather than in
imagination, and who write compositions for fifteen or twenty
voices in which not even Diogenes with his lantern could discover a drop of melody."

With such feelings and with such ideas, Telemann belongs entirely to the modern world.   He is not interested in the past;
his eyes are always turned toward the future.   One of his brav-
est sayings runs, "One never has to say to art, 'Don't go any
farther.'   One must always go farther, and one must go still
farther."   A spirit like Telemann's could not be satisfied with
writing elaborately contrapuntal music to impress his colleagues with his skill, and incidentally to honor the Almighty.
Telemann wanted to write for the whole world.   His creed was,
"He who writes music for the many does better work than he
who writes only for the few."   On another occasion he said,
"I have always aspired to facility.   Music ought not to be an

effort, an occult science, a sort of black magic." Though Telemann was a friend of Bach's and the godfather of K. P. E. Bach,
who was named Philipp after him, Bach's music and Telemann's
were worlds apart.

Telemann began his career as a child prodigy at the age of
twelve. Scores for church music and for operas had already begun to stream from his desk to church choirs and opera houses.
As a student in Hildesheim he first came into touch with French
music, and from that time on he remained an admirer of French
musical art. There must have been something radiant about the
young musician who represented modern taste with so much
vigor, for when he came to Leipzig in 1701 when Kuhnau was
cantor at St. Thomas's School, Kuhnau complained that the
choir singers of his church all ran to sing under Telemann's
baton at the Leipzig opera house. But the students continued
to sing for Telemann, and Kuhnau sat alone in the choir of the
dark, Gothic St. Thomas's Church.

Telemann arrived in Hamburg in 1721; he stayed there, working and writing, until he passed away in 1767, at the ripe age of
eighty-six. When he was appointed cantor of the famous city
school, the Johanneum, the whole city council of Hamburg
drove in stately carriages to the turnpikes at the city's limit to
accompany the new cantor to his office in the traditional manner. It was part of his duty to furnish the five great churches of
Hamburg with music, and, in addition, he conducted a public
concert every Monday and Thursday, wrote operas for the Hamburg theater, composed music for the court in Eisenach (of
which he was *Kapellmeister*), produced church music for the
city of Frankfurt, and wrote operas and instrumental music for
the court at Bayreuth. Scores flowed from his lodgings as if
from the assembly line of a giant factory. Even the composer
himself could not say how many scores he had written. A par-
tial list is overwhelming by sheer force of numbers: forty to
fifty operas, over six hundred suites, thirty-two compositions
for the installation of preachers, thirty-three captain's compositions (consisting of one sonata and one oratorio each, to cele-

brate the ship captains of the city), twelve mourning compositions for the deaths of kings, emperors, and Hamburg noblemen,
and forty-four Passions between 1711 and 1767 alone. During
his forty-six years in Hamburg, notes flowed from his pen like
water from a main.

In 1728 Telemann published a new kind of musical magazine
in Hamburg. It was called *Der getreue Musikmeister* ("The Faithful Music Master"), and it was the first magazine to publish
compositions. Telemann's plan was, rather than through theories and criticisms to influence the public directly by publishing new compositions in the modern manner. He did not
neglect his own music, for a collection of operatic arias from
his own works appeared in the journal. Only rarely did he
publish purely contrapuntal music in his magazine: one exception is a four-voiced canon by Bach.[1] Telemann also published
several articles on musical subjects in the *Musikalische Bibliothek*
("*Musical Library*") edited by Lorenz Mizler in Leipzig.

Telemann, like his contemporaries in musical criticism, was
a cultured man. He wrote librettos for some of his operas and
texts for some of his choral compositions. But he preferred
writing scores to writing articles. He wrote autobiographical
notices three times during his life (in 1718, 1729, and 1739) "to
show those who wish to study music that one cannot progress
in this inexhaustible science without great effort."

The indirect influence that Telemann exercised on the development of German criticism was of tremendous importance. With
Hasse and Keiser, who perhaps surpassed him in melodic charm
and delicacy, he was one of the inventors of a new, melodious,
and natural musical style. His compositions contributed to the
spread of French musical theory in Germany. He changed the
musical atmosphere of his country; the dusty air became clear
and bright. Mattheson loved French music because he thought
it was "a subtle imitator of Nature." Before Rousseau began
to preach his doctrine of the return to Nature, Telemann spread

---

[1] Bach esteemed Telemann's music highly; he even copied out some of his cantatas.
And Mattheson wrote that Telemann was "too high for praise."

the same watchword, which was thenceforth to be repeated in all the musical magazines, in all reasoning about music, and in all musical criticism.

IV. JOHANN ADOLF SCHEIBE (1708–76)

Johann Adolf Scheibe came to Hamburg in 1735. He had lived there only two years before he began to publish his magazine, *Der critische Musikus* (*"The Critical Musician"*). Thirty-six issues of the magazine were published in Hamburg. The first opens with a dedication to Scheibe's father, a well-known organ builder; this is followed by a general preface. Twenty-six issues were published between March 5, 1737, and February 18, 1738. A second series began on March 3, 1738, and continued until a total of fifty-one issues had been reached on February 23, 1740. A revised edition of both series was published in one volume in 1745, when Scheibe was court conductor in Denmark.

Young Scheibe studied at the university in Leipzig, and heard the lectures of Professor Gottsched, who at that time was the intellectual lighthouse whose rays lighted the whole of Germany with the bright French ideas of the Age of Reason. Those ideas were bread and wine to young Scheibe. He took up the new doctrines of reason and clarity with the enthusiasm of a neophyte; nor had his enthusiasm for them waned when he began to publish his own magazine.

Scheibe was a thoroughly cultivated man. Besides the articles in his magazine, he wrote theoretical books. One deals with the origin and the age of music, another with musical instruments and scales, a third with recitative. And when Scheibe died in Copenhagen in 1776, there lay on his desk — ready for publication — the first volume of a textbook of musical composition which he had planned to extend to four volumes.

Scheibe's ideas were like a breath of fresh air — even in Hamburg, where the atmosphere was constantly being cleared by the theories of Mattheson and Telemann, the melodious music of Keiser and Sigismund Kusser, and the lyricism of Handel's first operas. We shall hear more of Scheibe later, but we must leave him now on the streets of Hamburg, for it is there that we have met the first music critics. Dignified, weighty, ponderous men they were. And yet, for all their deep thinking and solid learning, they were not strewn with the mold and dust of pedantry. They are not pedants, for they feel themselves to be representatives of a new age in the history of mankind. They are proud of the human intellect, which has made music in the past and which is to shape its harmonies and melodies in the future.

BERLIN

I. THE BERLIN OF THE AGE OF REASON

As we have seen, modern rationalistic ideas first entered Germany through the port of Hamburg, and through the ancient gates of Leipzig where town officials anxiously inquired into the passports of foreign visitors. Nevertheless, Berlin was the most important of the German towns in which the new French ideas made themselves at home. Not until the middle of the thirteenth century had Berlin become a German town, a fortress of the conquerors who had subjugated the native Slavic peoples. At the end of the fourteenth century Berlin had nine thousand inhabitants: emigrants from Saxony and North Germany who had settled in the new country to become merchants and peasants. By the end of the seventeenth century more than one-fifth of the populace of Berlin was foreign. Saxon dialects mingled with those of Upper Germany, and Franconian and Slavic influences were not lacking.

In the eighteenth century, when the Electorate of Brandenburg became the Kingdom of Prussia, new settlers continued to arrive. Protestants from France and the Palatinate sought shelter in Berlin; in 1725, there were more than eight thousand French persons living there. In 1773 more than two thousand Jews were reckoned among the inhabitants of Berlin; from thenceforth they constituted an important element in the city's intellectual life. In the light of these facts it is safe to assume that this strong infusion of foreigners added something of critical acuteness to the mind of Berlin, for criticism has always been a prominent feature of the city's life. When the philosopher Moses Mendelssohn was summoned before Frederick the Great to vindicate a harsh judgment he had made on the royal attempts at poetry, he said to His Majesty, "He who writes poetry plays at bowls, and whoever bowls, be he king or peasant, must put up with the pinboy's criticism." And with intellectual pinboys Berlin was always well provided.

Frederick's own inclinations and predilections completed the French conquest of Berlin's culture. The king disliked speaking any language but French and seldom wrote in any other. He proudly told Gottsched, "I never read a German book when I was young, and I speak German like a coachman." French was the language of the court theater until 1778, as it was of the Berlin Academy of Sciences. In 1751 Voltaire accepted Frederick's invitation to Berlin and became a member of the intimate circle who discussed current philosophical questions at Sans-Souci. French scientists such as Maupertuis and Lagrange had their papers published in their native language by the Prussian Academy of Sciences. Thus French ideas lived in the letters and poems of the king, in the aristocratic palaces of Berlin, and in the magazines read by the middle classes.

When the English scholar Charles Burney came to Berlin, he observed, "Musical discussions are conducted in Berlin with more heat and animosity than elsewhere. Of course, as there are more theorists than practitioners in this city, there are more critics too." This critical spirit in Berlin created the musical schism between Berlin and Vienna: a split that first becomes evident at this time. The theorist Marpurg was spokesman for the northern city when he said that Vienna had no one from Fux to Haydn to compare with Bach, Telemann, Graun, or Hasse. Vienna was naïve, sensuous, and gay, while Berlin was sophisticated, intellectual, and sober. Berlin was fond of theories; Vienna, as of old, dreamed of wine, women, and song.

II. THE THEORISTS

In no other German city were there so many cultured and learned musicians capable of analyzing music as there were in Berlin. There J. J. Quantz wrote his *Versuch einer Anweisung, die Flûte traversière zu spielen* (*"Essay on Instruction in Playing the Flute"*) in 1752; and there Karl Philipp Emanuel Bach published the *Versuch über die wahre Art, das Klavier zu spielen* (*"Essay on the True Way of Playing the Clavier"*), in two parts, which appeared in 1753 and 1762. The year 1757 saw the appearance of J. F. Agricola's *Anleitung zur Singkunst* (*"Guide to the Art of Singing"*), a translation from the Italian of P. F. Tosi; Marpurg's *Kunst das Clavier zu spielen* (*"Art of Keyboard Playing"*) had already appeared in 1750–51. In 1755 the same author published his *Anleitung zum Clavierspielen* (*"Guide to Keyboard Playing"*), and in 1763 his *Anleitung zur Musik und Singkunst* (*"Guide to Music and the Art of Singing"*). Men like Marpurg and J. P. Kirnberger published their textbooks on harmony and composition in Berlin — works that offered solid nourishment to innumerable musicians. All these books rank as masterpieces of pedagogy that combine practical teaching with theoretical and esthetic instruction. Young classical musicians grew up with K. P E. Bach's book, just as the Greek youths of an earlier age grew up with the *Iliad* and the *Odyssey*.

Nor did Berlin lack men who were able to predigest the French ideas of the Age of Reason for the tender stomachs of the middle classes. One of these popularizers was Christoph Friedrich Nicolai, sober, narrow, and yet honest in his convictions. His *Bibliothek der schönen Wissenschaften* (*"Library of Arts and Letters"*) (1757–58), his *Allgemeine Deutsche Bibliothek* (*"General German Library"*) (1765–92), and his *Neue Allgemeine Bibliothek* (*"New General Library"*) (1793–1805) were the weapons with which he fought for religious and social enlightenment. This influential writer was a friend to Agricola, Marpurg, and J. F. Reichardt, the leaders of contemporary music theory in Berlin. Nicolai's magazines spread their ideas and influence throughout

Germany. When the Swiss esthetician Johann Georg Sulzer was preparing his *Allgemeine Theorie der schönen Künste* (*"General Theory of the Fine Arts"*), published between 1771 and 1774, he invited Kirnberger to write about musical matters. In 1773, however, Kirnberger was replaced by his pupil J. A. P. Schulz. Thus the musical doctrines of the Berlin theorists influenced the most important textbooks on esthetics in the second half of the eighteenth century.

III. FRIEDRICH WILHELM MARPURG (1718–95)

The greatest of the theorists in the time of Frederick the Great was Friedrich Wilhelm Marpurg. What Mattheson was to Hamburg, Marpurg was to Berlin: the standard-bearer of rationalistic ideas, a man of extraordinary learning, great in knowledge, in ability, and in pugnacity. When Marpurg attacked the other Berlin bigwig, Agricola, in his magazine *Der critische Musicus an der Spree* (*"The Critical Musician along the River Spree"*) or in the daily *Spener'sche Zeitung*, the effect was as if a mighty man-of-war had fired a broadside. As a young man, he had lived in Paris. Voltaire, D'Alembert, and Maupertuis were his friends. In 1749 he came to Berlin to become director of the royal lottery and counselor of war. In 1795, at the age of seventy-seven, he passed away in the city of his choice.

Marpurg might well be called a one-man academy of science, for he published books on all musical matters. Eleven of them dealt with theoretical questions; among them were textbooks on theory and composition, on piano playing, and on singing. And many of these enjoyed fame far beyond the borders of Prussia. His *Anleitung zum Clavierspielen* (*"Guide to Keyboard Playing"*), published in 1755, was translated into both French and Dutch; his *Abhandlung von der Fuge* (*"Treatise on the Fugue"*) — still, I think, the best book on the fugue — was also published in a French edition. In addition to these theoretical books, Marpurg published critical and historical works. Like all German scholars of the period, he was profound, thorough, and

precise. In the eighteenth century, it seems, only French scholars possessed the ability to give ease, charm, and lucidity to
scientific language, and only the English knew the secret of
writing simply and naturally. Marpurg, typically German in
his approach to scientific problems, moved slowly and ponderously like a great whale. When, in 1759, he published his
Kritische Einleitung in die Geschichte der Musik ("*Critical Introduction to the History of Music*"), he carried his work no further
than the ancient Greeks.

Among Marpurg's merits was his effort to promote the circulation of D'Alembert's *Eléments de musique théorique et pratique
suivant les principes de M. Rameau* ("*Elements of Theoretical and
Practical Music according to the Principles of M. Rameau*") in Germany. Marpurg published an annotated translation of it five
years after the essay first appeared in France.

We have already had occasion to mention his magazine, *Der
critische Musicus an der Spree*, which began publication on
March 4, 1749, and appeared weekly until February 17, 1750.
Articles by both German and French authors were included, the
latter in translation. Among the German contributors was
Lessing, who, incidentally, was also the author of a theatrical
satire on the Italian taste in opera, entitled *Tarantula*.

In 1754, Marpurg began the publication of another magazine,
the *Historisch-Kritische Beyträge zur Aufnahme der Musik* ("*His-
torico-Critical Contributions to the Appreciation of Music*"), which
ran to five volumes, each volume appearing in six numbers.
Every issue contained articles (including translations from the
French), reviews of musical books and compositions, biographies of musicians, reports on opera and concert activities in
Paris and on orchestral and other musical organizations in Germany, as well as anecdotes of the musical world. Among the
more significant items is a list of German operas, published in
the second volume, and a poem on Bach by Telemann, published
in the sixth issue of the first volume. Nor are musical supple-
ments lacking, for we find poems by Lessing set to music by
K. P. E. Bach and Agricola.

Marpurg began a third musical magazine in 1759, the *Kritische Briefe über die Tonkunst* ("*Critical Letters on Music*"). This was published in four parts, as was the second volume, which followed in 1763. Each issue contained a serious article on some theoretical question (for example, a theory of measure, instructions for composing a text, lessons on recitative, letters on the fugue, contributions to the history of music) as well as biographies and anecdotes.

The influence of Marpurg, Kirnberger, and their fellows was so great that Berlin long remained the center of theory and criticism. The musical magazines edited by Johann Friedrich Reichardt at the end of the eighteenth century reinforced the foundations laid by Marpurg.

While the other northern cities joined Berlin in active musical criticism, southern Germany and Austria remained lands of musicians; their air was full of sound and melody. The common people as well as the higher classes of society were musical. At the same time that the King of Prussia prided himself on speaking only French, the Empress Maria Theresia spoke the Viennese dialect of the common folk. So popular themes, folk songs and folk dances, made their way into the great music of the classics, where today we still enjoy them.

There was not in the north, as there was in the south, any connection between high society and the common people. The classes were separated by language, mentality, and manners. There was, in short, less nature in the north, and more intellect. Compared with K. P. E. Bach, Haydn was a man of the people. Musical theory prospered in the colder, dryer air of northern Germany, where pines grew in the sandy plains and where the sea air turned the sails of the windmills. Critical thinking had a larger place there than it had in the sensuous south. The Protestant beliefs of northern Germany sobered the mind, as the festive and splendid Catholicism of the south did not. Thus northern Germany became the center of modern critical ideas, of reason, of enlightenment, and the country of the first musical magazines and the first music critics.

LEIPZIG

I. LEIPZIG: THE CITY AND THE UNIVERSITY

If Hamburg was a great seaport, and Berlin the capital of the rising power of Prussia, Leipzig was the great fair of Germany, situated as it was on the border between the west and the Slavic east. In the Leipzig market one could see strange folk: Russians with high fur caps and tall boots, Poles with the timid air of an oppressed people, and Jews with the great curling beards of oriental patriarchs. But Leipzig was more than a market town; she was the center of the book trade, and her university was one of the most famous in Germany. There Christian Thomasius, the great champion of enlightenment, had dared to lecture on the new philosophy of reason dressed in modern clothes, with his golden sword at his side, instead of in the somber black traditionally worn by medieval scholars. And there the philosopher Leibnitz, a son of Leipzig, had studied.

From the day that Johann Christoph Gottsched began his lectures at the university in 1730, the old city became the most important outpost on the battlefield of new ideas. Young students felt still younger in the invigorating air of the town. In 1765 Goethe came to Leipzig from Frankfort to study at the university. In *Faust* Goethe reminds his readers of Leipzig, saying, "It is a little Paris and cultivates its people."

II. LORENZ CHRISTOPH MIZLER (1711–78)

In 1736, one year before Scheibe published the first issue of *Der critische Musikus* in Hamburg, Lorenz Christoph Mizler inaugurated his musical magazine *Neu eröffnete musikalische Bibliothek* [1] in Leipzig. The new periodical proved to be a great

[1] The full title, well suited to a more leisurely age, reads in English: "Newly Established Musical Library, or Thorough Report and Impartial Judgment on Musical Compositions and Books, in which All that Pertains to Mathematics, Philosophy, and Esthetics, and Serves for the Improvement and Explanation of Theoretical and Practical Music, Is Gradually Introduced."

storehouse of theoretical research and musical science. The first volume was published in six parts and appeared in 1736; three more volumes followed in 1743, 1752, and 1754 respectively. Each part is heavily laden with learned essays on musical history, acoustics, esthetics, and kindred topics, with reports of concerts and new books and musical news and anecdotes also occupying an important place. As in all contemporary magazines, argument and discussion played an important role. The century was not a polite one; music criticism was as rough in Leipzig as it was in Berlin, and Mizler vehemently attacked Scheibe, who as vehemently defended himself and attacked in turn. Mizler's special talent was in acoustics, a problem at that time being scientifically investigated by D'Alembert in France and Leonard Euler in Germany. An essay by the latter on new musical theory was published in Mizler's magazine. The chief contributor, however, was the great oracle of the Leipzig university, Professor Gottsched. Some of his most important essays — among them those on the origin and age of music and the quality of songs, on cantatas, and on the opera — appeared side by side with ponderously learned theoretical articles.

In the fourth volume Mizler published an obituary poem on Johann Sebastian Bach. When only nineteen years old and a student at the university, Mizler had been one of Bach's private pupils. He dedicated his dissertation, *Quod musica ars sit pars eruditionis musicae* ("*That the Art of Music is a Part of Musical Learning*"), to his master in 1734. This Lorenz Christoph Mizler was certainly a great scholar — not without that mixture of oddity and whim that characterizes so many scholars. At the university of Leipzig, he lectured on mathematics, philosophy, and music. Believing in the progress of science, he founded a society in 1738, called the "Association of Musical Sciences," from which he proudly expected the rise of a new period in music. Telemann was a member; Handel was named an honorary member; and Bach was invited to join. But Bach did not like discussions of music, since he believed that a true musician would be kept sufficiently busy writing scores, and hence ought not to waste his time on research. So he sent Mizler the score of his canonic variations on the Christmas song *Vom Himmel Hoch*, as well as a triple canon in six voices, in lieu of an application for admission. Thus, in 1747, he became the fourteenth member of Mizler's society.

The new magazine was the official journal of the society, so it was entirely fitting that it should publish this obituary poem, which appeared some four years after the composer's death. The poem was followed by a *Singgedicht*, the text of a well-meant but badly rhymed cantata deploring the passing of Bach. The text begins with the statement that Leipzig is mourning the death of the composer who has given so much to the city and the several countries of Europe and is now a corpse. After this preliminary lament, composers and lovers of music give vent to their grief in irregular verses — in which they are joined by the members of Mizler's musical society. The cantata ends with Bach's comforting the mourners by informing them that musical conditions in heaven are even better than they were in Leipzig.

Mizler, in whom the contemporary penchant for long-winded titles was well developed, published in 1739 *The Elements of Thorough Bass Treated According to Mathematical Method, and Distinctly Explained by Means of a Machine Invented for that Purpose.* In 1739–40, he edited another magazine, which bore the somewhat clinical title, *The Musical Operator on Cataracts, Wherein the Mistakes of Honest Musical Experts Are to Be Modestly Noted, but Wherein the Follies of the So-called Self-made Composers Are to Be Made Ridiculous.* In spite of its extensive ambitions, only nine issues of this magazine appeared. After translating Fux's *Gradus ad Parnassum* from Latin into German, Mizler went to Poland as court mathematician. The university of Erfurt conferred the title of doctor of medicine upon him, and in Warsaw he was ennobled as an Aulic counselor, physician in ordinary, and historian. When he died in 1778, he bore the proud title Mizler von Kolof in place of the unadorned, thoroughly bourgeois Mizler.

III. JOHANN ADAM HILLER (1728–1804)

At the end of the eighteenth century musical criticism in Leipzig was represented by one of the most amiable of musicians, Johann Adam Hiller, who established his musical magazine *Wöchentliche Nachrichten und Anmerkungen, die Musik betreffend* ("News of the Week and Notes Concerning Music") on July 1, 1766. Hiller was one of the most popular composers in Germany. The simple, heartfelt tunes of his arias met with the plain taste of the middle classes which formed the audience of the *Singspiele*. Hiller had the gift of understanding the needs and tastes of the modest shopkeepers and merchants who lived in the small rooms of bourgeois Leipzig houses, who furnished their homes with old-fashioned mahogany pieces, and from whose clean-curtained windows wives and maids occasionally peered, snatching a moment from their embroidering frames to let their longing thoughts wander. When these people went to the Leipzig theaters, they wanted to see simple plays with characters drawn from the people, with some humor, some sentimentality, and much love. Christian Felix Weisse's librettos, which Hiller set to music, followed the French *vaudeville* of Favart. These were idyllic plays, which contrasted the country folk with the aristocrats of the city. Weisse had been in Paris from 1759 to 1760, and had studied these works of Favart, which had so successfully expressed the feelings of the lower middle classes.

Hiller's music was admirably adapted to these librettos. His soul was the soul of a simple man with pure feelings — well evidenced, perhaps, in the many song books he published for children. Almost without trying, he found a natural and charming musical expression for the arias of his peasant girls and of his middle-class characters. The aristocrats in his *Singspiele* sang elaborate arias, but his middle-class lovers sang popular tunes, melodiously tender, and with that admixture of philistine feeling that is so necessary for popular success on the stage.

Hiller's *Singspiele* soon became popular in other German cities.

It was easy to sing the simple melodies, for they did not demand trained voices. Almost any actor could sing Hiller's tunes, and with them move the audiences in the barns and inns where the popular theater of the time was staged. In short, this kind of art was simple, unsophisticated, and clear, and Hiller's music impressed the German lower middle classes with the modern taste of the Age of Reason. This French taste was, of course, watered down with German philistinism, but even in this simplified form it represented the most modern contemporary taste.

Hiller (who had become cantor of St. Thomas's School in 1789) showed the same feeling for popular taste in his musical magazine. Until his time musical magazines had been written for theorists and by theorists. Hiller was the first editor who cared for the music lover as well as for the professional musician. The learned theoretical articles that filled the first musical magazines are missing. There are reports on musical organizations, opera houses and orchestras, and reviews of books and compositions. The reviews of compositions contain quotations from the music under review.

IV. MUSICAL CRITICISM IN THE GENERAL MAGAZINES

A clear sign that interest in music was increasing and that the musical public was growing is to be found in the fact that more and more musical articles appeared in general magazines. "*The German Museum*" published articles on music in many of its issues between 1776 and 1788. Two were by Johann Friedrich Reichardt, the Prussian court conductor; another, "Repetition in Music," was by Christian Gottlob Neefe, Beethoven's teacher.

Valuable articles on musical subjects also appeared in "*The German Mercury*," which was founded and edited by the poet Wieland. In it we find articles on Gluck's *Iphigenia in Aulis*, on Pergolesi's *Stabat Mater*, on Wieland's own opera *Alcestis* (the article, incidentally, is by Wieland himself), on the German *Singspiel*, on Italian music, and in fact on all manner of musical subjects. A striking feature of the magazine is its glowing enthusiasm for Gluck.

Political journals also began to open their columns to musical articles. Thus the *Frankfurter gelehrte Zeitung* ("*News of the Learned World*") published a series of articles on harmony, melody, orchestral instruments, accompaniment, etc. — all didactic in tendency. Among the subjects dealt with, the thorny one of criticism is not lacking. A book entitled *Truth about Music, Frankly Spoken out by an Honest German Man*, containing a collection of these articles, appeared in Frankfurt in 1770.

Knowledge of music, love of music penetrated the middle-class society that was superseding the aristocrats in supporting the arts. The musical magazines had consequently to adjust themselves to the taste of their readers. They had to become less learned, less stuffed with theory, less highbrow. This change began at the end of the eighteenth century. In the following years, the old-type music critic, the great theorist, the ponderous authority, the musical senator who wrote and thought with weight and profundity, became obsolete. They had been strong men, hard, coarse, and ready to fight. They had been men produced by the Protestantism of North Germany, molded by the thunderous preaching in the Gothic churches. The wrath of Bach was terrible. He is known to have threatened a student with his sword and to have shouted at his choir. Handel held the singer Cuzzoni on a window ledge and threatened to push her out if she refused to sing one of his arias. The King of Prussia shook his cane at his grenadiers when they faltered, and shouted, "You dogs, do you want to live forever?" The generations of men between 1650 and 1750 were vigorous and hearty. Bach wrote more than three hundred cantatas, Telemann more than six hundred overtures, Kuhnau fourteen annual sets of cantatas for Sundays and feastdays, Handel more than eighty operas and oratorios. The music critics were like the other great men of the day — boulders of men; like Mattheson and Marpurg — not elegant, pliant, and quick, like the modern journalists who whisk like lizards through the concert halls.

For these men reason, nature, simplicity, lucidity, intellectual greatness, and human feeling were not hollow catchwords. They believed in the power of the human intellect to create beauty. They did not indulge in skepticism. They had confidence in the artistic laws revealed to them by reasonable thinking. The words humanity, intellect, rationality, naturalness, sounded for them like the organ in a church.

Chapter Five

THE FIRST CONFLICT BETWEEN CRITIC AND COMPOSER

IT IS a strange fact in the history of musical criticism that, at the moment it first entered the world, the first clash between this new force and creative power occurred. Similar conflicts have accompanied the whole development of music, from Bach to Stravinsky and Schœnberg. Ever since the middle of the eighteenth century the world has been filled with the noise and fury of the struggle. Perhaps this is an inevitable and essential part of progress; perhaps it must accompany all great composers, just as military bands accompany an army into battle.

Such conflicts between great musicians and critics (both good and bad) do not interest historians as evidence of human narrowmindedness, stupidity, vanity, or vindictiveness. Nobody knows better than the historian that weakness is the common heritage of man, and that wisdom, justice, and understanding are commodities not to be found at every street corner. When a reader reproached Bernard Shaw with the injustice of a criticism, Shaw replied, "No doubt I was unjust; who am I that I should be just?" Conflicts between critics and artists can be profitably analyzed only when they are the necessary result of different outlooks on the world: conflicts, for example, between generations or periods. These are not personal matters, but matters of logic; one might say that they are conflicts produced by the development of historical trends, by God himself, it may be, as He struggles with his own critic, the devil.

The first conflict in modern musical history is of this type: it

was the product of historical development. The conflict between Johann Sebastian Bach and Johann Adolf Scheibe demands detailed analysis, for it proved to be typical of most sub-
sequent disputes between artist and critic. The conflict between
Bach and Scheibe was not — at least, not entirely — a personal
thing. Two great representatives of different epochs stood face
to face; the opposed mentalities of two great ages of history
clashed. The musician was the greatest composer of the Baroque period; the critic was one of the leading German expo-
nents of the Age of Reason, an age which had moved away from
the frenzied extravagance of Baroque art. The conflict between
the heated imagination of the Baroque artist and the rational
lucidity of the Enlightenment was inevitable, as were similar
struggles that appeared under different names in different ages.
In Bach's time it was the conflict between rationalism and
Baroque imagination; at the beginning of the nineteenth century, it was the struggle between classicism and romanticism.
It is a part of the everlasting struggle between fantasy and reason, between imagination and intellect, between the forces of
the unconscious and of consciousness.

Ernest Newman, in his spirited book, *A Musical Critic's Holiday*, has attempted to minimize the importance of these conflicts between creative fantasy and critical sobriety. He uses a
wealth of historical knowledge, a polished style, wit and
common sense to whitewash Scheibe and the other critics of
great composers. He says, in effect, that Scheibe was not wholly
wrong as against Bach; that there is some truth in the charge
that Bach was labored, intricate, and over-elaborate. So, too,
the critics of Mozart, Beethoven, Wagner, and other great
artists were not entirely wrong in their analyses — a fact that
may comfort all imprudent critics as well as the public at large.

But the truth about Scheibe is that he was wrong, totally
wrong, when he found Bach's music labored, intricate, and over-
elaborate. He was wrong, as Hanslick was wrong about Wagner, Liszt, and Bruckner. But Scheibe had to be wrong, for he
was the representative of an epoch that preferred clarity to ex-

uberant fancy. He could not understand the floridity of Bach's music. He would have been insincere had he pretended to comprehend Baroque opulence and emotion.

Scheibe's inability to understand Bach's music need not be excused, but it must be explained. To explain it, we must know the tendencies of the age, its musical taste and conflicts, its critical and esthetic trends. We must know the leading contemporary figures in musical society and the rapid transformation which that society was undergoing. And we must know these things as they influenced or made up a part of the musical life of Leipzig.

II

Bach's long connection with Leipzig begins on May 31, 1723, for on that day he was inducted into his new office as cantor of St. Thomas's. On that day, for the first time, he entered his apartment in the left wing of the St. Thomas schoolhouse: a three-story, squat, heavy building. From the windows of his new lodgings, Bach could look out at the fountain in the small square, and at the adjacent church, with its high Gothic windows and its steeple with the Baroque cap. Here Bach lived for twenty-seven years; here, at the age of sixty-five he died, and from here his body was carried to St. John's Cemetery.

Every morning the Cantor of St. Thomas's went to the school in the same building and taught singing and theory, and, for some time, Latin as well. Every Saturday afternoon after vespers, he rehearsed his choir in the new cantata he had written for the Sunday service. All in all, Bach wrote about three hundred of these cantatas, in addition to the Passions, oratorios, and motets performed at Mass and vespers. He sat at the organ every Sunday and feastday, conducting both his choir of thirteen voices and his orchestra of about twenty pieces. Occasionally he would grow angry with the choir, pull his great wig from his head, and hurl it at the boys.

The service was opened with the powerful voice of the organ, and it was closed with a mighty fugue. Bach played wonderful preludes to the chorales, which the parishioners sang standing, and between the hymns, sermon, and anthems he improvised, letting his fancy soar in the jubilant counterpoint of his organ. When a parishioner died, Bach, bareheaded, led the mourners' procession and conducted one of his pensive motets at the grave. Thus Bach's music wove itself into the religious life of Leipzig, both in its sad and in its festive moods. He was a religious man himself, perhaps even a mystic, who struggled his whole life with thoughts of life and death, of redemption and sin. His last work was a touching chorale prelude entitled *Before Thy Throne, My God, I Stand.*

Cantors like Bach lived in every town of Protestant Germany. Bach looked like them, and they looked like him. They all seemed to be dignified middle-class men, dressed in black, with big, heavy wigs falling to their shoulders and billowing neckerchiefs under their chins. They, like Bach, begot a multitude of children and educated their sons to be musicians. They sat at the organ and played chorale preludes, fantasies, and fugues. They composed cantatas for every Sunday and every feastday, for Good Friday vespers they wrote Passions, and for funerals they produced motets to glorify the eternal life. In some cities the office of cantor seemed almost hereditary. It went from father to son or to son-in-law. All these cantors and organists in German cities belonged to one great family of musicians, connected by one strong tradition. They were different from the opera composers, the Italian virtuosos, and the French harpsichord and viol players.

For men of this kind, music was connected with religion. Bach wrote "S.D.G." (*Soli Deo Gloria*) on many of his scores. And on the front page of his *Orgelbüchlein* he wrote the couplet, "Dem höchsten Gott allein zu Ehren, dem Nächsten draus sich zu belehren." ("For the glory of the most high God alone, and for my neighbor to learn from.") "The end and goal of thorough bass is nothing but the honor of God," he wrote on the manuscript of the rules of accompaniment that he had sketched out for his pupils. It is not strange to discover, then, that none of the great works he composed for the church, none of his Passions, magnificats, or oratorios (and only one of the more than three hundred cantatas) was ever published by Bach. Like all German church music of the seventeenth and eighteenth centuries, they were written for the honor of the Almighty.

Bach and his fellow organists and cantors belonged to a closed society. Whether to join that restricted group or to leave Germany was the question that confronted young German musicians. Handel, for example, could have succeeded the famous organist Buxtehude in Lübeck, on condition of marrying his predecessor's daughter. Had he agreed, he might have written innumerable cantatas, motets, and Passions, and might, perhaps, have begotten plenty of children. But Handel's personality was too keen, too much in love with freedom, too powerful. It demanded more room than Protestant Germany could offer, it demanded fresher air. So Handel declined the Lübeck position and went to Italy, where he began his European career. We say "European," because the music in which the European spirit expressed itself at that time was operatic and worldly, not ecclesiastical. All the new moods, all the new feelings of the new period, all its passions, were to be found in the arias of its operas and in the instrumental works played by its orchestras. No other music was so thoroughly appreciated in the great centers of Europe as that of Hasse, Telemann, Scarlatti, Handel, Stamitz, and Rameau.

Bach, however, did not belong to this larger world. His reputation as an organist was widespread, but it was a provincial fame, far from the European reputation that Handel enjoyed.

III

Leipzig, as we have pointed out in the last chapter, was one of the German cities most receptive to new ideas. Bach must have felt himself a stranger there, for on every side he met with uncongenial modern ideas. The world was changing from day to day before his eyes, and Leipzig was enthusiastically welcom-

ing the new French music, so different from the great polyphonic
compositions of the past. The year 1736 saw the publication in
Leipzig of a most successful song collection, the *Singende Muse
an der Pleisse* (*"Singing Muse on the River Pleisse"*), edited by
Johann Sigismund Scholze who assumed the more gorgeous
appelation of "Sperontes." In the engraved frontispiece we
see the Leipzig of Bach's time, with its walls that served as
promenades, and St. Thomas's church and School. The songs
in the book were set to instrumental tunes after the French manner — a fact which pleased the students of the university town
mightily. They were children of the times, and when Telemann
founded his Collegium Musicum right under Bach's nose, the
students ran straight to the modernist who stripped music of all
the weight of counterpoint.

Even Bach's own sons regarded their father as if he belonged
to an outmoded world. K. P. E. Bach spoke ironically about
canons "which are always dry, pretentious music." "Music,"
he said, "need not be a great party where all the people speak
simultaneously." Bach's son had traveled so far from the contrapuntal art of his father that he was able to call him "an old
bigwig." All of the old man's sons had plunged into the fresh
stream of new, melodious, homophonic music, which carried
them far from the high shadowy mountains of polyphony on
which their father had spoken with God in sublime loneliness.

Everywhere in old Leipzig new and popular melodies were to
be heard. An orchestra player in Koch's theatrical company in
Berlin, J. S. Standfuss by name, wrote new tunes for Coffey's
The Devil to Pay, a comical picture of marriage. Christian Felix
Weisse, a friend of the poet Lessing's, had written a new German
text, and in this revised form the comedy was played in Leipzig
in 1752. It was an immediate hit. The whole town sang its
tunes, which were inspired by the songs of the French *opéra
comique* that Weisse adored. When, some years later, Hiller
began writing his pleasant tunes, Leipzig became the center of
this kind of music.

Thus the lonely island on which Bach had been writing his

scores was surrounded by the inexorably rising waters of a new music. This music ranged from the simple songs of the people, through the glittering Italian coloratura arias, to the great recitatives that painted all human emotions. There was sweet and sensuous music, as in Keiser's operas; there were solemn, broad melodies, as in Handel's, or lovely tunes as in Hasse's. The Mannheim masters wrote symphonies changing in mood and flaming with passion, or chamber music in which temperament exploded in energetic rhythms. Telemann and Mattheson brought the vivid colors and the dramatic melodies of the new age to the oratorio. Musicians felt that the world was changing and progressing from day to day.

Critical ideas followed the same pattern as music itself; they too developed from day to day. Leipzig was no exception. There Gottsched, the dictator of German literary taste between 1730 and 1740, ruled as a professor in the university. He had come from Prussia, where the recruiting officers had shown an unwelcome zeal in trying to make him a squad-leader in the Prussian Guard. Notwithstanding his flight, Gottsched proved himself a valiant warrior in the struggle for modern French ideas. He did his part in spreading Boileau's rationalistic ideas throughout Germany. He glorified clarity, and attacked the extravagant bombast of Baroque poetry and Baroque music. His *Handlexicon der schönen Wissenschaften* (*"Dictionary of Arts and Letters"*) sowed the seeds of French philosophy and esthetics; and his *Redekunst* and *Kritische Dichtkunst* (*"Art of Rhetoric," "Critical Approach to the Art of Poetry"*) were influential all over Germany.

Gottsched was an unwearied fighter. He fought for the French theater, made regular by the unities of time and place. He opposed, as was to be expected, the German popular theater, where Harlequin, the improvising fun-maker, displayed his theatrical fancies much as the Broadway comedians of the present day display theirs. He was the adversary of the ostentatious Baroque opera, which covered the whole of Europe like a gorgeous spreading plant. "The opera," he echoed innumerable

French authors in saying, "is the most stupid thing that human reason ever produced. Reason may be left at home if only the ears are tickled and the eyes dazzled." [1] Or, "Opera is a senseless hodge-podge of poetry and music where poet and musician take equal pains to produce a bad work." [2] Or "Leave your reason at home and take only your ears with you when you go to an opera house . . . . In operas no one speaks in such a way as to express his nature, his profession, or his personality. For the sake of a long shake, an otherwise quite reasonable person must often do a most stupid thing by singing in Italian what might better be told in German." [3]

A generation later Gluck, in his famous Preface to *Alceste*, was to expand Gottsched's ideas, when he wrote, "I tried to remove all the abuses against which good taste and reason have long raised their voices. I believed that I should dedicate the greatest part of my work to aspire to beautiful simplicity and to avoid boasting of artificial devices at the expense of clarity."

Gottsched founded one magazine after another, in order to attack Baroque taste on all sides. He was fighting for the French ideal of reasonableness and clarity. His importance lies in the fact that he was the most efficient propagandist for the new epoch of reason.

And Scheibe, the critic of Bach, was Gottsched's pupil. Hence he measured Bach according to his master's standards. He weighed Bach's music in the scales of contemporary French rationalism and found the music too heavy, too full of religious mysticism and polyphonic thoughtfulness, too massive in construction, and too passionate.

Bach had no connection with that world of revolutionary ideas which was soon to destroy the last trace of the Middle Ages and was to create a new society and a new way of life. He kept at a distance from Gottsched and his group. Once, in the autumn of 1727, he set one of Gottsched's cantatas, the *Trauerode* ("*Mourning Ode*"), to music for the funeral service of Queen Christiana in St. Paul's church at Leipzig. In 1737 Gottsched

[1] *Kritische Dichtkunst.*   [2] *Der Biedermann.*   [3] *Kritische Dichtkunst.*

wanted his beautiful young wife to study music with Bach, but the master was not interested and recommended her to his pupil Krebs, who grew enthusiastic over the beauty to which the domestic Bach had been indifferent. This seems to be all that is known about the relationship between Bach and one of the most influential personages in Leipzig. Bach and Gottsched lived on different planets.

Bach, refusing to change, was the last and greatest of a long line of musicians who had developed the polyphonic style, and the successor of the great contrapuntists who had written their Masses and motets for the Netherlands churches. Just as in the music of Josquin Desprez, Ockeghem, or Orlandus Lassus, so in Bach's music the voices majestically resound, not as the songs and voices of single men, but as the music of the universe. And the older Bach grew, the more abstract his musical form became. His *Art of the Fugue* and *Musical Offering* display a contrapuntal art distinctive not so much for the color of life as for the spiritual form of thought.

Thus Bach disappeared on the heights of music, a lonely figure. His work was not essentially connected with the work of the day; hence his contemporaries could not see the real Bach. He was to them a great organist, whose pedaling let loose the thunder. There is a list in Mizler's *Bibliothek* (published in 1754) of the famous German composers. They are set down in this order: Hasse, Handel, Telemann, the two Graun brothers, Stölzel, Bach, Pisendel, Quantz, and Bümmler. Bach stands in the seventh place; the first six are representatives of the modern movement. Bach, of course, was too great to be completely ignored, yet how small was his reputation in comparison with the fame of Hasse, Handel, Telemann, and the Grauns!

IV

We must acquaint ourselves with Scheibe's ideas in order to understand why he could not judge Bach otherwise than as he did. Under the perspective of rationalistic ideas, he almost had to see Bach, the polyphonic master, in distorted proportions.

To evaluate him properly, Scheibe would have to have understood the contrast between Bach and the age, and this he was incapable of doing. His model was Gottsched, his ideas were the rationalistic esthetic ideas of the new era. He preached with fervor on behalf of a return to simple nature, and he predicted that the opera of the future would be music drama. No doubt Scheibe impressed Gluck, just as Gottsched had, and was partly responsible for some of Gluck's reforms.

"A musical composition," Scheibe wrote, "must not only be pleasant and tickle the ear, it must also please the reason." Again, "The creative faculty is the quality of a composer which enables him to think musically in a reasonable way." Or, "Musicians must think naturally, reasonably, and sublimely, and possess enlightened reason. . . . Reasonable thinking, knowledge of true beauty, sublimity, and knowledge of the science of beauty combined create good taste in music." He continues, "Musicians must be equipped with strong fantasy and with reasoning power."

Like Gottsched, who followed the lead of the French Encyclopedists in his attacks on the Italian opera, Scheibe furiously assailed Baroque opera, vehemently criticizing librettos, ornate arias, and the lack of connection between words and music. Here also he demanded more reasonableness. "One should aim in opera," he wrote, "more at noble simplicity than at the evil debauchery of Italian opera." He hopes to live to see the epoch "when naturalness, which has until now been banished from music, will be raised to the throne it deserves." He points out that instead of reasonable tragedies, senseless operas are performed, crammed with "machines" and "sorceries." "In our operatic plots," he adds, "almost nothing is coherent. Persons come on the stage without knowing why, and they leave the stage for no better reason than that the role is written so." Scheibe blames "the eternal repetition of words, . . . the long shakes on some syllables," and insists that if one has to speak in musical terms, the meaning of words must not lose its importance. Sounds must fit words, for the expression of meaning is one of the most important problems to be considered by the composer. He adds specific examples to his indictment: "In opera we see those who are supposed to be unhappy shake the words 'dolore,' or 'morire,' their mouths laughing so that the words seem strange when trimmed with these flourishes. . . . It is absurd," he concludes, "for many singers to think that they need to use nothing but their voices."

Scheibe, in reality, is fighting for the musical tragedy. As a pupil of French esthetics, he naturally demands that the unities of time and place that ruled French tragedy should also rule opera. He asks for a "reasonable imitation of nature" on the stage, as well as for proper understanding of the words, for sense, for coherence, and for the natural expression of passions. In short, for the beautiful simplicity and clarity set forth by Gluck in his Preface to *Alceste* as the goal of his work.

Scheibe was neither a stupid nor an insignificant man. He represented his age with knowledge and with conviction. His aim was to promote more naturalness, more reasonableness, more simplicity in music. Reason was the deity of the mid-eighteenth century. Only a few decades later, Reason, represented by a beautiful woman, was set on an altar and adored by the Parisians as the deity of modern times. Reason was the slogan, the battle cry, and the password of the age. And music like Bach's, which mastered irrational forces, was thoroughly unintelligible to a rationalistic age, which was as proud of its critical postulates as we are of our scientific habit of mind.

v

Now the stage is set for the conflict between Bach and Scheibe. The bell rings and the curtain rises, with the audience hissing, in accordance with naïve theater usage, when the villain appears on the scene: the villain here, it goes without saying, is the music critic. Even in 1737 music critics were always to have personal motives for adverse criticism — as critics, it was of course impossible that they should have objective reasons for their judgments. In Scheibe's case, it was whispered through

Leipzig that he was angry at Bach because the older man had rejected the younger's application to become organist at St. Thomas's. Thus gossip in 1737, thus gossip today. Everywhere and eternally one can hear gossip about music critics, whether it be at a party, in a dressing room, or in the privacy of a singer's bedroom.

Scheibe's criticism of Bach was first published in the columns of *Der Critische Musikus* in Hamburg on May 14, 1737. Scheibe was a young man of twenty-eight when he wrote the article, and had, as we have seen, the right to regard himself as one of the representatives of modern taste and as a champion of modern music. Bach's music, judged from that point of view, appeared to Scheibe to be almost purely an example of technique:

The gentleman is the most distinguished of musicians. He is an extraordinary artist on clavier and organ. . . . I have heard him play on several occasions. One is astonished at his craftsmanship. One wonders how it is possible for him to move his fingers and feet so rapidly without entangling them, or how he can stretch them to make the widest leaps without producing one false tone and without distorting his body with such vehement movements.

This great man would be admired by the whole nation, had he more agreeableness and did he not keep naturalness away from his compositions by employing bombastic and intricate devices and darkening beauty with overelaborate art. He judges the difficulties of his music according to his fingers. His compositions, therefore, are difficult to perform, as he demands that singers and instrumentalists perform with their throats and instruments the same feats he can perform on the clavier. This, of course, is impossible. All the ornaments, all the little grace notes, and all that are known as *agréments* are written out in full. Therefore his compositions are deprived of beauty, of harmony, and of clarity of melody, since the song is unrecognizable. All voices must work with each other, all with the same weight, so that it is impossible to recognize the principal voice. In short, Bach is to music what Lohenstein [1] is to poetry. Their inclination toward bombast led them both from naturalness to artificiality, from sublimity to want of clearness. With both one admires the laborious effort and the except-

---

[1] Lohenstein was a bombastic dramatist of the seventeenth century.

ional work expended in vain because they are not conformable to reason.

Reason is, as always, the last word, Scheibe's *ceterum censeo*.

Two men stand on the stage opposite each other: the composer and the critic. Behind them are two different ages, different mentalities, different ideas. The scene might be compared to the scenes of the *Iliad* in which the gods appear behind the fighting heroes to protect their own by interposing a shield or by hurling a spear. There is more to this fight between Scheibe and Bach than the usual quarrel between a critic who opposes either his principles or his intellectual deficiencies to a great musician.

After the first lightning flash of the critical thunderstorm that drove from Hamburg to Leipzig, other strokes followed, though of diminishing strength. One of Bach's friends, Magister Birnbaum, published an anonymous pamphlet answering Scheibe and defending Bach. Scheibe replied that the writer did not understand anything about music. Whereupon Birnbaum published another pamphlet defending himself against the charge that he was an uneducated man. Scheibe answered again, without saying anything of importance. And, indeed, later on, Scheibe used the columns of his magazine to praise Bach's *Italian Concerto*, written in the contemporary homophonic style. But Scheibe was unable to repress the remark that, as a composer of cantatas, Bach was surpassed by Telemann and C. H. Graun.

Bach read Birnbaum's pamphlets with the pleasure every artist takes in seeing his critics answered, and even distributed copies to his friends. But this was not the only way in which he reacted to the annoying criticism. He was an artist, and true artists use all their experience of life in their work; thus did Bach make use of his encounter with Scheibe.

In 1732, he wrote the satirical cantata, *Der Streit zwischen Phoebus und Pan* ("*The Quarrel between Phoebus and Pan*"). Phoebus and Pan compete for a prize offered to the best singer. The judges, Tmolus and Midas, do their best. Tmolus chooses

Phoebus, the god of music; Midas chooses Pan, whose easily remembered melodies "fell on his ear." As the result of his error, Midas is awarded a pair of donkey's ears, and the cantata ends with a chorus praising the music enjoyed by gods and men, music able to withstand all sneers and all criticism. Humor was the means Bach used to relieve his feelings. He enjoyed gibing at the incompetence of critics, and was happy laughing at the dull souls who prefer stupid ditties to beautiful melody.

Three times only in later years have great musicians had the superiority and freedom of mind to dissolve the bitterness of adverse criticism in humor and satire. Eduard Hanslick's fussy vanity and vindictiveness suggested the character of the vain, malicious Beckmesser to Richard Wagner. As a matter of fact, Wagner, in the first version of *Die Meistersinger*, gave the character the all too transparent name of Hans Lick. Hugo Wolf managed to turn the tables on the critics in the composition of the last of his *Mörike* songs. When, in the song, the critic has been thrown out of the artist's room and falls down the stairs with a great crash, Wolf intones a jubilant waltz. And in our own time Richard Strauss put the critics in their place with his *Heldenleben*, in which one can hear the critical voices hissing, screaming, buzzing like wasps, squeaking like toads, and croaking like frogs — a witty use of the orchestra in musical criticism. Thus Bach, Wagner, Wolf, and Strauss saw criticism in its proper perspective, incorporating it into their life and art, and transfiguring its narrow malevolence by means of fantasy, intelligence, and humor.

VI

Why did Scheibe fail in his criticism of Bach? It is not that he was dull; on the contrary, he was a cultured man who thought seriously and honestly on musical problems. He knew his business well, since he was a composer himself — though, like many composers who turn to criticism, he was not a particularly successful one. But he failed because he judged Bach from a point of view that did not fit Bach at all. It did not make the least particle of sense to miss qualities in Bach's music which Bach had never intended to put there. Bach did not want to write music according to contemporary taste. He was essentially a man of the Baroque epoch, and he wrote his music in the Baroque style. It was his misfortune that the Baroque style had gone out of fashion with the rise of the Age of Reason.

The only possible standpoint from which to judge Bach's music is the historical standpoint. Had Scheibe looked upon Bach as a representative of the Baroque age, he would have understood all that he opposed. He would have seen Bach against the whole background of a period that wanted to grasp infinity. He would have understood the pompous style of the polyphonic music — everything that he called bombastic was really only a different way of achieving greatness of expression.

It is not mere chance that all music critics who have used the standards of a formed taste instead of historical standards have failed as Scheibe failed. Musical life is always changing, fluctuating to and fro. There are always new forms, new styles of expression, and new personalities. Any new or uncommon feature of artistic life gives the lie to a formed taste, which, after all, is the wisdom of yesterday.

Does this mean that the critic has to dance every dance, to swing, to turn, to jitterbug without pause? Not at all. But it does mean that he must be enough of a historian to analyze every new fact of musical life, to study the peculiar conditions of each special event. He must think historically.

There must be a reason why history, on the whole, is just, while criticism, on the whole, is unjust. Historians are accustomed to study different times with the same zest, with the same impartiality and objectivity. Historians judge the ages of the Greeks and the Egyptians, the Renaissance and Baroque periods, the Romantic and Industrial eras with impartial eyes. The life of a tribe of cannibals is no less interesting to the true historian than the life of a present-day European country. He analyzes customs and morals, religion and war, in the same spirit in which a naturalist observes the lives of lions, beetles, and infusoria — that is, with equal interest, conscientiousness, and objectivity in either case.

One objection remains to be answered. Is the historical viewpoint adequate to the study of the present? Is there not an essential difference between the evaluation of the events and ideas of the past and the evaluation of contemporary artists who are working for the future? Is not the gaze — the quiet, impartial gaze — of the historian turned backward, and is not the gaze — the passionate gaze — of the critic turned forward? Can the critic make use of historical methods, methods that perhaps inevitably weaken his vigor and his sensitivity at a time when he needs all his imagination and vision to judge music that has just emerged from the steaming kettle of the present and is being served for the first time?

The answer is that there is no present independent of the past, and no new music unconnected with the music of the past. An old oak with huge branches like Bach's music must have had roots deep in the music of the past. Over a century of Protestant church music, the whole development of organ music in Italy, Holland, and Germany, the Italian concertos and chamber music, all helped to provide the rich soil in which Bach's music grew.

The musical life of any period is partly a product of the past. Sometimes, when an old and glorious tradition has been built up, modern composers regard themselves as the heirs of the past. They grow up within the boundaries of settled tradition, as Mozart and Beethoven did. They take over the musical forms and technique of their ancestors, as the heirs of great fortunes take over the property of their fathers and try to enlarge it. Other composers seek shelter with the great men of the past in order to find shelter from the blowing storm. Brahms was such a man. From time to time composers endeavor to run away from the past; for example, the Florentine composers who lived around 1600 detested the contrapuntal music of their predecessors. Though they lived in the same age with Palestrina, whose polyphonic compositions filled the Sistine chapel with splendor, they regarded counterpoint much as Debussy was later to regard it: as the artificial and complicated lock to a strongroom. They hated the forms and techniques of the past, and preferred their dry, primitive recitative to the elaborate masses of Palestrina, Josquin Desprez, and Orlandus Lassus. In like manner, the composers of the Age of Reason ran away from polyphonic music; and today we see the same panicky fear of the past in Arnold Schœnberg, a fear which led him to detest the colorful romanticism of his first compositions and to destroy the harmonic, technical, and formal foundation of classical music. All musicians of these revolutionary schools that deny the past have written music, one might almost say, with a negative sign. They have not stopped to think that negative and positive are but different aspects of numbers, and that one complements the other. No living composer can escape history. Even he who thinks to destroy the past or to escape from it remains chained to it by hatred or contempt.

Only a thorough understanding of this fact enables the critic, aided by full historical knowledge, to understand the musical life of his contemporaries. Thus equipped he has a strong foundation for his analyses. There are always similarities and relationships between the past and the present which help us toward a better understanding of contemporary music. Ernest Newman was right when he said, "Teach me rightly to admire Bach and Mozart and I will find my own criticism of living composers. Help me to enjoy, however feebly, Palestrina or Purcell, and I will promise not to lose my head over Puccini's *Manon*. Fire my enthusiasm for Wagner or Brahms, and I shall be able to distinguish between the muses of Darius Milhaud and Erik Satie." Seen from the height of a historical watchtower, the musicians of the present do not seem greatly different from those of the past. The struggles and the quarrels of the present belong to the same family as the struggles and quarrels of the past. Musical life, with its enthusiasms and hatreds, its admirations and its skepticisms, remains much the same in all ages. Musical criticism needs the wider field of vision that only the historical approach can afford.

Chapter Six

THE BATTLES AGAINST THE BAROQUE: THE MUSIC CRITICS IN THE FIGHT

I. BAROQUE AND THE AGE OF REASON

THE CONFLICT between Bach and Scheibe was but one small action in the great battle between the old and the new which was being fought throughout all Europe between 1720 and 1750. It was the same struggle: scientific clarity against religious emotion, lucidity against mysticism, natural feeling against extravagance, simplicity against bombast, reason against exaltation, and a sense of proportion against floridity. All these conflicts characterize the transition from the Baroque period to the classicism of the eighteenth century. The chief actors were the statesmen, philosophers, scholars, artists, journalists, critics, and even the people themselves, whose voice can be heard in the choruses of Handel's great oratorios and Bach's chorales.

On October 19, 1739, Frederick (who was then Crown Prince of Prussia) wrote to Prince William of Orange: "Please give assurances of my esteem to your wife. She honored me too highly in thinking of me when mentioning the operas of Handel. I am infinitely obliged to her for her touching attention. But please tell her that Handel's good days are over. His brains are exhausted and his taste is out of fashion." And, indeed, the Baroque taste was going out of fashion. It had dominated Europe for one hundred and forty years, and the might of its style had been demonstrated by men as diverse as Velasquez, Rembrandt, Milton, Rubens, Van Dyck, Bernini, Calderon, Purcell, Carissimi, Lully, and others no less important. Michelangelo's treatment of the dome of Saint Peter's in Rome is sufficient evidence that the Baroque manner has never been surpassed in abundance, power, and magnitude.

The Baroque style may be said to have been inaugurated in 1568, when Vignola began building the Gesù church in Rome, employing a new theatrical and ostentatious mode. It rose to its greatest heights in the seventeenth century, when the Thirty Years War set central Europe ablaze. But by the beginning of the eighteenth century the first signs of decadence had appeared. The great lines became graceful. The feeling for great spaces diminished and dissolved into refined delicacy. The picturesque, impressionistic fancy of Rococo art spread through Europe like a new fragrance, and painting, music, and the other fine arts were affected, together with the applied arts. The giant canvasses on which Rubens and Tintoretto had painted their great historical allegories shrank to more human dimensions; and the discovery of porcelain as a suitable material for small statuettes began the vogue for little images of shepherds watching their flocks, of shepherdesses with their staffs in their pretty hands, and for representations of mannered dancers measuring the affected figures of their dance. The giant of the Baroque style had been transformed into an effeminate worldling with refined taste and impotent longings.

The middle of the seventeenth century saw the beginning of the French struggle against the pomposity and ostentation, the festooned splendor and the showy decoration, which characterized the French phase of the Baroque style. The noise of this conflict filled the remainder of the seventeenth and the first half of the eighteenth century with the clash of arms. As might be expected, the music critics played their part in these great battles against the Baroque taste. They were in the vanguard of that army of philosophers, estheticians, and writers who marched against the mighty forces of an older day — a day that had given free rein to all passion, all lavishness, and all abundance of artistic fancy.

The music critics in Hamburg, Berlin, and Leipzig took up the doctrines of the French estheticians: the theories of Boileau who enjoined mankind to love reason; the advice of the Abbé Pluche in his *Art de la poésie* ("*Art of Poetry*"), "And music, like painting, ought to represent the truth of nature to our senses." This belief that the function of art is to imitate nature dominates the whole eighteenth century.

"Reason" and "Nature": these were the battle cries in the struggle between the Age of Enlightenment and the Baroque epoch. In his *Essai sur le beau* ("*Essay on Beauty*"), Père André analyzes his musical impressions and describes the musician reading a score in these words, "He is reading his score which is written in notes that are eternal and inextinguishable in the book of reason." It follows that since music is to be a reasonable imitation of nature, it must reveal the structure of speech. Music is, according to Fénelon's *Dialogue sur l'éloquence* ("*Dialogue on Eloquence*"), a "kind of passionate declamation" since "it must paint things and express passions." When Lully wanted to create a national French style of opera, he studied the declamation of the great actors of the Comédie Française, Champmeslé, Duclos, and Baron, as they recited the lines of Corneille and Racine before King Louis XIV and his court. He wanted to imitate the intonation of their passionate declamation, which a contemporary account described as a "kind of singing." [1]

All these concepts of music's being a manifestation of speech or an imitation of nature, as well as the other doctrines of the rationalistic approach to music, appeared in the criticisms of Mattheson, Scheibe, and Marpurg, in the musical magazines, and in the periodicals edited by Gottsched. The chief contribution of these first music critics lies in the fact that they gave currency to the ideas of French rationalism, and thus helped to form a new style of music, which finally unfolded its musical and spiritual greatness in the compositions of the "classics."

II.   ITALIAN BAROQUE OPERA IN FRANCE

French opposition to the music of the Baroque period began

---

[1] *Entretiens galants*, 1681.

with criticisms of the profuseness and lavishness of the Italian opera. The seventeenth century is unique in the esteem in which it held opera. Opera houses, of course, have always been filled with enthusiastic audiences roaring applause, but neither the operas of Rossini nor the operas of Meyerbeer, however well they may have been received by jubilant audiences, exercised such an influence as the Baroque opera. The opera of this period was a lavish display of all the arts, a mixture of such diverse elements as light, color, decorative fancy, coloraturas, the voices of *castrati*, colorful pageant scenes, luxurious fancy-dress balls, ballets, and concerts. The world has never since experienced a pyrotechnic display of fancy equal to that of Baroque opera, for in those days opera was not restricted, as it is today, to the opera house. Performances were given in the pompous halls of palaces, where kings, emperors, and princes were accustomed to walk; they were given in parks surrounded by statues of Greek gods and mythological nymphs; they were given on ships in artificial lakes, in castles — and even in theaters. Coloratura arias, choruses, ballets, overtures, recitatives, and *ritornelli* invaded all festive life. Operatic scenes formed the prelude to fireworks. Ballets were intermingled with arias and choruses; and in the famous ballet performed on the occasion of the marriage of Leopold I and the Infanta Margaret Theresa of Spain, which took place in Vienna in 1667, the Goddess of Fame stood on shipboard with a golden trumpet in her hand, and sang the aria of the Prologue. Sweet choruses from the Temple of Diana alternated with the action of the ballet; golden carriages glided from the clouds; and choruses hailed the appearance of the emperor, dressed as a Roman *imperator* in golden armor, with a crown on his head and a scepter in his hand, and riding a black horse whose saddle and bridle glittered with jewels.

There was no dividing line between the opera (which was musical festival, dream, fairy tale, and circus, rolled into one) and life. The two fused and flowed into each other. Cantatas were sung by costumed singers at wedding banquets, while Greek deities congratulated the bridal pair in the name of Jupiter by means of elaborate arias and ensembles. Even the church was not immune from the contagion, for performances were given in the schools and universities of the Jesuit, Augustinian, and Benedictine monks, in which mythological personages appeared on the stage and sang laudatory arias in Latin to the officials sitting in the front row. In Catholic churches on Good Friday a stage was set up representing the Holy Sepulcher, on which Mary, the saints, and other allegorical figures appeared and sang operatic arias on the themes of redemption and resurrection. And secular hunting parties were often regaled, when they stopped to rest, by the appearance of antique deities who sang a cantata.

Even the sandstone statues in the parks of the great looked like opera singers and ballet dancers. Mars and Apollo in the part at Versailles look exactly like the tenors in Lully's operas, the nymphs like the prima donnas. The statues of saints in Baroque churches or on Baroque bridges remind one, because of their theatrical movements, of the saints who were represented in the Lenten oratorios.

Music, religious or secular, vocal or instrumental, was dominated during the seventeenth century by the opera. The overture of the opera was moved to the concert hall and became a symphony. Even in the eighteenth century one can see how tyrannical the form of the three-part *aria da capo* was in Bach's cantatas and Passions. Even an independent and creative genius like Handel was hampered by the operatic forms of his time, which had already been fixed in a formula.

In the middle of the seventeenth century the Italian Baroque opera began its conquest of Europe. It came over the Alpine passes to Vienna and Munich, to Dresden and Hanover, to the great and small cities of Germany as far as the seaports on the stormy North Sea. Vienna, the capital of the Holy Roman Empire, became an Italian city: Italian was the language of the court and the aristocrats. The greatest Italian poet of the period, Metastasio, wrote the librettos of the Italian opera for the Viennese court. Some of the greatest Italian composers of

Baroque opera, Cesti, Ziani, and Caldara (to name only a few), became court composers. Singers, instrumentalists, and stage designers like the famous Burnacini were imported for Vienna's operatic stage. Operatic music sounded in the court opera house, in the Redoutensaal, in the Burgtheater, in the garden of the Favorita (the summer residence of Charles VI), in the castle parks of Schönbrunn and Hetzendorf — in fact, wherever the Emperor spent the night when he traveled.

Munich and Dresden also became centers for Italian opera. In all such cities money was lavishly spent for settings and lighting, for machines and instruments. The performance of Cesti's *Golden Apple* which took place in Vienna in 1666 cost the equivalent of a hundred thousand dollars; the performance of *Paride* in Dresden in the same year cost the equivalent of three hundred thousand dollars. What the eighteenth century paid for the services of *castrati* and prima donnas cannot be reckoned. Farinelli had an annual income of more than three thousand pounds sterling in London alone. Men like Caffarelli, Matteuci, Senesino, Crescentini, and others of no less importance were among the wealthiest of their time.

Cardinal Mazarin imported Italian singers, stage architects, and ballet masters from Florence and Rome to Paris, and Goulas says in his *Memoirs* that people were embittered by the waste of money on Italian singers and theatrical machines. The ascendancy of the Italian opera was complete almost throughout Europe. Only the French opera of the court of Versailles succeeded in developing a style of its own. It was characterized by festive solemnity, stylish magnificence in the declamatory recitative, great choruses, and gorgeous ballets. The influence of this French style penetrated Germany as far as Hanover, Hamburg, and Brunswick, but the domination of the Italian opera was not seriously threatened. It was so closely connected with the life of the ruling classes of Europe that the two could not be separated.

Traveling companies carried Italian opera in all its forms through Europe during the eighteenth century. Girolamo Bon introduced the Italian opera to St. Petersburg in 1742 on the occasion of the coronation of the Empress Elizabeth. Mingotti's company had Gluck for a conductor; he was with them when they played at Copenhagen. These performances were a sort of annex to the solemn palace of the great Baroque opera; they introduced *opera buffa*, the laughing child of the Italian streets, to Europe.

It is impossible to understand Baroque opera from a twentieth-century point of view. It was not, like today's opera, a realistic or romantic play performed by singers; it was festive decoration. Imagine an Italian triumphal arch erected to honor a princely guest. It is profusely decorated with mythological statues. Festive decoration of a similar nature can be found in the mighty frescoes on the ceilings of Baroque palaces, where antique deities sit, enthroned on clouds. Baroque operas spring from the same source: they were part of the general festive pleasure of the heroic period of the Counter Reformation, in which the power of the princes reached its height.

The settings for these operas, designed by great painters, show vast halls with giant staircases and mighty columns, gardens with clipped hedges, statues, and fountains, landscapes with stormy skies and threatening clouds, and tossing seas. The imaginations of the painters did not stop with this world: one might see the nether world with the forges of the Cyclops, or with the three-headed Cerberus standing guard and breathing fire. Or one might see the grove of the Gods, where all is serene peace. The buildings represented were ornate structures, set at a bold diagonal, so that the art of perspective could be most effectively employed.

Where there are Gods, there must be machines; hence we find that these theatrical machines were often considered to be the most important part of the performance. A book entitled *The Newly Opened Armory, Arsenal, and Machine House* appeared in Hamburg in 1710 which openly maintained in the fourth chapter that "machines are the best part of an opera," for they "fill the souls of all the spectators with admiration." And in the preface to the opera *Diana* by Johann Ulrich von König, which appeared in 1712 (also in Hamburg), one may read that the French take their operas only from the works of poets, "because such poems gave occasion to many beautiful machines and transformations on the stage."

The festive character of the Baroque opera meant that unhappy endings were not popular. Only a relatively few works in the seventeenth and eighteenth centuries permit their heroes to die.[1] The audience was opposed to tragedy, no matter who the author might be. Mattheson tells in his autobiography how the audience "started a great shouting" when, as the character Antony in his opera *Cleopatra*, he killed himself with his dagger. Even Gluck bowed to the tradition by reviving his dead heroes as gods, and that great innovator was forced to conclude his operas with brilliant choruses and ballets.

This was the adversary that philosophers, writers, and critics had to fight for over half a century. The battle began in France, a fact that can easily be understood in view of the early development of the French spirit, with its lucidity and charm, its brightness, and its grace. In the simple and cheerful prose of Descartes, in the common sense of Boileau, in the neat and felicitous poetry of La Fontaine, in the majestic verses of Corneille, and in the tender measures of Racine, French genius had succeeded in creating the appropriate language for its joy in clarity and interest in highly finished perfection of form. Simplicity, naturalness, clarity, and nobleness became the indelible characteristics of the French spirit. Corneille and Racine created a new, logical, and simple form for tragedy. Unity of time and place concentrated the action. The number of persons in the drama was restricted according to the demands of the plot. Only one passion was depicted, growing and struggling between the first rise of the curtain and its final fall. Corneille early began to ignore the external spectacle, the material movement of the stage, and to concen-

---

[1] Quinault, *Atys* (1676), *Phaeton* (1683), *Armide* (1686); Danchet, *Idoméné* (1712); Metastasio, *Didone abbandonata* (1724), *Catone in Utica* (1727), *Attilio Regolo* (1740); Houdar de la Motte, *Marthesie* (1699); Verazi, *Sofonisba*.

trate on the representation of human passion in abstract sur-
roundings. With Racine, the tragedy becomes moral action,
which lives by itself in a kind of ideal space.

Between the festive, colorful lavishness of the Baroque opera
and the logical simplicity of French tragedy there existed a gulf
too wide and too deep to be successfully spanned. They were
like two continents separated by the sea. Lully tried to recon-
cile French Baroque opera with the tragedy of Racine, but it was
only a compromise. Much later, Gluck was inspired by Racine's *Iphigénie* to advance much further toward heroic simplicity. There was no doubt, however, that there was no room
for both art forms in a changing world. One of the two must
prevail, either the tragic spirit of Corneille and Racine or the
decorative pomposity of the Baroque opera.

III. FRENCH CRITICS

The French writer who fired the first shot was the Abbé
François Raguenet. He contrasted the characteristics of the
Italian and the French operas in his pamphlet *Parallèle des François et des Italiens en ce qui regarde la musique et les opéras* (*"Parallel
between the French and the Italians in respect to music and operas"*),
which first appeared in 1702. He proved the superiority of the
French opera in the choice of its librettos, in its recitative, in
the significance of its choruses, in the pomp of its ballets, in its
machines, and in the precision of its orchestra. He accomplished all this without denying the musical splendor of the
Italian opera, the virtuosity of Italian singing, and the power
of the stringed instruments.[1] As he put it, the Italian opera was
a spectacle that never bored, while the French opera was a play
that always hit the mark.

This booklet gave rise to a heated discussion. Jean Laurent

---

[1] Raguenet was an admirer of the librettos Quinault wrote for Lully. He thought, on
the other hand, that Italian librettos were "pitiful rhapsodies without any connection,"
and that the scenes in these operas were nothing but "discussions or monologues to which
arias are affixed without any connection with the true plot." Quinault's librettos were,
he said, "regular and connected," and the language derived from the characters. In the
background of Raguenet's arguments, Racine's influence is everywhere apparent.

le Cerf de la Vieville de Freneuse answered with an essay entitled *Comparaison de la musique française et de la musique italienne* ("*Comparison between French and Italian Music*"), which was first published in 1704. He blamed the monotony of expression in the Italian opera as its greatest fault, and maintained that Quinault had purified the style of the French opera by removing its platitudes. His essay culminates in the praise of Lully as the great master of opera. Raguenet retorted with his *Défense de la Parallèle* ("*Defense of the Parallel*") in 1705. Both Vieville's essay and Raguenet's were reviewed in the *Journal des savants*, and thus the fight of the two musical enthusiasts spread to the society of scholars. One physician added oil to the flames by contributing an essay to the same journal called "The Art of Cursing What One Does Not Understand." This essay used Raguenet's article as a starting point.

The sparks of the fire Raguenet had lit on the roof of the Baroque opera flew to Germany. Mattheson was the first to publish Raguenet's book. It appeared in the *Critica musica* in 1722, in translation and with commentary; and in 1760 Marpurg published it once again in his *Kritische Briefe*. In this way, German music critics took up the fight against Italian Baroque opera.

In Lully's day, no one hated the Baroque opera more passionately than Saint-Évremond. He gave expression to his hatred in a letter addressed to the Duke of Buckingham, which was published in the third volume of his works in 1705. To this spirited writer, opera was only "a stupidity, loaded with music, dancing, and mechanical contraptions." He gave vent to his poisonous hatred not only in his essay *Sur les opéras* ("*On Operas*") but also in a comedy, *Les Opéras* ("*The Operas*"). He saw in opera the pattern of superficial pomp, inner hollowness, and boredom.

Boileau, the most respected esthetic judge of the period, was his supporter. He attacked the opera in two of his classical "Satires." He did not restrict his attack to the institution, but turned his big guns on a specific target as well — Quinault.

He assailed his librettos as senseless, and accused his work of
being "commonplaces of lewd immorality which Lully warms
up with the sound of his music."

The doctrines, the hatred, and the mockeries of Saint-Évremond were gladly taken over by Gottsched in Leipzig. This
herald of French rationalism, whose trumpet was heard over the
whole of Germany, translated *Les Opéras* and had it performed
in the Hamburg theater.

In France Raimond de Saint-Mard accepted the challenge of
Saint-Évremond, and spurred his charger against him. He defended the slandered opera in a pamphlet, *Réflexions sur l'opéra*
("*Reflections on the Opera*"), first published at The Hague in 1741.
He assailed Saint-Évremond as a "pedant . . . a man of rank
who has intelligence, but is a superficial judge." He went on
to maintain that opera had the form of a tragedy except for the
divertissements, the ballets which ended each act of the French
opera. The main characteristics of the opera ought to be miraculous; that is, the text of an opera ought to be planned so as to
bring about miraculous events. What an effect, he pointed out,
when the hero, after wandering over the whole world, arrived
in an enchanted palace ! The noble and majestic, in his opinion,
did not suit the opera as well as the sweet and passionate: this
was the reason why Quinault was great. The librettist's duty
was to touch the audience; he must, therefore, take his rules
from nature, which alone could tell him what was touching.
It might perhaps be possible for poet and composer to be "united
in the same person. . . . If settings, dances, machines, and good
singers were added to these two arts, in order to give more
power and veracity to the performances, the ideal art work
would be created."

The crest of the rising opposition to the Baroque opera as the
most alluring form of Baroque pomposity was reached in the
middle of the eighteenth century. The struggles between the
admirers of Italian *opera buffa* — the Buffonists — and the admirers of the French opera tradition — the Anti-Buffonists —
and the literary controversy about Gluck are all but details in

the great picture. When the French philosophers Diderot, D'Alembert, Grimm, Holbach, and Rousseau joined the forces opposing the artificial and luxuriant style of seventeenth-century opera, the battle between the old and the new became the battle between the leading ideas of the epoch before the French Revolution. It was fought over the question whether reason and nature should prevail in the opera, or stylized, artificial solemnity.

For these men there was no doubt that the Baroque opera was just as outdated as the society which had enjoyed its flattering prologues, its stiffly formal recitatives, its coloratura arias, its senseless ballets, its hollow mechanical tricks, its hodgepodge of antique mythology and history. For these men the beautiful and the natural were one. Therefore they loved the Italian *opera buffa*, with its reflection of the noise and bustle of Italian market places, its humanity, grace, and unspoiled life.

The speaker who expressed the ideas of the parliament of French philosophers was Baron Grimm, the son of a clergyman of Ratisbon. Grimm had studied with Gottsched in Leipzig, and when he arrived in Paris in 1748, he soon became one of the most influential critics of his day. He commenced his criticism of the Baroque opera with an article published in the *Mercure de France*. With his criticism Grimm not only demolished the opera of Destouches and his entire musical output, but the whole of French music as well. Grimm's criticism caused a sensation in Paris, and he was recognized as a critic who wielded a sharp pen. In 1753, he exploded another bombshell in the French opera house with the publication of an essay entitled "The Vision of the Little Prophet of Boehmischbroda," a satirical, humorous sketch. The story concerns a lutenist and composer of minuets named Waldstorch ("Stork of the Forest") who is bewitched and flies through the air to Paris from his native Prague. Here he sees a performance in the opera house and mistakes it for a puppet show. The possibilities for irony and mockery are great, and Grimm makes the most of them in his attacks on the Baroque opera of Lully and Rameau. The essay met with great

success. Voltaire was enthusiastic about it, and elegant gentlemen carried the issue of the *Mercure de France* about, to have it
ready to show to the ladies they were courting.

This sketch may have been the key that opened the door of
literary success to Baron Grimm, for he soon became editor of
the *Correspondance Littéraire* ("*Literary Correspondence*"), a sort of
eighteenth-century literary service favored by high society, its
subscribers including most of the German princes as well as
Frederick of Prussia and Catherine of Russia. The contents of
the journal consisted of articles on science, art, social evolution,
and the latest shop talk, no matter what the field. There were
also reports on new books, discussions of universities and acad-
emies, reviews of expositions of painting; opera first nights were
described, and accounts of world travel printed. It was, in
short, a chronicle of all the events that interested cultured
people between 1753 and 1773. Only politics were excluded
from its columns.

Grimm's career as an active critic encompasses the period between Rameau and Cherubini. He was an adversary of the
Baroque opera and of the Académie Royale, the opera house in
Paris. Once, after the building had caught fire, the critic pub-
licly wondered how a fire could have started "in a glacier." To
him, the opera house was infected with the disease of boredom.
It was an "old den," to which one went only through "careless-
ness and want of judgement." Another time Grimm referred to
it as the "Academy of boring memory." A paragraph on the
death of two famous ballet dancers began with the words, "A
place of desert and boredom has suffered a loss."

When Lully's *Persée* was revived in 1770 on the occasion of the
marriage of the Duc d'Aumont, Grimm wrote: "The opera
Persée was splendidly boring. The only interesting moment was
when the actor who played the part of Persée slipped and fell by
mistake at Andromeda's feet." He summarized his opinion of
Lully in a few words: "We have praised this Lully as a genius
for more than half a century, though his gloomy, cold works
never radiated the warmth of a real fancy. . . . Habit is indeed

the strongest power in human life, and it provokes the strangest phenomena."

Grimm's judgments on the operas of Rameau were not different from his criticisms of Lully. His predecessor in the editorship of the *Correspondance Littéraire*, Raynal, had however treated Rameau's operas with esteem and understanding and had defended the composer against reproaches. When the overture to *Zaïs* was derided because of a roll of covered kettledrums, which the critics jeered at as more fitting for "funeral music for an officer of the Swiss Guards" than for an overture, Raynal explained that this orchestral effect had its dramatic reason. He praised the imagination displayed in Rameau's use of the orchestra, and wrote most accurately, "Rameau is the only one of our musicians who is endowed in the highest degree with the faculty of translating the phenomena of nature into music."

Grimm, when he took over the magazine, changed its critical course. Rameau, to Grimm and to his epoch when the storm clouds of the French Revolution were gathering, was the representative of an antiquated taste; and there was no essential difference between Rameau and Lully. Both represented the outmoded art of the courts, not the realism of the new period, which Diderot proclaimed in his plays based on the life of the middle classes. The solemn recitatives of Lully and Rameau, the stylized, artificially pompous imitation of the declamation of the French tragedians, did not express the feelings of the men of the age of Rousseau. In 1753, the same year that Baron Grimm started his far-flung correspondence, Rousseau published his *Lettre sur la musique française* ("*Letter on French Music*") in which he tried to prove that the French language was unfit for musical composition. To men of this stamp, the recitative operas of Lully and Rameau could mean nothing.

Grimm referred to Rousseau's pamphlet in his own criticisms of two of Rameau's operas, *The Lyrical Talents* and *Hymen's Festival*, which were performed in 1753. He repeated the opinion that Frenchmen made themselves ridiculous when they regarded Rameau as one of the first composers of the age. One aria by

Hasse or Buranello, he concluded, was more valuable than all Rameau's operas put together. No doubt there were personal reasons for these harsh criticisms, for Rameau and the foremost Encyclopedists were on bad terms. Diderot described Rameau's character in most unpleasant terms. Rameau retaliated with a pamphlet, *Erreurs sur la musique dans l'Encyclopédie* ("*Mistakes on the subject of music in the Encyclopedia*"). The pamphlet was directed against Rousseau, who had taken the composer to task in the *Encyclopédie*. He had complained that Rameau's orchestra was "confused and overloaded," and he had failed to find any connection between the several episodes of Rameau's operas. Apart from these personal frictions, Grimm's opposition to Rameau was based on objective contrasts of ideas and convictions. His hatred for French opera was genuine. He never tired of holding forth on this "sophisticated and empty art." His wit seemed to grow sharper as each new opera appeared. Let the malicious epigram that he wrote on Laborde, who composed operas for the court in Fontainebleau, bear witness: "After Rameau you have appeared, Laborde. What a successor! Lord, have mercy on us!"

When Gluck reformed the French opera, leading the pompous spectacle back to the sublime simplicity of Racine's tragedies, Grimm hailed the innovator. After the performance of Gluck's *Iphigenia in Tauris* in 1779, Grimm wrote, "Without interfering in the famous fight [between Gluckists and Piccinists] I must confess that Gluck's work seemed to leave an extraordinary impression. . . . I do not know if this is singing, but it is perhaps something better than that. Hearing this *Iphigénie* I forget that I am in an opera house and think I am hearing a Greek tragedy." He praised Sacchini, three of whose operas were produced in Paris between 1783 and 1784, *Renaud*, *Chimène*, and *Dardanus*. The spirit of Gluck was a moving force in these productions, as well as in his powerful *Oedipus at Colonus*, first staged in 1786, but which continued to move its hearers for many years with its tragic greatness.

Grimm also acclaimed Cherubini when that composer appeared for the first time on the stage of the *Académie Royale* with his opera *Démophon*. Thus, Baron Grimm whom Sainte-Beuve praised as one of the most distinguished of French critics, who "had that enthusiasm and that love of beauty which is the inspiration of real criticism," was a true leader of the public taste between 1750 and 1790. As a critic, he had a lively feeling for music. Madame d'Épinay reported in a letter, "He loves music passionately; we made music with him, Rousseau, and Francueil the whole afternoon." Grimm was also the composer of a little *opéra comique* called *Nanette*, and included one of his arias in his journal. He was, in brief, much more than a mere enthusiast, though enthusiasm certainly caused his critical flame to burn more brightly. In a letter that he wrote attacking the opera *Omphale* in 1752, he confessed, "I regard the admiration and respect that I feel towards all who possess true talent, in whatever field it may be, as my greatest good beside love of truth." German by birth and education, Grimm became one of the most influential men in the shaping of the French spirit in the decisive four decades before the French Revolution. He fought in the field of musical criticism for modern ideas, for reason, for nature, and for simplicity.

When Mozart's father came to Paris with his child prodigy in 1763, Baron Grimm was in the forefront of those who greeted the genius of the seven-year-old boy with acclaim. Mozart's father acknowledged Grimm's efforts in a letter: "He did all. He brought our case to the court. He took care of the first concert, and will take care of the second. See what a man can do who has intelligence and a good heart!" Baron Grimm could not have known at that time that the little boy from Salzburg who cracked childish jokes with Mme de Pompadour and played hide-and-seek with the King's children at Versailles would some day rank with the great creative spirits of the world.

IV. THE SPIRIT OF PARODY

The conflicts indulged in by the philosophers, critics, and writers of the eighteenth century were accompanied by the laughter of the comedians. The pompous gravity of the Baroque opera had no more dangerous foe than these fun-makers. They followed the solemn *opera seria* much as Sancho Panza followed his master Don Quixote, chattering, laughing, and talking common sense.

As early as the end of the seventeenth century, Italian comedians had played before the King of France and the society of his court. Gilles and Scaramouche, Scapin and Arlequin have all been painted by Watteau in a typical canvas, exhaling the charm of refined colors. Pantalone appeared on the stage, clad in armor, with a waving plume on his helmet, like an operatic tenor, and Arlequin strutted about in the crinoline of the prima donna. They were burlesquing the *opera seria* of the court, and jeering at the librettos of Lully's operas. Merry songs, like those sung by ballad singers on the Pont Neuf, took the place of formal recitative and sophisticated aria.

Other parodies of opera as it was performed at Versailles or in the opera house at Paris were staged in small wooden huts at the various fairs. There was a small "orchestra" and there were comedians who amused the audience with popular songs and jests. Le Sage wrote librettos for many of these burlesques, which were really criticisms acted out. Every new opera was ridiculed. In one of these parodies, the Opera descended as Orpheus to the Underworld. Arlequin, the Orpheus, began to sing some recitatives, and everyone on the stage, from Pluto to Cerberus, began to fall asleep. Baron Grimm and the Encyclopedists must have been delighted to see their criticisms of the court opera made popular in this way — that is, if they ever attended performances of the Théâtre de la Foire. Out of these little wooden huts, surrounded as they were by the noise of the fair, eventually grew the French *opéra comique*: Rousseau's little musical play, *The Village Soothsayer*, and the operas of Duni, Monsigny, Philidor, and Grétry. Le Sage, the chief poet of these theaters of the Parisian fairs at Saint-Germain and Saint-Laurent, wrote the libretto of the *Pilgrims of Mecca*, later set to music by Gluck.

Groups of Italian comedians roamed through Europe. Wandering through Germany, they eventually reached England. This was the time of elaborate operatic ventures in London, backed by the court and by the aristocracy, but looked upon with dismay if not disgust by the populace. The visitors' travesties found an appreciative audience. Healthy laughter filled the theater. The hollow pomp of the great operas was unmercifully parodied. As in Paris, the comedians made the stylized pathos and the artificial affectation of the *opera seria* ridiculous. At about the same time that the Italian comedians were making even the stiff Londoners shake with laughter, a book appeared in Italy which ridiculed the Baroque opera and showed that in the very homeland of the *opera seria*, its clock had run down. The author was Benedetto Marcello, and the title *Il teatro alla moda* ("*The Fashionable Theatre*"). This famous composer of psalms made fun of composers, librettists, singers, *castrati*, managers, sponsors, and even the mothers of the prima donnas. This book is a kind of parody itself, written with the humor of a comedian. Almost certainly influenced by the jokes of the Italian comedians, the fun and vivacity of the Venetian popular theater gleamed from every page. It was identical in spirit with the opera parodies performed by the Italian comedians in London.

The efficacy of these farces was great. Opposition to the *opera seria* had already begun in London. In 1711 Addison had published three articles in his *Spectator*, which turned his critical fire against the *opera seria*. He ridiculed its unnaturalness:

Every actor that comes on the stage is a beau. The queens and heroines are so painted, that they appear as ruddy and cherry-cheeked as milkmaids. The shepherds are all embroidered, and acquit themselves better in a ball than our English dancing-masters. I have seen a couple of rivers appear in red stockings; and Alpheus, instead of having his head covered with sedge and bulrushes, making love in a fair full-bottomed periwig and a plume of feathers, but with a voice so full of shakes and quavers, that I should have thought the murmurs of a country brook the much more agreeable music.

Swift joined the battle in 1726 with his *Gulliver's Travels*; in 1728, Pope took up arms with the *Dunciad*. All three great English writers followed the lead taken by the Italian comedians. They were friends, and they were accustomed to talking things over in a satirical vein when they sat in the leather chairs of their Scriblerus Club.

Among the members of the Scriblerus Club was another man destined to contribute his bit to the downfall of the Baroque opera, John Gay. He was the poet who wrote the libretto for the *Beggar's Opera*, which was performed for the first time on January 29, 1728. This was the knockout blow to *opera seria* as it was conceived in the seventeenth century, and signifies the greatest victory that the spirit of musical comedy ever obtained. It is likely that the subject of the *Beggar's Opera* was suggested to Gay by Swift, and it is sure that Pope was consulted. In a certain sense, the *Beggar's Opera* is a common product of the Scriblerus Club and the lasting document of its satirical spirit.

The *Beggar's Opera* is essentially a satire on the *opera seria*: much the same sort of thing that the Italian comedians played in their own theaters. The satiric spirit makes its first appearance in the Prologue. Instead of the usual deities of the Baroque opera, a beggar appears, explaining that beggars have the same right to play their parts on the stage that mythological characters have. The heroes of the play proper are contrasted with the mytho-logical or historical characters of serious opera. Highway rob-bers, thieves, prostitutes, and all sorts of criminals make their way onto the stage to Handel's march from *Rinaldo*. The hero is Macheath, a captain of brigands. The music consists of popu-lar songs, adapted for the stage by the German musician Pepusch.

The noble English society which stormed the theater sixty-two times recognized the *Beggar's Opera* as the satire it was in-tended to be. Everyone knew and understood the mocking ditty on Walpole, the Prime Minister, which was foreshadowed in the overture. Nor was it difficult to recognize the corrupt poli-ticians of Walpole's ministry in the gang of thieves. Social satire was never more mordant and venomous than in Gay's dialogue. The dialogue fairly crackles with sharp repartee and epigram. The morality of the play is expressed in the Beggar's epilogue, in which he observes that throughout the play the audience my have observed such equality of manners in high and low life that it was difficult to decide whether in the dominating vices the noblemen imitated the men of the streets or the men of the streets imitated the noblemen.

Satire on society and criticism of morals made the *Beggar's Opera* a masterwork of the modern critical spirit. It was the work of a courageous journalist. In its pages a modern realistic outlook was opposed to an out-of-date society, which had mis-used power, money, and politics, and which relied for its amuse-ment on French and Italian opera music that had outlived its time. The laughter of Gay and the other members of the Scrib-lerus Club was already a revolution on the march.

Modern criticism took different shapes and forms. It was never more efficient than when it adopted the stage as its me-dium. The *Beggar's Opera* by Gay, the *Marriage of Figaro* by Beau-marchais, Schiller's *Robbers*, Beethoven's *Fidelio*, and Gerhardt Hauptmann's *Weavers* had the impact of as many revolutions. The reverberations from the *Beggar's Opera* affected a whole so-ciety and its musical tastes. And in London's Westminster Abbey no epitaph is more appropriate than Pope's on Gay:

> Life is a jest, and all things show it.
> I thought it once, and now I know it.

English ballad opera lost no time in crossing the Channel and wandering down the highway to Leipzig. There comedians performed *The Wife's Metamorphosis, or the Devil to Pay*, a typical ballad opera whose English folk tunes delighted the Leipzig bourgeoisie. C. F. Weisse rewrote the successful play, and Stand-fuss furnished it with new tunes; and thus the German *Singspiel* entered the German theater, in which it was to become so great a success when Hiller wrote his popular tunes and homemade lyrics designed for the palate of the average middle-class man. The laughter of the English ballad opera and the French *opéra comique* echoed in the Leipzig theater.   There was only one man in the theater, tall and self-conscious, sitting in a box with his coquettish young wife, who disliked the successful ballad operas, and this was Professor Gottsched. He hated opera in every form, and not least the *Singspiel*, against which he wrote articles. Koch, the manager of the Leipzig theater, answered these articles from the stage, to the great amusement of the audience, who laughed and applauded his sallies. Rost, a former pupil of Gottsched's, published a witty letter that the Devil was supposed to have written to the Professor ridiculing him as literary dictator. Gottsched ran to Brühl, the prime minister, to complain of Rost's insolence, but it was to no avail. The audience of German burghers kept on going to the *Singspiele* and singing their simple melodies.

Italian comedy, English ballad opera, French *opéra comique*, and Viennese farce combined to form the popular suburban theater in Vienna, ruled over by the Austrian incarnation of the old English jester and the Italian Harlequin: Jack Pudding, or Hans Wurst. Ringing laughter echoed through the small wooden theater on the Graben in Vienna when Stranitzky first appeared as Hans Wurst, dressed like a Salzburg peasant, a green hat on his head with an enormous cock's feather stuck into the band. He sang popular tunes, and joked with the audience in Viennese dialect. For this popular theater Haydn wrote his first comedy with music, *The Crooked Devil*. The libretto is based on a pantomime by Le Sage, originally written for the Théâtre de la Foire in Paris. But the most accomplished work to come out of the Viennese popular theater was Mozart's *Magic Flute*. Papageno was the successor to the older Hans Wurst.

V. THE BERLIN SCHOOL, A PRELUDE TO THE CLASSIC ERA

Between 1720 and 1750 the taste of the whole of Europe had imperceptibly changed. About 1750 (the year in which Bach died) the Baroque taste was so thoroughly dead that it seemed as if even the greatest Baroque music had vanished from the earth. Forgotten were the Bach cantatas and Passions. His six

Brandenburg Concertos were sold as waste paper, one concerto bringing six groschen. His pieces for solo violin were found in a butter shop, where they were destined to be used for wrapping-paper.

The French estheticians of the eighteenth century and the music critics of Hamburg, Berlin, and Leipzig had performed their task. They had spread the ideas of the Age of Enlightenment. Scheibe had won his victory over Bach. Reason and lucidity, naturalness and clarity, had become the esthetic ideals of the period, and were echoed in all the magazines. Addison and Grimm, Gottsched and Scheibe, Mattheson and Marpurg had become the spiritual rulers of society. Rationalistic ideas were proclaimed in the stuffy lecture rooms of German universities. Leibnitz, who had never cared much for opera, anticipated the doctrines of the French Encyclopedists in 1681 when he wrote to Henfling, "I was often aware that what experts used to esteem the best had nothing touching. Simplicity often makes a greater effect than grafted ornaments."

The Baroque opera was a deposed monarch. Gluck's operas renewed the "quiet simplicity and noble greatness" that the gifted archaeologist Winckelmann had declared to be the characteristics of Greek art. The Baroque opera had played with antiquity, had transformed its gods and heroes, its religion and mythology into a colorful spectacle. Now, in 1748, real antiquity began to rise out of the earth when Pompeii was discovered in her grave of ashes. In 1740 Piranesi began to work on his engravings of Roman ruins, with his inimitable use of mighty light and shade. Great humanists like Ernesti and Christ (with whom Lessing studied) in Leipzig and Rector Damm (with whom Winckelmann studied Greek) in Berlin all spread the doctrine of the greatness of the antique world. The rationalism of the eighteenth century allied itself with Greek antiquity; the French tragedy of Racine with Greek tragedy; and both united gave the great style to the opera of Gluck. Opera lost its courtly pomposity and its fairy-tale variegation and became a lyrical tragedy.

It would be erroneous, nevertheless, to attribute the changed situation solely to Gluck's reforms. Already, a generation earlier, real Baroque opera had had to give ground to the new ideas of melodious simplicity and natural feeling. Composers like Reinhardt Keiser, Hasse, and Giovanni Bononcini (Handel's London rival), and even Handel himself, owed their success to the more flexible and sensitive melody, which, in the great orchestrally accompanied recitatives, gives a natural expression to the storms of passion, and, in the operas of Keiser, descends to the simplicity of folk tunes. Le Cerf de la Vieville praises Bononcini for his sparing use of "fugues," and Sere de Rieux glorifies the "reason and charm" which relate Handel's music to the French taste. And, of course, the comic operas attain complete naturalness, for the melodies of the Italian *opera buffa* are open-air melodies. Their home is the Italian street, the blue sea, and the orange groves. Their tunes are as naïve as folk songs; their accents and rhythms are Italian accents and rhythms. French *opéra comique* plucks flowers on the meadows of French villages and puts them into cut-glass vases. English ballad opera is fond of Scottish broadside ballads, and the German *Singspiel* admires the sentimental atmosphere of German folk songs. During the eighteenth century, Europe was flooded with popular melodies.

Under the influence of such melodies, the Berlin composers created a new style of composition, the Berlin *Lied*. The city saw the publication of the first volume of these simple songs, *Odes and Melodies*, in 1753. Almost all of the composers represented were native Berliners; among them were K. P. E. Bach, Nickelmann, Agricola, and Benda. Besides Berlin, only Hamburg is represented — with Telemann. In the Preface to the book French songs are highly praised as models, and the French are referred to as "born friends of song."

Marpurg called time and again for more simplicity in songs. In the Preface to his *Odes*, which appeared in 1761, he said, "He who always disfigures songs with many ornamental notes has no taste. He confirms once again the already well-known truth that it is more difficult to invent a simple and easy tune than an overloaded and complicated one." The period in which highly ornate cantatas flourished was over. In fashion were new melodies in the style of folk songs, like those J. A. P. Schulz published in Berlin in 1785. Schulz boasted that he had tried to write his songs "as simply and clearly as possible." In Leipzig Hiller was composing songs for children. Scheibe, like Hiller a champion of modernity, added morality to music with the publication in 1766 of *Little Songs for Children for the Promotion of Virtue*. Simplicity became as cheap and common as blackberries in the spate of song books that were published during this period. There were songs for soldiers (some by K. P. E. Bach), songs for women, and songs for peasants. There were plenty of *Lullabies for German Nurses*. Reichardt brought out *Lullabies for Good German Mothers* in 1798; and the next year saw the publication of a thoroughly inclusive affair called *Songbooks for Good Men in Hours of Melancholy and Cheerfulness*.

The taste of the new epoch also invaded the instrumental field. Here, too, the melodic lines lost their Baroque redundance and their grave tread. They became agile and plastic, and, carried by the flowing stream of feeling, they became simple and natural forms of expression. Popular music began to usurp the domain of serious music. There was dancing and feasting, loving and praying.

I have always regretted that the history of modern melody has not yet been written. It was one of the greatest accomplishments of the human mind, to grow from the themes of the Gregorian chant and the songs of the minnesingers to the symphonies of Haydn, Mozart, and Beethoven. One of the most important stages of this development is the epoch when the heroic Baroque music became pliant and was melted into smaller, more variegated, and more fluid forms. The thorough bass, which gave so much character to the older music, disappeared when instrumental music became the reflection of the changing emotions of men. In the first three decades of the eighteenth century, the textbooks of Quantz and K. P. E. Bach introduced the new, expressively tender instrumental music, which has been called the *style galant*. They contrasted it with the so-called *gearbeitete* style (*i.e.*, "strict," or contrapuntal, style), which had bound the voices with contrapuntal devices and which had stalked on the stilts of the thorough bass as gravely as a courtier had walked over the parqueted floor of a castle. The old contrapuntists shrugged their shoulders, while the first music critics were advocating the new style. Scheibe wrote in his *Critische Musicus*: "The beauty of that manner of composing consists in the melody being very clear, vivacious, fluent; and, in addition to this, easily using some nicely invented ornaments, and flowing freely, unaffectedly, and always delicately." Marpurg, in his *Treatise on the Fugue*, defended the new style from the charge of superficiality in these words: "Is not the free style of composition connected with exertion? Did the excellent composers who are daily enriching the world with their tasteful, delicate works write their scores standing on one leg?" Mattheson, speaking of small pieces done in this *style galant*, insists that their production requires just as much mastery as the production of "mighty concertos and proud symphonies." Marpurg praised Telemann because "his masterpieces refute the false opinion" that the so-called *galant* style of writing could not be combined with some contrapuntal traits.

The *gearbeitete*, or strict, style became altogether dated at the end of the eighteenth century. In a criticism published in the *Mercure de France* on the occasion of the revival of Rameau's opera *Castor and Pollux* in 1772, the overture was attacked as lacking variety as compared with the instrumental music of the Mannheimers: "We do not wish to commit the injustice of comparing the overture to *Castor* with the symphonies that Germany has given us in the last twelve or fifteen years, with the works of Stamitz, Holzbauer, Toëschi, Bach [K. P. E. Bach, of course.] . . . The nuances of piano and forte used alternately or gradually increasing are delicacies of art of which Rameau makes little use. His pieces are monotonous. . . ." The development of the modern instrumental style was so rapid that the advanced masters of the *style galant* of yesterday became tomorrow's reactionaries. It is always the same story: as Alphonse Karr used to say, "The Blacks are the Reds who have arrived; the Reds are the Blacks on the march."

With the composers of Mannheim, who already represented the "Storm and Stress" of the age of Rousseau; with K. P. E. Bach, who declared in his *Versuch* that "the mixture of brilliancy and simplicity . . . sadness and joy, of the singable and the instrumental style" were the essence of orchestral music; with Gluck, we have approached the portal of so-called classical music. The whole development of music, from the Baroque to the Classical period, was accompanied by music critics. Like sappers, they cleared the way by removing the ruins of an obsolete style, and set up signposts at crossroads to indicate the modern way. The portly theoreticians like Mattheson, Marpurg, and Scheibe, who were the first music critics in Europe, may seem old-fashioned today. They were slow, profound, combative, quarrelsome, pedantic, conceited, and rigid like all dogmatists. But when they had done their work, trumpeting with the paper trumpets of their magazines the signals of a new day — nature, reason, clarity, humanity, and simplicity — there *was* a new day on the horizon. Haydn wrote his symphonies and chamber music — music that was lucid and fluent, as naïve as a folk tune and yet ingenious, singing and dancing — music that was intelligible to everyone, middle-class music that reached to the heavens — music that was related to forest and field, to neat villages and churches, and even to rural inns where fiddlers played the dances of the people. Mozart wrote his music, dramatic yet angelic, the purest music that any human being had yet written. It was a music of golden harmonies and silver melodies, in which humanity sang the choruses of *The Magic Flute* in their joy and took leave of the world in the transfigured melodies of the *Requiem*. And after the golden age of Mozart came Beethoven, who was expelled from the paradise in which Mozart had wandered and came forth to fight the battles of mankind on earth. Beethoven was the heroic warrior, victorious in his struggle against tragic fate and singing the choruses of a triumphant and jubilant mankind.

There was a new world and a new music. And neither Mattheson, nor Scheibe, nor Telemann could have imagined the new beauty. They had dull, narrow minds compared with the imagination that created the new music. But it will remain their merit that they opened the portal of that gorgeous new palace.

Chapter Seven

MUSICAL CRITICISM AND THE CLASSICS: THE ATTITUDE OF THE COMPOSERS

Two of the three German cities in which the first musical magazines were published maintained their positions as musical centers in the period of the so-called classical composers. These cities were Berlin and Leipzig. Hamburg lost her importance soon after K. P. E. Bach died there in 1788. The musical magazines published in Berlin by Reichardt and Marx between 1790 and 1830 were among the leading journals of the period, while Leipzig's importance was assured when the first issue of the *Allgemeine musikalische Zeitung* ("General Musical Journal") was published there on October 3, 1798.

In this first issue, the editor, Rochlitz, poses the question: Why should Leipzig be the home of a musical journal, when the city is not to be compared with the great musical centers of the day such as Berlin, Vienna, Prague, Dresden, and so forth? He answers by maintaining that it is doubtful if any other German city has done so much for the science of music. He says that the very lack of composers and virtuosos in Leipzig may be an advantage for a critical magazine, since "preachers speak more freely in places where there are no consistories." By the time that Robert Schumann founded his *Neue Zeitschrift für Musik* ("New Magazine of Music") in 1834, the city that boasted of Schumann, Mendelssohn, and Richard Wagner could not be regarded any longer as a place where consistories were lacking.

In the classical period, musical magazines were the only vehicles of musical criticism. Dailies did not give much space to critical articles until after Beethoven had written his greatest compositions. From time to time, however, the dailies did publish short paragraphs on the first performances of musical works, but these were more in the nature of reports and advertisements than criticisms. The entire report on the first performance of Mozart's *Marriage of Figaro* as reviewed in the Vienna *Zeitung* consisted of three sentences: "On Monday, May 1, a new Italian musical comedy called *Le Nozze di Figaro* was performed for the first time in the National Theater, arranged in imitation of a French comedy of Beaumarchais by Abb. da Ponte, poet of the theater. The music was composed by Conductor Mozart. Mrs. Laschi, who recently arrived, and Mrs. Bassani, a new singer, appeared for the first time as the Countess and the Page." The Prague *Oberpostamtszeitung* gave the event even briefer notice: "Yesterday Mozart's opera *Figaro*, that work of his genius, was conducted by himself." That was all. And in 1787, when Mozart gave a concert in Prague, the same journal wrote: "On Friday, January 1, Mozart gave a piano concert in our National Theater. He accomplished all that one could have expected from this great artist." This is a detailed criticism in comparison with the Vienna *Zeitung*'s report on the first night of *Don Giovanni*, which merely stated that the opera had been performed.

The London dailies were no better. When Haydn was achieving his greatest successes in England, the *Morning Chronicle* of December 30, 1791, saw fit to announce: "A concert is planned under the auspices of Haydn, whose name is a tower of strength, and to whom the amateurs of instrumental music look as the God of the science." On March 12, 1792, the *Morning Advertiser* reported: "Salomon gave his fourth concert in which Haydn shone with more than his usual lustre. The new Concertante [1] was performed for the first time with admirable effect. The new overture [2] is one of the grandest compositions we ever heard, and it was loudly applauded: the first and last movements were encored. It was 12 o'clock before the concert was over."

[1] *New Concertante for Violin, Violoncello, Oboe, and Bassoon.*
[2] The "overture" was the symphony in B-flat major. *Complete Haydn Edition*, No. 98.

Occasionally the writer attempted to justify the brevity of the comment. The *Oracle*, for instance, on the day after the first Haydn concerts of 1794, wrote, "We must of necessity be brief. And after all it may be the best thing when the chef d'œuvre of the great Haydn is the subject. 'Come then, expressive silence, muse his praise.'" This same expressive silence had, unfortunately, to cover the music of good and bad composers alike.

Regular musical criticism in the dailies did not begin until Haydn and Mozart had died and Beethoven had established his fame. The daily newspapers, therefore, neither contributed to the greatness of the classic period nor demonstrated their own shortcomings as critics. The musical magazines bore the whole burden of forming public opinion. The editors of these great magazines knew their responsibilities. Most of them were among the most important musical personalities in Germany. We find the names of historians like Forkel and Marx, of composers like Reichardt, and of literary men like Rochlitz. The correspondents were mostly elderly, experienced men who, since they received no pay for their articles, wrote entirely as music lovers. Anonymity assured complete independence. There was often narrowness, of course, but never frivolity; lack of judgment and stupidity, but never the audacious ignorance so characteristic of much of our present-day criticism.

The influence of these musical magazines was great. The *Allgemeine musikalische Zeitung*, which we have already mentioned, was so highly respected in 1820 that the French critic Castil-Blaze sadly exclaimed: "Why have we not in Paris a journal exclusively dedicated to music like the Leipzig *Musikalische Zeitung*?" These magazines were read by musicians and amateurs who were as yet neither guided nor misguided by the often inadequately trained musical criticism of the daily papers. The musical society of the classical period was relatively homogeneous. It was connected by a common taste, a common experience of many years standing, and a common reaction to music. The members of such a society were like members of a club or of a community, and the criticism of the leading magazines enjoyed an authority similar to that which the London *Times* enjoyed in England during the Victorian era.

Although the criticism in these magazines had mostly a narrow, dry, and banal character, the critics themselves were honest men, whose judgments, however much they may have lacked imagination, were solid and simple. Musical criticism had what might be called a middle-class character; it was a kind of handicraft. The eighteenth-century theoreticians had been transformed into honest bourgeois. Scholars of Mattheson's type turned into modest schoolmasters. The rationalistic critics who had believed in the sovereignty of reason in matters of taste dried up and became barren pedants. At the end of the eighteenth century the insignificant type of music critic had been born who still exists as a fossil in modern times. We meet, almost for the first time, the foolish, dull critics, the endless varieties of little men who occupy a big office. Experts like Mattheson and Marpurg had a certain kind of greatness. They represented their age with dignity; they were priests of the religion of enlightenment. The average writer for the magazines, on the other hand, was no longer the conscious expert of the eighteenth century, nor had he yet developed into the literary man of the later nineteenth century. Often an expert without experience and a writer without the power to write, he stood in the middle of that evolution.

The average critic of the time of Haydn and Mozart was a middle-class philistine. One looks in vain through all the published criticisms on the music of Haydn and Mozart for one significant word: one finds nothing but trivialities. Even the praise is conventional. When Goethe (who is usually characterized as unmusical) wrote concerning Haydn, "His works are an ideal language of truth, connected in all their parts by necessity, and full of life. They may perhaps be outmoded, but never surpassed," he produced a judgment whose equal cannot be found in all contemporary musical criticism on Haydn. The keen assurance with which Goethe put Mozart with Raphael and Shakespeare, and said, "Mozart would have been the man to write music to my *Faust*," finds no equal in the published criticisms of Mozart in the periodicals. Not until the Romantic period can one read truly thoughtful evaluations of Mozart and Haydn.

Yet even great composers like Haydn and Beethoven took the criticism of the musical magazines seriously. The letters of both attest this fact. When Haydn sent the finished score of his oratorio *The Creation* to the Leipzig publishers Breitkopf and Härtel (who also owned the *Allgemeine musikalische Zeitung*), he asked that the gentry of music criticism might "not treat his work too severely and hurt him in so doing." The year before he died, Haydn complained to the musician Nisle that the critics had often treated him very harshly and that it was impossible for him "to satisfy all of them." Later he calmed himself with the thought, "You will write what your heart dictates to you." When Haydn heard that he was reproached for some incorrect harmony, he said, "The gentlemen think themselves very wise with such discoveries. Alas, how much would I find were I to begin criticizing!" He wrote to Neukomm, mocking at the "pointed and witty pens" of the critics. And in 1778 he wrote an extraordinarily touching autobiographical sketch for the *Gelehrtes Österreich* ("*Learned Austria*"). Already a famous composer, he complained of the critics in Berlin: "I had the good fortune to please almost everyone except the people of Berlin with my chamber music: the public journals and the letters I received will prove this. I wonder that the Berlin critics, generally so sensible, have no middle standard in their criticisms of my works. They raise me as high as the stars in one weekly. In the other they beat me sixty fathoms into the earth, and this without argument. I know very well that the reason is that they are not capable of performing my pieces, or do not take pains to study them because of their self-love and of other motives that I will explain in time with God's help."

Where the mild and kindly Haydn relieved himself by his sad complaints, Beethoven roared like a thunderstorm. He too wrote a letter to Breitkopf and Härtel about the criticisms in the

Allgemeine musikalische Zeitung. His letter runs: "I recommend more caution and judiciousness to your critics, especially with regard to the works of younger authors. . . . I myself can say that I am far from believing myself so near perfection as not to endure blame. Nevertheless, the shouting of the music critics against me was so humiliating in the beginning that I could hardly find fault with them, but remained quiet and thought: they do not understand. . . ." In a letter to the publisher Hoffmeister, Beethoven expressed his opinions about the critics of the *Allgemeine musikalische Zeitung*: "As for the oxen from Leipzig, they may say what they will. They will make nobody immortal with their talking, and, likewise, they will not take immortality from that man whom Apollo has destined for immortality."

Such philosophical resignation was not the usual reaction with Beethoven. When the correspondent of the *Allgemeine musikalische Zeitung*, in his account of the first performance of the oratorio *Christ on the Mount of Olives*, complained about the high prices charged for admission, Beethoven hurled a thunderbolt at the head of the editor. He wrote to Breitkopf and Härtel that their correspondent lied and treated him infamously, and added, "How much magnanimity is justly demanded from a true artist! But how low and detestable is one who is permitted to attack us without any exertion." Three years later, in 1806, Beethoven again had reason to complain about a criticism of his music which appeared in the same luckless magazine. The occasion of the criticism was the *Eroica*, and the composer wrote, "I hear that somebody on the *Musikalische Zeitung* has run down the symphony. . . . I did not read the criticism. When you think you do me harm, you are mistaken. On the contrary you bring your journal into discredit."

But Beethoven was not always the gray lion who shook his mane and roared threateningly. He could joke about his critics too. The critic Kanne wrote in the Vienna *Allgemeine musikalische Zeitung* that the symphony in A major was "a symphony difficult to perform." This provoked Beethoven's clumsy humor, and he wrote a letter to the publisher Steiner, whom he had nicknamed "the Lieutenant General." He said, in part, "As to the title of the new sonata [the *Hammerklavier*], nothing is necessary but to give it the title that the symphony in A was given in the *Wiener Musikzeitung*, the 'sonata difficult to perform.' My dear Lieutenant General will of course wonder, and think that difficulty is a relative notion — what is difficult for one may be easy for another — therefore nothing has been said; but the Lieutenant General must know that everything is said with this, for what is difficult is beautiful, good, grand, etc. Everybody understands that it is the fattest praise one can bestow, for what is difficult produces perspiration."

In spite of his demonic nature, Beethoven understood the value of publicity. He was generally skillful in his relations with influential critics. Neither Haydn, who was a timid peasant, nor Mozart, who flew over the world on Ariel's wings, dared to approach the music critics. Beethoven, however, knew how to handle them. Most of the editors in Vienna, both of the magazines and of the dailies, were Beethoven's friends. He used the familiar "*du*" in addressing Kanne, the editor of the Vienna *Allgemeine musikalische Zeitung*. He read the *Allgemeine musikalische Zeitung* of Leipzig regularly, and when the *Musikalische Zeitung* of Berlin was founded in 1825, he wrote the editor a letter asking that the journal be sent to him regularly, and adding his compliments for the "spirited editor, Mr. Marx" who would "continue to discover the higher and truer territory of art." In his letters to his Berlin friends Beethoven seldom forgot to ask them to convey his compliments to Marx. Rochlitz and Rellstab, the two most influential editors and critics of Beethoven's day, were his personal friends and admirers. Like Jupiter of the myths, he was not always engaged in hurling his thunderbolts; he occasionally visited among mortals. Beethoven was the first great composer who understood the importance of the press. Even here he looked into the future.

Chapter Eight

HAYDN AND THE CRITICS

THE EARLIEST critical mention of Haydn is to be found in a 1766 issue of Hiller's musical magazine, *Wöchentliche Nachrichten* ("*Weekly Notices*"). There "Our Josef Heyden [*sic*]" is mentioned in the same breath with such long-forgotten symphonic composers as Hofmann, Thuma, Orsler, Ordonitz, and Ziegler. At this time Haydn was thirty-four years old; he had written his "first symphony" in 1759, and the symphonies he wrote between that year and 1766 were already known, both in Vienna and elsewhere. Forty symphonies by Haydn are listed in the catalogue of Breitkopf and Härtel between 1766 and 1769.[1] His string quartets were also popular, for no less than eighteen of them were published in the five years between 1764 and 1769. The first Amsterdam edition of the quartets was published in 1765, and in the same year a London publisher advertised the first six string quartets as available. In 1766, when Haydn's name was first mentioned in Hiller's magazine and in the Vienna *Diarium*,[2] he was already a European celebrity. Yet no musical criticism had contributed to his fame. There was no publicity. His scores flew over the world like birds in springtime. Wherever four musicians tuned their stringed instruments and sat

[1] These symphonies had already been played in Paris and London.

[2] The notice in the Vienna *Diarium* was most favorable: "Mr. Joseph Haydn [is] the darling of our nation; his gentle character is impressed on every one of his compositions. His writing has beauty, order, purity, and a fine and noble simplicity. . . . The manner of coupling voices in octaves was originated by him, and it gives a charming impression when used rarely and in Haydn's way. He is both . . . strong and inventive in his symphonies. He is charming . . . in his cantatas, and naturally playful and alluring in his minuets. In short, Haydn is in music what Gellert used to be in poetry." This notice was reproduced in the *Gelehrtes Österreich* of 1778.

down to play chamber music, Haydn's quartets lay on their desks. It was the same in Vienna, in Paris, and in London. Musicians and music lovers said to one another, "You must play Haydn; you will enjoy it," with the appreciative smile of a connoisseur recommending a wine of particularly choice vintage.

The sheer quantity of symphonic and chamber music published around 1750 is astonishing, and still more amazing is the rapidity with which the compositions became known throughout Europe, even though they did not have the benefit of today's publicity methods. Breitkopf and Härtel's catalogue of 1762 enumerates over fifty composers of symphonic music: among them famous or well-known names such as Galuppi, Conti, Scarlatti, Locatelli, Gluck, Graun, Hasse, Hiller, Holzbauer, Mozart's father, Stamitz, and Gyrowetz. The publishers of Vienna, Berlin, Amsterdam, and Paris threw great numbers of symphonies on the market, so it was no wonder that Haydn's symphonies were published by this time in Germany, France, and Holland. Gyrowetz, a contemporary of Haydn and Mozart, was only eighteen years old when his symphonies were played in Viennese concerts. Mozart, too, performed one of the young composer's symphonies in his Mehlgrube concerts. When Gyrowetz left Vienna for Naples, he heard his chamber music played in the drawing room of Ferri, a rich farmer, whose custom it was to have chamber-music concerts three times a week at his home. Gyrowetz's music was heard as well at the house of Count Razumovsky, the Russian ambassador to Naples. And when the composer left for Paris, he heard his symphonies played as works of Haydn; and when he came to London as Haydn's rival, he found his symphonies and chamber music equally popular in England. The music seems to have traveled faster than the composers themselves, no matter how fast they urged the postilions of the mailcoaches to drive their horses.

In 1767 we find a two-voiced andante by Haydn published as a supplement to Hiller's musical magazine. Thus, without any help from the critics and without any praise from the magazines, Haydn had become a musician of European fame. The earliest detailed criticism of Haydn's works that we are acquainted with was written by Hiller himself in 1770 for his magazine. The discussion deals with the six symphonies printed by Baileaux in Paris (*Six Sinfonies à huit parties*). They were dealt with in the narrowly pedantic manner characteristic of the age's critical approach. Hiller wondered if all six symphonies were composed by Haydn since "there are more composers of that name." He believed numbers one, five, and six to be the best; in the others he missed "Mr. Haydn's peculiar and original style." The second symphony, according to Hiller, was "a miscarried and disgusting imitation of the manner of Filtz."[1] The third had "quite a nice allegro at the opening; in the andante, the composer divides the melody in a ridiculous way between the first and second violins. . . . The last movement of the symphony carries the direction *Presto Fuga*: anyone who will let the thing pass for a fugue may do so." The fourth symphony, so Hiller tells us, had been rewritten by a Leipzig composer who reshaped it into tolerable form. "The last movement is missing in the printed score.[2] It would have been better if the stupid trio with the whole minuet were missing too." And the music critic concluded, "Mr. Haydn, for whose genius we have all due regard, may see if he recognizes all these symphonies as his compositions, or if the publishing of them did him any good."

A criticism on Haydn's string quartets (Nos. 39–44) and his six symphonies published as *opus* 18, written by Reichardt and published in his *Musikalisches Kunstmagazin* ("*Musical Art Magazine*") in 1782, shows how the outlook of the musical magazines had changed in the fifteen years between this criticism and Hiller's.

Both works of Haydn [Reichardt wrote] are full of thoroughly original humor, and vivacious, pleasing wit. There was surely never a composer who combined so much originality and variety with so much charm and popularity as Haydn does. And there are few composers at once so pleasant and so popular, who have a good technique

---

[1] Filtz was a composer of the Mannheim group.
[2] It is missing in the autograph too.

of writing. It is very interesting to look at the sequence of Haydn's compositions with a critical eye. Even his first compositions, which were known to us some twenty-odd years ago, demonstrated his peculiar good-natured humor, but it was mostly youthful frolicsomeness and buoyant gaiety with simple harmonic development; by degrees his humor became manlier and the development more balanced, until finally the mature, original, and purposeful artist expresses himself in all his compositions, through increased feeling and more profound studies of art, especially the art of making an effect. Had we only Haydn and Ph. E. Bach, we Germans could boldly say that we have our own style and that our instrumental music is the most interesting of all.

In another musical magazine which was supposedly read by many music lovers, the *Magazin der Musik* ("*Magazine of Music*") of Karl Friedrich Cramer, one may see similar opinions on Haydn, published in 1783. "His compositions are praised and deserve praise, since in them the most original humor and the most vivacious and most pleasant wit prevail." In the same year, this magazine published a criticism on Haydn's first twelve songs, in the worst schoolmaster style. "These songs are not worthy of Haydn. I suppose he did not intend to increase his fame with them but to give pleasure to certain amateurs of either sex. Nobody will doubt, therefore, that Mr. Haydn would have been capable of making better songs if he had wanted to. Whether he should not have done so is another question." Cramer's magazine contained still more criticism of Haydn's work; in 1784 one of the sonatas, *opus* 37, was reviewed. Here Haydn was called "the famous man." Another criticism on Trios Five and Six in 1787 praised them as one of the "highest stages among Haydn's works." In yet another article the third trio, in E flat, was praised as the "most beautiful among the beautiful ones . . . where Haydn's genius takes its highest flight." A criticism in the *Musikalische Real-Zeitung* ("*Technical Musical News*") of 1789 maintained that "Haydn's original writing, his beautiful modulations, and his wealth of ideas are already so widely known that it is unnecessary to say

anything in their praise here." And in 1799 the critic of the
Allgemeine deutsche Bibliothek ("*Universal German Library*" —
Nicolai's Berlin magazine) spoke of the known originality of
the author of these same three string trios. He added that for
a long time he had not seen anything that could compare with
them. The development was excellent, the modulation praiseworthy, but the critic warned would-be players about the difficulty of the music, yet made amends by saying that if the pieces
were played neatly and expressively in all the voices, they would
give the greatest pleasure "that music of this type can produce."

When these criticisms were written, Haydn was already the
most celebrated composer in Europe and had been crowned with
the fame of his London concerts. He was approaching his seven-
tieth birthday and was becoming the "grand old man" among
the composers. Compared with his fame and his success, what
praise he did get from the musical magazines was dry and insignificant. This dry critical tune did not change before the beginning of the nineteenth century.

In the period of transition between pedantic criticism and the
genuine enthusiasm of the Romantic movement, we meet the
criticism that was published in the influential Leipzig *Allgemeine
musikalische Zeitung* in 1800. The magazine's Berlin correspondent expatiates on the "sense of well-being" conveyed by Haydn's
music. It inspires him with "an impulse to do good" in the
same way that Sterne's writing does.

On this very evening, I had an argument with W . . . . He found
the symphony only funny . . . you know, of course, his seriousness.
He wants great passion and gravity everywhere. He holds so fast to
Mozart's genius that, like many Christians, he forgets the Son for the
sake of the Father. It is true that one can find more passion in Mozart
on the whole, but is it necessary to find all salvation in outbreaks of
vehement passion?

This was written in 1800. At that time Mozart was the musical representative of passion. It would not be long before he
was supplanted by Beethoven and endured a transformation into
a serene, Olympian god. This transformation was effected in

the critical and popular mind in spite of the tragic clouds that overshadow *Don Giovanni*, the melancholy dreams of the G Minor Symphony, and the D Minor Piano Concerto, which taught Beethoven how to gather tragic thunder.

This musical criticism in the *Allgemeine musikalische Zeitung* was the first of its kind to step out of the fenced garden of music into the wider domain of literature. The comparison between Haydn and Sterne was the first tentative exploration, but it was quickly followed by others. Haydn was compared with Wieland, Gellert, and Richter as well. Carpani likened him to Tintoretto; and during a discussion with Emperor Josef II the composer Dittersdorf compared Mozart with the poet Klopstock, and Haydn with Gellert. Mozart's father said his son was the Klopstock among musicians, and this comparison with a poet who resembled Milton in his austerely solemn style proves that at the end of the eighteenth century Mozart was esteemed as the representative of greatness and gravity rather than of charm and paradisiac happiness. Haydn's jokes and popular cheerfulness were something very new and unusual in music and consequently met with much opposition.

Haydn stepped into the full limelight of his European fame when he made his two concert tours in London. London was the center of the musical world at the end of the eighteenth century, and its most important market. Haydn's success resounded through Germany in a report published in 1794 in the *Journal des Luxus und der Moden* ("*Journal of Luxury and Fashions*"), a society journal published at Weimar. After an enthusiastic account of Haydn's string quartets, the correspondent goes on to say:

But what would you say about the new symphonies he composed for this concert and conducted at the piano! It is admirable what sublime and original ideas the great master weaves into his compositions. There are often moments when it is impossible to listen quietly; one is transported with admiration and applauds with clapping and shouting. This happens chiefly among the French, of whom there are so many here that every place is crowded with them. They are, as you know, highly sensitive and cannot restrain their excitement, so they applaud noisily in the midst of most beautiful passages in sweet adagios, and in this way interrupt the impression. In every symphony by Haydn the adagio or the andante is repeated upon urgent demand. At such moments the good Haydn, whose personal acquaintance I enjoy, always remains very modest. He is, of course, a very kind, frank, and honest man, esteemed and loved by all.

Another report on Haydn's London concerts was published in the Berlin *Musikalische Zeitung* of March 18, 1793. To this correspondent we owe our knowledge of the size of Haydn's London orchestra: twelve to sixteen violins, four violas, three violon cellos, four double basses, flute, oboes, bassoons, horns, trumpets, and kettledrums.

On his return to Vienna Haydn enjoyed the admiration bestowed upon success. In an advertisement of a concert by a Mrs. Auernhammer in 1795, "the great symphony by Mr. Haydn with the popular andante"[1] was the main attraction. In the same year, a concert by the Tonkünstler-Societät threw out the same bait of a performance of "the great symphony with the popular andante." Haydn himself conducted three of his London symphonies at a concert where Beethoven, then only twenty-five years old, played his own piano concerto in B flat. This event took place on December 16, 1795, and the Vienna *Zeitung* announces, "The tickets are to be had from conductor Haydn at his apartment in the Neuen Markt at the house of the Court fruitdealer, third floor, at all hours."

The most welcome mark of respect for old Haydn was the order Prince Esterhazy, his master, gave to the wine-superintendent to deliver "one quart of officer's wine" to him daily. Haydn was fond of wine, and the chorus of the grape-gathering that he was soon to compose for his oratorio, *The Seasons*, with its realistic description of drunken peasants, was an echo of the days he had spent at Eisenstadt, where the vineyards stretched from the little village to the Esterhazy castle.

The two oratorios, *The Creation* and *The Seasons*, mark the high

---

[1] The *Surprise Symphony* in G.

point of Haydn's life and work. These, his most popular compositions, were written when the master was close to seventy, with the light of his mastery and fame shining on his wrinkled face. *The Creation* was performed on April 29 and 30, 1799, in the vast palace of the princes of Schwarzenberg in Vienna. The aristocratic audience came in sedan chairs and in carriages. The crowd was so dense that eighteen mounted and twelve unmounted policemen were needed to keep order. The magazine reports were enthusiastic, especially that of the *Allgemeine musikalische Zeitung. Eipeldauers Briefe* ("*Eipeldauer's Letters*"), [1] a popular contemporary Viennese journal, which glossed its reports with dialect jokes, wrote:

When the music began, there was instantly such a silence that you could have heard a little mouse run; and had people not clapped their hands, one would have thought that no one at all was in the theater. But, my dear, I shall never hear such beautiful music again in my life. I should not have been sorry if I had been forced to sit three hours more, even if the stench and the Turkish bath had been still worse. I should never have believed that the human bellows, the gut of sheep, and the skin of calves could produce such miracles. The music alone expressed thunder and lightning, and you could hear the shower of rain and the new water, and the birds really sang and the lion roared; and you could really hear how the worms crept in the earth. In short, I never left a theater so delighted, and I dreamed the whole night of the creation of the world.

In this way even Viennese malice paid homage to Haydn.

While Haydn was composing *The Seasons*, the magazines seethed with rumors about what he was doing, developing, and planning. News, both true and false, alternated with human-interest stories about the composer. The first performance took place in 1801 at the Grosser Redoutensaal in Vienna, but in this case even Haydn's great fame did not save him from criticism. The realistic tone paintings of the oratorio aroused critical scorn and esthetic censure. The tone painting that should have made

[1] Eipeldau is a village near Vienna. Hence, an *Eipeldauer* is the Viennese equivalent of a hill-billy.

the oratorio popular, and have given it the character of a colorful picture book with its realistic portraiture of croaking frogs,
made the croaking musical critics furious, and they leaped to
the defense of music. A. G. Spazier, the editor of the *Zeitung
für die elegante Welt* ("*Journal for the Fashionable World*"), started
the drive by the guardians of music. He had already published
an unkind criticism of *The Creation*; he now took up the cudgel
against *The Seasons* by complaining about the badness of the
text. "Good taste," he observed, "must oppose some passages."
In fact, he went on to suggest, the whole work should be opposed because it attempted to describe what ought not to be described. In deference to those who enjoyed the oratorio, the
critic pointed out that in a fair, no matter how bad some of its
parts might be, people always find something to please them.
And so it was with *The Seasons*. Praise was due to the "unsur-
passable beauties, and wonderfully worked out details, the true
mastery in the choruses especially," but poisoned seasoning was
liberally mixed in with this praise.

A detailed review of Haydn's new composition was also published in the *Journal des Luxus und der Moden* in August, 1803.
The critic wrote: "As great and unanimous as the applause was,
it would have been still greater had the subject treated by
Haydn's art been chosen with more musical taste." This judgment was followed by a long lecture on what is proper for musical representation and what is not. The critic objected to the
many realistic descriptions. The Hunt, for example, was "common"; the Vintage was "too long." And, finally, the critic
delivered his parting shot: "Notwithstanding its characteristic
perfection, the music has not quite the same value as the music
of *The Creation*."

Still more peremptory was the criticism by F. T. Mann in the
Musikalisches Taschenbuch ("*Musical Pocketbook*"). This critic
held that in "the judgment of a cultured judge of art . . . the
work is, in accordance with its libretto, a detailed imitation of
nature, but common and unworthy of an artist of this rank, and
possesses as such no totality. It is therefore tiring and does not
produce the pure and unified effect of real art."

The most famous performance of *The Creation* took place on March 27, 1808; this was Haydn's last appearance in a concert hall. The hall still exists in Vienna, the great hall of the old university, decorated with colorful frescoes, supported by gorgeous marble columns, and illuminated with covered lights, which make the colors shine magically. Here Haydn sat, an old man of seventy-six, hearing his music for the last time. He was comfortably seated in an armchair, and was surrounded by beautiful Viennese ladies who vied with each other in trying to make him comfortable. He was already so frail that he had to be carried out of the hall after the first part of the oratorio.

The music was applauded frantically, and enthusiastic reports appeared in the *Allgemeine musikalische Zeitung*, in the *Prometheus*, in the *Zeitung für die elegante Welt*, and in the *Vaterländische Blätter* ("*National Magazine*").

A year later, during the occupation of Vienna by Napoleon's army, Haydn died. At Napoleon's order French soldiers kept guard at the door of the composer's house. Haydn's critics were forgotten. Haydn was immortal.

Chapter Nine

MOZART IN MUSICAL CRITICISM

No GREAT musical genius was simpler, more modest, or more human than Haydn. Where the music of other great composers tried to raise the audience to its own lofty heights, Haydn's seemed to remain firmly rooted in the earth, kindly and familiar as Haydn's own character. His happiness, humor, and religious feeling conspired with his delight in composing, as well as with his clarity and friendly urbanity, to make music that was closely connected with the feelings of the common man. His music was not at all difficult to understand — not even the music critics found it hard.

It was otherwise with Mozart, whose music was more complex, more aristocratic, a precious mixture of tragic and comic mood. There was, of course, sensual beauty in his music; splendor of sound and angelic purity; but it was neither so simple nor so healthy as Haydn's music. Mozart was a nervous child, easily brought to tears. He lived in a world of fairy tales, and all his life he remained a child who enjoyed the gaiety of masked balls, and who, when there was no fire, danced with his wife around the stove as two children dance around a Christmas tree. When he composed, his wife had to sit beside him and tell him tales of Snow White and Cinderella. The mood of Mozart's music is the mood of fairy tales. The listener moves into a world where lights are brighter and colors more vivid than those on earth. Like Shelley, he had "luminous wings."

Mozart, like Haydn, arrived at the summit of musical achievement without the help of musical criticism. Criticisms of his work were infrequent before the *Marriage of Figaro* appeared.

When *Idomeneo* was first performed in Munich on January 29, 1781, the report of the *Münchener Staats gelehrten und vermischten Nachrichten* ("*Munich News of the State, Science, and Various Matters*") consisted of these few lines: "On the 29th of the past month, the opera *Idomeneo* was performed for the first time in our new opera house. Libretto, music, and translation originated in Salzburg. The decorations — of which the most inspiring are the view of the seaport and the temple of Neptune — are masterpieces by our theater architect, Mr. Corent Quaglio, and aroused the admiration of all." That is the entire text of the notice. The first real criticisms of Mozart appeared after the first night of his great masterpiece, *The Abduction from the Seraglio*. This opera, the monument to Mozart's love for Constanza Weber, was first performed on July 19, 1782, in the National Theater of Vienna, where Gluck had once been conductor and where *Orfeo* and *Alceste* had been performed for the first time. The theater, small but high, with the Emperor in the first box on the right, flanked by all the aristocrats, was overcrowded. "The opera," reported Cramer's *Magazin de Musik*, "is full of beautiful music. It surpassed the expectation of the public. The striking taste and ideas of the author enjoyed the loudest applause of all." The same magazine also published a detailed, highly laudatory article on the opera. Another flattering article written by B. A. Weber in 1788, appeared in the *Dramaturgische Blätter* ("*Dramatic Magazine*"). Weber, noted as pianist, composer, and conductor, had been visiting Vienna and was present at a performance of the opera. Mozart, who liked the sweet smell of praise as well as any other artist, was so pleased with both these articles that he kept copies of them. After his death they were found in his small library.

In 1783 Mozart gave a subscription concert in the National Theater, playing two new piano concertos of his own composition. His success as a pianist is well documented. Haydn said with tears in his eyes that Mozart's playing was unforgettable because it touched the heart. Clementi testified that nobody else could play with as much spirit and grace as Mozart, and

Dittersdorf found an unequaled fusion of art and taste in his playing. "Mozart·is the best, the most accomplished pianist I ever heard," reported the Vienna correspondent of Cramer's *Magazin der Musik* in 1787. And Rochlitz wrote in the *Allgemeine musikalische Zeitung* that he would never forget "the heavenly delight that Mozart evoked with the spirit of his compositions and the splendor and heart-affecting delicacy of his rendition."

On March 29, 1783, Mozart wrote to his father about the concert in the National Theater. He was happy — he said — that His Majesty the Emperor was present and that he enjoyed the concert and that he applauded so enthusiastically. . . . The concert was reviewed in Cramer's magazine:

Today the famous Chevalier Mozart[1] gave a musical concert for his own benefit in which some of his favorite compositions were performed. The concert was distinguished by an unusually large audience, and the two new concertos and other fantasias which Mozart played on the piano were given much applause. Our Emperor, contrary to his habit, honored the concert with his presence, and the whole audience applauded so unanimously that no similar case comes to mind.

The clarinetist Stadler, for whom Mozart had composed the charming clarinet quintet, gave a concert in Vienna in 1784. On the program was Mozart's serenade for two oboes, two clarinets, two basset horns, four horns, two bassoons, violoncello, and double bass. The Hamburg music critic Schink expressed his opinion of the concert in a series of exclamations: "Today I heard a piece for wind instruments composed by Mr. Mozart, in four movements . . . wonderful and splendid! . . . Every instrument was played by a master. . . . . Oh, it makes an effect! . . . wonderful and great, excellent and magnificent!" The concert was reviewed by the Vienna *Zeitung*. The critic wrote, "A great composition for wind instruments of quite a special kind was performed, composed by Mr. Mozart."

From 1785 on, the laudatory criticisms of Mozart were inter-

[1] Mozart was a Knight of the Golden Spur. The order had been conferred upon him by the Pope when the boy visited Rome in 1770.

mingled with unfavorable and malevolent criticisms. It almost seems as if the dullest critics had a fine feeling for the exact point at which an artist begins to develop the new and personal forces of his genius. When Beethoven began to expand Haydn's symphonic framework, or Wagner to free himself from the romantic operatic form of Weber, Marschner, and Meyerbeer, the music critics scented that something new was in the air, and began to shout that the future of music was imperiled. So the critics scented — and they were right — that the Mozart of 1785 was about to reach heights from which his view of the world was wider. They suspected that he was leaving the sunny, happy days of youth for a different world, where his mastery would become more conscious. Three new accomplishments proved Mozart's new outlook on life and art. The first was his use of the full symphonic orchestra for the first time in *The Marriage of Figaro*. The second was his new use of chromatic harmonies and of dissonances on a chromatic basis. And the third was his Shakespearean mixture of tragedy and comedy. The critics of Mozart's time smelled a rat; and the more conservative they were, the more they cautioned the public against Mozart's innovations. Their unfavorable and indignant criticisms were merely their own way of saying that a genius was beginning to create new art forms. Their intuition was correct.

Criticism turned really sour in 1785 when Mozart published his six string quartets dedicated to Haydn. These quartets had not been composed to order. Mozart wrote them to try out the strengthened forces of his imagination, and his mature technical mastery. This was music to please his own sense of beauty and to meet his own highest ideas of art. In the touching dedication to Haydn by which Mozart introduces these compositions, his children, to the "famous man and dearest friend," he speaks of "his long and industrious work." As a matter of fact, Mozart worked over five years on these quartets. They were written for himself, and this explains the boldness of their style, the novelty of their harmonies, and the joy in experiment which is so evident in them.

The last of these six string quartets is in C major. Sharp dissonances are used in the introduction, and major and minor clash. Dissonant anticipations are so cutting that at each hearing one feels that one is being struck with a knife. Never before had tragic pain been expressed in music with such directness. The artistic expression is almost naturalistic.

It stands to reason that these dissonances met with opposition. Boldness of harmony has always been exciting. Neither eccentric melodies nor strange rhythms are as stirring as new harmonies. To Hanslick, for example, the opening bars of the Prelude to *Tristan and Isolde* were only "chromatic whining." In point of fact they were the heralds of a new age of harmony. Mozart's chromaticism met with the same opposition — and with reason, for Mozart was daring. He used chromatic turns and changes of harmony to express differentiated mental states, to give slight shades and delicate colors. These chromatic mixtures and oscillations impart rich coloring to his harmonies. Even Haydn could learn from Mozart. Witness the chromatic chords that conclude the prelude to *The Creation* and so strikingly anticipate the harmonies of *Tristan*. Even today the dissonances of the introductory measures of the quartet in C major prick the ears of the critics.[1]

In January, 1787 the Viennese correspondent of the *Magazin der Musik* reported of Mozart: "He is the best and cleverest piano player I have ever heard; but it is a pity that in his ingenious and really beautiful compositions he goes too far in his attempt to be new, so that feeling and sentiment are little cared for. His new quartets, dedicated to Haydn, are too strongly spiced — and what palate can stand that for long?" Another guardian of the public taste wrote in the same magazine, "The works of Kozeluch [a forgotten composer] remain alive and are welcomed everywhere, but Mozart's compositions do not unanimously please. It is true, and his new quartets dedicated to Haydn

[1] One finds them stinging the ears of such an intelligent and witty critic as Ernest Newman, who defends his fellow critics as a good uncle defends the conduct of his naughty nephews. See his book, *A Musical Critic's Holiday*.

prove it, that he has a decided inclination for the grave and unusual."

The main characteristic that impressed the critics of the day seems to have been his daring harmonies. The *Allgemeine musikalische Zeitung* advises its readers to regard a composition as Mozart's "especially when one audacious transition closely follows another." As late as 1809 J. B. Schaul [1] found Mozart's harmonies "hard and sophisticated"; Mozart led his hearers "between steep rocks into a thorny forest in which flowers grow but thinly," whereas Boccherini led one "into serene country with flowering meadows, clear, rushing brooks, and thick groves"; Mozart was "a musical Daedalus" who knew "how to construct great, impenetrable labyrinths" but the writer lamented that he knew no Ariadne to provide the thread which should guide him out through the tortuous passages.

How bizarre some critics found Mozart's music is demonstrated by J. G. K. Spazier's review of a concert by the pianist Rick. The review appeared in Reichardt's *Musikalisches Wochenblatt* ("*Musical Weekly*") in 1791. The reviewer wrote: "He played a concerto by Mozart and brought out effectively the sensitive passages and the peculiar traits of this rich artist, who like every great genius must command the most bizarre flights of the soul and who often indulges in the strangest paradoxical turns." Even as late as 1826 Nägeli was lamenting "the exaggerated, debauching contrasts" in Mozart's music. In this last case, it was the Prelude to *Don Giovanni* that aroused the critic to protest.

Mozart's harmonies were not the only elements of his art which offended critical ears. His use of the symphonic orchestra in the opera weighed heavily upon them. This new orchestra was not mere accompaniment, as the orchestras of the earlier Italian *opera buffa* had been. It was the painter of all moods and of all the details of the dramatic action. Out of the orchestra rose Cherubino's enamored sighs, the Countess' noble laments,

---

[1] Court musician in Stuttgart and a writer whose book, *Letters on Taste in Music* (1809), enjoyed considerable authority.

and the clear laugh of Susanna. The orchestra contained the possibility of the merry movement of a musical comedy as well as the calm of the night where only whispers thronged the air. The voices of the orchestra, as in the symphony, were richly tinted. The strings sang tender melodies, or perhaps chirped and chattered like a guitar, scurrying and running , laughing or joking. The wind instruments uttered only a breath, the delicate sound of longing. The horns shouted in mockery. Dittersdorf writes in his autobiography that the Emperor Josef II said after a performance of *The Marriage of Figaro* that Mozart completely blanketed the singers with his full orchestra. In the *Journal des Luxus und der Moden* of 1791, we read that Mozart's operatic orchestra is "artificial, weighty, and overloaded with instruments."

No other reproach is so often met with in contemporary criticisms of Mozart as the charge that his music is overloaded and overstuffed. The impact of this music on indolent ears must have been similar to that which the music of Richard Strauss made on conservative hearers between 1890 and 1910. When *Don Giovanni* was performed in Berlin in 1790, Spazier wrote in the *Musikalisches Wochenblatt* that Mozart was hurling such large masses of sound at his audience that it was almost impossible to survey "the excellent whole." And B. A. Weber maintained in the same journal that if Mozart were to be reproached, "this would be the only blame: that the wealth of beautiful detail almost crushes the soul."

The mighty stride which carried Mozart from *The Marriage of Figaro* to *Don Giovanni* left the critics far behind. They attacked both the immorality of the libretto and the complexity of the music. After the first performance of *Don Giovanni* in Berlin, the *Chronik von Berlin* ("*Berlin Chronicle*") thundered from the critical pulpit that in this opera the eye was satiated, the ear charmed, reason grieved, morality offended, and virtue and feeling trampled upon by vice. "Oh!" cried the critic to unperturbed Mozart, "had you not so greatly wasted the power of your mind! Had your feeling been more in correspondence with your fancy!" The Munich censor even prohibited the showing of the opera. Other critics took exception to the overloading of the music. The *Chronik von Berlin* declaimed to the effect that

music for the theater knows no other rule, and no other judge than the heart. . . . What the composer must express is, not an overloaded orchestra, but heart, feeling, and passion. Only as he writes in a great style, only then will his name be given to posterity. Grétry, Monsigny, and Philidor prove this. Mozart in his *Don Giovanni* intended to write something uncommonly, inimitably great. There is no doubt: the uncommon is here, but not the inimitably great! Whim, caprice, ambition but not heart created *Don Giovanni*.

Again and again the critics chant their the song, that Mozart is not a tasteful composer. In 1793, the *Allgemeine musikalische Zeitung* carried an article that said among other things: "Mozart was a great genius, but he had no real taste, and little or perhaps no cultivated taste. He missed, of course, any effect in his original operas." The critic challenges anyone to come forward and "prove that Mozart understood how to treat a libretto correctly!" When B. A. Weber expressed his admiration for Mozart in the columns of the *Musikalisches Wochenblatt*, an irate reader sent a letter to the publisher, saying, "Weber's judgment on Mozart is highly exaggerated and one-sided. Nobody will overlook the talented man in Mozart and the experienced, rich, and pleasant composer. But I never heard a single profound expert praise him as a correct, much less a perfect composer. Least of all will the tasteful critic believe him to be a composer who is correct in regard to poetry, and sensitive." In 1801 the Parisian correspondent of the Leipzig *Allgemeine musikalische Zeitung* wrote of Mozart as Haydn's rival, but not a serious rival since "he possesses more genius than taste."

One can easily realize how the libretto of *The Magic Flute*, which fused popular humor with nonsense and wisdom and raised the Viennese popular theater to its greatest heights, displeased the tasteful critics. Like Shakespeare's *Winter's Tale*, the opera combined colorful imagination, naïve jokes, and solemnity. Jack Pudding jested before temple walls ornamented with magic signs, while behind them sounded the choruses of the priests. Sublime symbols of light and darkness were to be seen in the background, while in front the animals listened enchanted to the magic flute and wagged their tails. No rationalist could understand this free play of imagination, which so charmed the mind of Goethe. Hence we see in Koch's *Journal der Tonkunst* ("*Journal of Music*") of 1795 a critic lamenting that one "has in this very century to see the fugue, the greatest masterpiece of art, parodied in an opera intended to be half comical and half serious. In that opera, clowns and sages, together with animals and all the other elements, form a chaos in order (as I suppose) to make the miraculous in the serious part of the opera comprehensible, and to make war on good taste and sane reason in a spectacle that dishonors the poetry of our age." Rationalism has here come to the border line beyond which begins the realm of free imagination, where the comedies of Aristophanes, the *commedia dell' arte*, the *Midsummer Night's Dream*, the *Winter's Tale*, and *The Tempest* of Shakespeare, and *The Magic Flute* of Mozart are all at home.

Men like Reichardt and Rochlitz, around 1800, began to inaugurate new and serious forms of musical criticism in their magazines, and began to do justice to Mozart as they had already done to Haydn. The new, enthusiastic style of Rochlitz may be seen in one of his articles, published in the *Allgemeine musikalische Zeitung* in 1800, which praised the quartets for piano, violin, viola, and violoncello that Mozart had composed between 1795 and 1786.

That these quartets enjoyed an immediate success and were played both in drawing rooms and in concerts, we learn from an article entitled "On the Newest Favorite Music Played in the Great Concerts," written in 1788 by a Viennese correspondent of the *Journal des Luxus und der Moden*. This article is of the greatest interest. It shows not only the wide circulation obtained by new music without the benefit of present-day advertising methods, but also that Mozart's music could not be instantly and easily understood. It was complicated music — complicated both from the player's standpoint, and the listener's.

Some time ago there was published [wrote this Viennese correspondent] a quartet (for piano, violin, viola, and violoncello) which is very artfully composed. Its performance requires the greatest precision on the part of all four players, but even in perfect rendition the music can be enjoyed only by musical experts. . . . The rumor that "Mozart has composed a new quartet, that this and that princess owns it and plays it," spread quickly and caused this particular composition to be senselessly performed in great noisy concerts. . . . Many other pieces are impressive even in a mediocre rendition. But this work of Mozart's is intolerable . . . when carelessly executed. This happened last winter in innumerable cases. Almost everywhere I went . . . a lady, or middle-class girl, or some saucy dilettante appeared with the quartet . . . and insisted that one must enjoy the music. One could not enjoy it. Everyone was bored and yawning at the incomprehensible hodge-podge of instruments which did not harmonize in a single bar. . . . But the music had to please. It had to be praised. I can hardly describe with how great obstinacy people took pains to obtrude this music everywhere. It means nothing to dismiss this folly as a passing craze of the day, because it lasted almost the whole winter and was to be met — as I have been told — everywhere and any time.

There we have in one picture the popularity of Mozart's music around 1788, and the ambition of amateurs to play it. We see Viennese society and the difficulties of understanding this modern music. Rochlitz's criticism of these same compositions is serious, enthusiastic, and intelligent, in spite of the many flowers he puts into his critical vase.

In those compositions [he wrote] which are intended only for select, smaller groups, the spirit of the artist appears in a strange, rare form, great and sublime like an apparition from another world. When he softens into sweet melancholy or for some moments dallies with a merry mood, they are but moments only, after which he pulls himself together — if only for moments too — to bold, sometimes wild force; or perhaps he writhes in bitter, cutting agony, triumphant after victory or dying in battle. In order not to believe these words to be mere empty enthusiasm . . . it is necessary to hear an accomplished performance (which is only attainable by persons who possess, besides the necessary great skill, a heart and mature intelligence). . . . One may hear it, then study it and hear it again.

Romantic critics produced the finest evaluations of Mozart, who was most certainly a Romantic himself. To prove the point one need cite only the veiled melancholy of the quintet in G minor, the tragic storm of the piano concerto in C minor, the ghost voices in *Don Giovanni*, the ironic ball game of *Così fan tutte* ("*So Do All Women*"). Mozart's chromatic harmonies were romantic, as were the changing colors of light and shadow that were intensified by Chopin and Debussy. Romantic likewise was his sense of the tragic meaning of life. E. T. A. Hoffmann, musician, poet, and critic, revealed Mozart's romanticism in his fantastic short story *Don Juan*, which he wrote in 1812. And in his *Phantasiestücke* he sang a hymn of praise to the symphony in G minor. "Love and melancholy sound in the sweet voices of ghosts. Night rises in shining gleams of purple. In ineffable longing we follow the apparitions, who beckon in friendly wise. We may join their round dance and fly through the clouds in the eternal dance of the spheres." It was Hoffmann too who first uncovered the romantic irony in *Così fan tutte* in the pages of his collection of tales and novels, *Die Serapionsbrüder*. In 1792 the *Journal des Luxus und der Moden* had called the opera "the silliest thing in the world." Twenty years later, Hoffmann praised the same work as "the essence of comic opera in the fantastic mood that depends on the fanciful flights of the characters, and partly on the bizarre play of chance." The epoch of rationalistic criticism was drawing to an end. The age of poetical criticism was beginning.

Chapter Ten

BEETHOVEN AND THE CRITICS

1. BEETHOVEN'S FIRST YEARS IN VIENNA

SOMETIME in November, 1792, the stagecoach carrying passengers from Passau and Linz to the old fortress town of Vienna stopped at the gate where uniformed officials scrutinized passports and cast suspicious glances at stamps and registrations. One of the travelers was a youth of twenty-two, a small, slender young man with a dark pock-marked face, black eyes, and black hair streaming in the wind. This young man, with his high domelike forehead, flat nose, and teeth that pushed his lips outward, was one of the many musicians who came to this famous city to study with the great composers who made Vienna their home. "Ludwig van Beethoven, musician of His Highness the Elector Max Franz of Cologne," read the official as he looked at the passport. His reading was not unmixed with awe, for he knew that the Elector was an uncle of His Majesty the Emperor of Austria, that same Emperor whose arms were affixed to the officer's hat.

Beethoven disappeared into the stream of passers-by which noisily flowed through the narrow streets of Vienna. There one might see elegant men dressed in silk, with their thin stockings and buckled shoes, army officers fresh from Balkan, Italian, or Belgian campaigns, commoners in sober, black clothes, and Capuchins in brown cowls. One was jostled by carriers of sedan chairs in which sat distinguished ladies; one was importuned by toy-sellers whose wares had been carved in low huts on the Slovakian mountains. There were Italian merchants, Hungarians in the tight trousers and feather-tufted hats of their national costume, smiling girls selling violets in baskets — all forming an uninterrupted medley streaming to and fro and kept in order only by the efforts of the constables, conspicuous by their cocked hats and the tasseled sticks they carried in their hands. When Beethoven emerges from the crowd, we meet him in the Alserstrasse, seated at the drawing-room piano of Prince Carl Lichnowsky. Close to Beethoven sits the Princess Christiana, while behind her chair stands the Prince himself, a great lover of music as well as something of a pianist. Around the piano cluster noted Viennese musicians, among them the violinist Schuppanzigh, a Falstaffian figure. They all stare at the young musician at the piano, whose hands storm over the keyboard awakening masses of sound in broad chords that presently quiet into the charm of a heavenly melody as fervent as a prayer or as simple as a folk song. All of them had heard Mozart, but here was something new. After Mozart's playing, this piano music seemed like a thunderstorm at the close of a long summer's day. The pianist himself, with his shaggy hair almost falling over his dark, ugly face, reminded his listeners of some exotic aborigine. He was as gloomy as a demon endowed with elemental forces; while Mozart, small and graceful, always neatly dressed, had had the charm of a child of genius.

Beethoven gave his first public concert on March 29, 1795. He played his piano concerto in B flat at the National Theater during the intermission of an Italian oratorio. On the following day he gave a second concert in the same hall. This time he improvised, displaying his fancy, wrestling with the demoniac forces in his mighty soul, finally winning his way through to the peace and transfiguration of heaven. A day later, Beethoven again played in a concert, this time an affair arranged by Mozart's widow. He was to play in the intermission after the first half of Mozart's *The Clemency of Titus*, and performed, as befitted the occasion, not his own work, but Mozart's concerto in D minor.

It had taken Beethoven only three years to conquer Vienna — no small matter, for here Mozart had died only four years earlier, and here, in the suburbs, Haydn still lived, surrounded by the humble people whose dialect he spoke. The first Viennese criticism of Beethoven appeared in the Vienna *Zeitung* of April 1, 1795. The article indicated that the composer had won his first battle, for it said in part: "During the intermission, the famous Ludwig van Beethoven, in his first evening, reaped the general applause of the audience with a new piano concerto of his own composition."

In the same eventful year Beethoven published in Vienna the first of his compositions that he deemed worthy of printing, the three trios, *opus* 1. These works had been performed for the first time at Prince Lichnowsky's, in the presence of Haydn. With the three concerts we have mentioned, and the publication of the trios, Beethoven's career was definitely launched.

II. CRITICAL REACTION TO BEETHOVEN'S EARLY WORKS

Beethoven dedicated his first three piano sonatas to Haydn. Consequently he passed in the eyes of Prince Lichnowsky and of Viennese musical society as Haydn's pupil. This was a natural impression, for he seemed to continue that master's work. His first trios and string quartets, the first piano sonatas, the first two symphonies were all written within the framework that Haydn had created and that Mozart had inherited. Thus it was not unreasonable to hope — as the music lovers and musicians of Vienna did hope — that Beethoven would receive and cherish the symphonic forms entrusted to him by the trembling old hands of Haydn.

Few of Vienna's music lovers had much sympathy for the new and revolutionary elements in Beethoven's music, which already, even in the most Haydnesque of his compositions, had begun to seethe like boiling metal in a pot. Beethoven, though using Haydn's forms, had endowed them with a new energetic rhythm, with the strength of marching soldiers. There were in the restless dynamics repressed forces that every moment threatened to erupt like lava from the crater of a volcano. The beginning of the First Symphony, with its unusual opening on a dominant

seventh chord, announces the dawn of a new century of passionate struggle. Surprising harmonic turns point the way toward
romantic feeling. Vehement contrasts express dramatic conflicts
within the soul..

No longer did this music contain the harmonic balance of all
the moods and forces of the soul, as had the music of Haydn. No
longer could one find Mozart's gloriously transfigured beauty
shining through melancholy shadows. In place of these things
there are the excited feeling of Rousseau and the passionate eloquence of Mirabeau, Byron's melancholy, and the storm of
the attack on the Bastille. In the same year in which Beethoven composed these first Viennese works, he wrote in the
album of a friend, "Be charitable where you can; love freedom
more than all; never renounce truth, not even before a throne."
Thus spoke the new citizen of the age of the French Revolution.
Here is a new pride in humanity, a new will to fight. And all
this is to be found in these first compositions, so restricted by the
eighteenth-century forms into which it is cast as to be almost
ready to explode and destroy them. The eruptions of the *Appassionata*, the Third Symphony, and the string quartet in F
minor are here foreshadowed.

The conservative music critics were the first to suspect that the
music of this pupil of Haydn concealed powder kegs on the verge
of exploding. The first criticsms of Beethoven's music are most
interesting human documents. They demonstrate how quickly
and accurately the new elements in it were ferreted out by reactionary minds at a time when ordinary music lovers believed
themselves to be listening to a talented pupil of Haydn. These
critics decried all the novelty of dynamics, rhythm, harmony,
and sound as dangerous to the peace of music. Apparently, reactionary critics are just as sharp-sighted as progressive ones, for
they seem always to be ready to attack what is new, just as a
good policeman holds himself ready to discover every crime almost the moment it is committed.

It would be a poor business merely to quote these reactionary
criticisms of Beethoven, because they are ridiculous. There are

more important documents on human narrowness than stupid criticisms, and more dangerous ones. It is much more essential to analyze the uncanny accuracy with which these critics always hit the exact point where the new music began to progress to new beauty, new expression, and new value. They achieved their goal with the infallible sureness of a head-hunter. The sagacity of a reactionary critic to detect, and, having detected, to check progress with implacable determination — these qualities are so well developed that not the slightest advance of music escapes the attention of these guardians of art. Perhaps the habit of constantly looking backward sharpens the sight.

In 1799 there sprang up a crop of criticisms on the work of Beethoven in the pages of the new musical magazine, *Allgemeine musikalische Zeitung*, published in Leipzig. At the date of its first publication — October 3, 1798 — Beethoven had already printed many compositions: eight trios, ten piano sonatas, one quintet, and the popular serenade, *opus* 8, whose success infuriated the composer. Almost the whole of Beethoven's creation was reviewed in the magazine, and the complete story of the road it traveled from unwilling resistance to admiration and enthusiasm lies open before our eyes. The first of these criticisms appeared in March, 1799. The critic busied himself in tearing to pieces the variations on *Ein Mädchen oder Weibchen* [1] and *Mich brennt ein heisses Fieber*. Time has pulled the cloak of anonymity from the author of the review, though his article, in accordance with the common practice of the day, appeared unsigned. He was Johann Nepomuk Möser, a high Austrian official, well known in Viennese musical circles as a man who judged with the double authority of critic and government official. He seems to have specialized in imprudent attacks on Beethoven. The first review comes straight to the point:

It is well known that Mr. van Beethoven is an excellent pianist. Were it not so well known, one could surmise it after looking at his variations. It is a question, though, if he is as accomplished as a com-

[1] From Mozart's *Magic Flute*.

poser; and this is a more difficult question to answer by judging the present samples. The critic does not mean to say . . . that he did not like some of the variations. He gladly confesses that the variations on *Mich brennt ein heisses Fieber* are better than those of Mozart who worked on the subject when he was young.[1] Beethoven has succeeded less well in the variations on the second theme. Here he permits himself modulations, shocks, and a recklessness that are not at all beautiful. . . . When I look at such transitions and hear them, they are common and remain common, and the more pretentious and contrived they are, the commoner they become.

Möser's final bit of advice to Beethoven is to study the variations of Haydn and Vogler if he really wants to write good music and not music that is nothing more than sounding brass and tinkling cymbals.

Thus the critic perceives, with truly astounding sagacity, the elements of Beethoven's new style in what are really only comparatively simple harmonic progressions. In the following issue of the magazine, one meets with a criticism of the clarinet trio, *opus* 11, in which the critic says that Beethoven ought to be able to write many good compositions, since he evidently possesses an unusual knowledge of harmony as well as a love for serious composition, if he would only "prefer to write naturally instead of affectedly." In June, 1799, our critic took up the three sonatas for piano and violin, *opus* 12, and produced the following judgment:

The critic, who was not until lately familiar with the piano compositions of the composer, worked through these peculiar and overloaded sonatas and has to confess that, after playing them with much care and strain, he has the impression that he had spent his time walking through an alluring forest in the company of a talented friend, delayed every moment by impenetrable thickets, and emerging tired and exhausted. There is no doubt that Mr. van Beethoven goes his own way. But what a bizarre, toilsome way it is! Studied, always studied! No nature, no singing melody! Indeed, even with thorough consideration, one finds only studied masses without good method,

[1] This is apparently a mistake on the part of the critic; for to the best of my knowledge, no such variations exist.

oddities in which we are not interested; striving after rare modulations, hatred for the usual combinations, heaping up of difficulties upon difficulties until we lose all patience and pleasure. . . . If Mr. van Beethoven would control himself more, and go the way of nature, he could with his diligence and talent certainly write many fine compositions for an instrument which he seems to command so excellently.

Is this acknowledgment of Beethoven's oddity, rare modulations, and unusual combinations anything but an acknowledgment of Beethoven's genius? One must understand the special language of reactionary music critics — later-day Joshuas who want the sun to stand still — in order to appreciate the justice of their judgments, their sagacity, and their fine feeling for new artistic values.

In the next criticism (which deals with Beethoven's variations on the duet *La stessa, la stessima*) the critic confesses himself "not to be at all content" with the music. The variations are "stiff and affected" and full of "unpleasant passages where hard tirades in half-tones are in bad relationship with the bass, and conversely. Nay, Beethoven may be able to improvise, but he certainly does not understand how to write good variations." In October, 1799 *opus* 12 was again the object of critical consideration. "The critic does not deny that Mr. van Beethoven is a genius and goes his own way. His wealth of ideas, however, often induces him to heap up his ideas wildly." In his efforts to "adjust himself gradually to the manner of Beethoven," the critic cannot suppress his wish that "the fanciful composer may try to be guided in his work by a certain economy." The critics are already beginning to waver. They are beginning to doff their hats to Beethoven, even though their criticism continues to blunder. Still, it is already obvious that the young Beethoven has been recognized by musical critics as a spiritual force who is expected to revolutionize music.

III. CRITICISMS AFTER 1800

The period when Beethoven could be regarded as essentially a pupil of Haydn's ended at the beginning of the year 1880. At

the turn of the century and at the same time that the French
Revolution was committing the old structure of feudal society
to the flames, Beethoven began to transform the symphonic
forms he had inherited from Haydn. He enlarged the framework
of the symphony with the composition of the *Eroica*. He had a
new feeling for greatness and for masses of sound. He clothed
symphonic forms in a dramatic atmosphere. The delicate, chamber-music style of the symphony, which had originated in the
candle-lit rooms of palaces, gave way to a new abundance of
chords, to music that no longer chattered but spoke in the thunder tones of a mighty speech. Broad, arching planes appeared
in his work, and mighty chords struck the ears of his auditors.
Passionate feelings were tossed up as the sea tosses up waves in
a storm. Dynamics were charged with explosive energy, as if
man had become once more an elemental being, passionate and
wild; like Prometheus, defying the heavens and quarreling with
Jove himself. Within the music we find also new poetical forces:
symphonic music had become the language of humanity, for now
were heard funeral marches and fantastic scherzos with Shake-
spearian overtones, as well as prayers and hymns whose solemnity had never before been equaled.

Rationalistic musical criticism, especially in the reduced state
in which it found itself at the end of the eighteenth century, was
incapable of appreciating the sense of ecstatic feeling, the knowledge of the pathetic struggles of the soul, and the consciousness
of the worth of humanity that Beethoven had discovered. The
minor critics of the period found disquieting signs in both the
First and the Second Symphony. The Viennese correspondent of
the *Allgemeine musikalische Zeitung* found the superabundance of
brass unpalatable in the Frst; while the Second came in for more
severe criticism.

Apparently even the slightest forward step does not escape the
sensitivity of conservative minds. There was certainly no such
striking difference between the First and the Second Symphony
as there was between them and the *Eroica*. Both works (the First
appeared in 1800 and the Second in 1803) seem at first glance to

be on the same plane: they are both in the style of Haydn — that is to say, energetic, vigorous, and buoyant. Nevertheless, conservative criticism was aware of the progress from the First to the Second Symphony with a sureness that seems almost instinctive. The critic of the *Zeitung für die elegante Welt* did not hesitate an instant in condemning the Second Symphony, even though the difference between it and the First does not seem great to us. He maintained that the First Symphony was more valuable than the Second because it was "written with unaffected ease, while in the Second Symphony the striving for new and striking movement is more conspicuous." The critic of the *Allgemeine musikalische Zeitung*, although recognizing its power and originality, its effective instrumentation and careful working out, suggested that it might be greatly improved by "cutting out some passages and a few overstrange modulations."

What else was to be expected from these and similar experts when the *Eroica* appeared? Its first performance took place in Vienna in the winter of 1804-05 at a concert sponsored by the bankers Würth and Fellner. This first, semipublic performance opened a new age of symphonic music: the critics, however, received it in their own inimitable fashion. Thus we read in the *Allgemeine musikalische Zeitung* that the new symphony "is a lengthy, wild and bold fantasy, very difficult to perform. Strikingly beautiful passages in which one can recognize the energetic and talented spirit of the author are not lacking; very often, however, it goes astray into complete irregularity. The critic certainly belongs among the most sincere of Beethoven's admirers, but he has to confess in regard to this composition that there is too much shrillness and bizarreness; this makes it difficult to survey the whole, and one almost entirely loses any sense of coherence."

When the first public performance of the symphony took place in the Theater an der Wien on April 7, 1805, the same critic said that he saw no reason to change his judgment: "The symphony would gain greatly if Beethoven would make up his mind to cut it, and to bring more light, clarity, and unity into the whole." [1]

[1] This critic is the same Möser whose acquaintance we have already made.

The Viennese correspondent of *Der Freimüthige* ("*The Candid*") (edited in Berlin by Kotzebue, the famous playwright) divides the audience into three groups: The first, made up of Beethoven's friends, asserts that the music is masterful, that its style is the style of great music, and that if the public dislikes the work it is because the public has not sufficient culture. After a few thousand years, however, the public will learn to be greatly impressed. The second group denies that the symphony possesses any artistic merit at all. It is of the opinion that there are no traces in the work of beauty, sublimity, or power; that it is, on the contrary, a wholly uncontrolled striving after effect and novelty. This group believes that Beethoven has accomplished a certain undesirable originality by means of odd modulations and forced transitions, and by the combination of heterogeneous elements. It would, for example, be possible to write a Pastoral, working it out in the most exalted style, with a good deal of "jerking in the basses," the use of three horns, and so forth. But genius manifests itself, this group maintains, not by producing things unusual or fantastic, but things beautiful and sublime. The third — and much smaller — group is somewhere in the middle. It concedes some beauties to the symphony, but holds that there is no real unity and that the seemingly infinite duration of the music is tiring for experts and intolerable for amateurs. It hopes that Beethoven may use his great talents to produce works like the first two symphonies, like the charming septet in E flat, and "the spirited quintet in D major." [1] More work along these lines will put Beethoven in the first rank of instrumental composers. This third group, however, does not rest from its labors at this point. It goes on to fear that music can become so complicated that no one but experts will be able to take any pleasure in it; that everyone will leave the concert hall with a feeling of "fatigue, depressed by plenty of incoherent

[1] The critic means the quintet in C major, op 29.

and overstuffed ideas as well as by the perpetual noise of all the instruments." [1]

It seems that neither the audience nor Beethoven were entirely pleased by that first performance. For the audience, the symphony was too long and too difficult and the composer too impolite, for he did not even condescend to nod to his hearers when they applauded. Beethoven, on his side, did not find the applause sufficiently flattering.

The critic whose remarks have just been paraphrased stands guard over the realm of music like a policeman. He shakes his bludgeon at the composer who wants to cross over the boundaries of Haydn's music. He shouts at the criminal, "Stay where you are!" It is his business to see that order is maintained, and it is the business of the composer of genius to destroy the old order and to create a new one. Brahms used to say, "It would have been possible for Beethoven to become a great criminal." He was just such a criminal in the eyes of the policeman who guarded the domain of music.

Beethoven did not confine his trespassing on forbidden ground to the field of the symphony. At the same time that the *Eroica* was shaking the world with its passionate storm of feeling, the Razumovsky string quartets, the violin concerto, and the *Appassionata* were produced. When Schuppanzigh and his colleagues tried to play the new music of the Razumovsky quartets, they laughed at it, convinced that they were not real quartets at all, but a practical joke on Beethoven's part. The correspondent of the *Allgemeine musikalische Zeitung* reported on the new quartets as follows: "Three new, very long and difficult quartets . . . which are profoundly invented and well worked out, but not intelligible to everyone." This criticism appeared on February 27, 1807. The violin concerto, which had been played by Clement in the Theater an der Wien on December 23, 1806, was criticized

---

[1] Two years later there appeared in the same periodical a very detailed and appreciative article on the same symphony. In the issue of February 18, 1807, the critic discussed "the strange and colossal work, the vastest and most artistic created by Beethoven's original and wonderful fancy."

in the *Theaterzeitung* ("*Theater News*") of Vienna by Möser. That
learned judge reported that the opinion of all the experts was
the same: "They concede many beautiful details to the composition, but state that the coherence is often disrupted and that
the perpetual repetitions of some vulgar passages may easily
tire." The thunderstorm of the *Appassionata* drew from the
critic of the *Allgemeine musikalische Zeitung* the pronouncement,
"In the first movement Beethoven again released many evil spirits whose shape we already know from other of his great sonatas,
though it is worth while to overcome the great difficulties and
one's indignation over affected oddities and eccentricities." This
comment was published in the April 1, 1807, issue. In the
Journal des Luxus und der Moden of February, 1807, one can read
that even at this period many blamed Beethoven's "neglect of
noble simplicity, and the exaggerated accumulation of ideas
that, because of their abundance, are not sufficiently connected
and developed, and therefore produce the same effect as uncut
diamonds."

The same year in which Beethoven's *Eroica* cast its shadow on
the sunny landscape of Haydn and Mozart saw the first performance of *Fidelio*. On November 20, 1805, officers of Napoleon's
army sat in the orchestra of the Theater an der Wien and heard
the new music. The court, the aristocrats, the bankers, and the
other well-to-do people of Vienna had fled from the city. French
grenadiers kept guard in front of the palace of Schönbrunn, in
whose rococo rooms Napoleon dictated his orders. Consequently the theater was nearly empty and the applause thin.

Fidelio was another *Eroica*. The opera glorified heroism, freedom, justice, and love. Only six years earlier, fanatical Parisian
crowds had stormed the Bastille and released its prisoners. Now
the French officers could see another Bastille on the stage. They
saw the dusky walls of a prison, subterranean cells where prisoners starved, longing for the blue sky and the fragrance of growing things. Heroic courage and a woman's love open the prison
doors, while jubilant choruses praise the brotherhood of man.
In Leonore's aria one hears again the exulting horns of the

Eroica, fanfares of battle and victory. And in the gloriously ecstatic choruses at the end of the opera Beethoven is already close to the hymns of the Ninth Symphony. The opera was a personal confession. The subject was Beethoven's own; its expression, the expression of his own ideals, his enthusiasm for humanity, his hatred of oppression, his ardent desire for love, his morality, and his religion. The stream of his symphonic music flowed in the opera; and it was, in fact, the prison scene from *Fidelio* that kindled the flames of Wagner's dramatic genius. Brünnhilde and Isolde could not have existed without Leonore. This opera, Beethoven's only effort in the field, was to affect the whole evolution of nineteenth-century German operatic music. It was the real "Music of the Future."

It stands to reason that a creation of this kind, with its dramatic passion and its moral sublimity, was incomprehensible to contemporary critics. Music critics did not yet exist who possessed the critical vision that Romanticism was to produce. The critics of Beethoven's day were the impoverished descendants of the great rationalist critics of the eighteenth century, who believed that all the phenomena of the artistic world could be judged by reason. These pedantic heirs of a dead past thought themselves expert enough to judge art works by the worn-out standards of traditional criticism. The report published in the most distinguished musical magazine of the time, the Leipzig *Allgemeine musikalische Zeitung*, on January 8, 1806, well demonstrates the narrowness of the critical outlook and the distance between unimaginative criticism and highly creative imagination:

The strangest among the musical products of the last month was certainly Beethoven's long-expected opera, *Fidelio*. . . . It was performed for the first time on November 20, but was received very coldly. I shall discuss it somewhat fully. Whoever has followed with interest and serious scrutiny the march of Beethoven's otherwise uncontested talent, must expect something different from what we were given. Beethoven has often sacrificed beauty to novelty and strangeness. One ought, therefore, to expect, first of all, peculiarity, novelty, and some original creative splendor from his first theatrical creation. And just those qualities are not to be met. The whole, regarded calmly and without bias, is neither conspicuous by invention nor by performance. The overture [*Leonore*, No. 2] consists of a very long adagio debauched into all keys, followed by an allegro in C major which cannot bear comparison with Beethoven's other instrumental compositions, not even with the overture to the ballet *Prometheus*. Most of the arias are not based on new ideas; they are generally too long, the words being repeated incessantly; and, finally, they are strikingly lacking in characterization. I quote as an example the duet in G major in the third act that follows the recognition scene. The incessant accompaniment of the highest chords of the violins seems rather to express loud, wild jubilation than the quiet, sad feeling of finding each other in these circumstances. Much better is the four-voiced canon in the first act, and an effective aria in F[1] where three obbligato horns and one bassoon form a nice though somewhat overloaded accompaniment. The choruses are without effect, and one of them which expresses the delight of the prisoners in enjoying the fresh air is a manifest failure. The performance was not a good one either. Mrs. Milder does not possess enough passion or life for the role of *Leonore* in spite of her beautiful voice; and Demmer almost always sang flat. All together (and partly as the result of circumstances) the opera was given but three times.

In Kotzebue's *Der Freimüthige* we read that the opera did not please, that the melodies lacked character, and that the whole opera was far from being an accomplished, let alone a perfect, work. The *Zeitung für die elegante Welt* called the third act too long, and the music repetitious and without effect. Even after Beethoven had rewritten the opera and the new version was performed in 1806, the critic of the same magazine said in the issue of May 20, "Beethoven lacks the ability to survey and to judge the text with a view to its effect on the whole work. . . . The overture displeases almost completely because of its incessant dissonances and the overloaded whirring of the violins, and is more affectation than real art."

The great symphonic overture, the ancestor of the great sym-

---

[1] It is always more cautious not to mention keys. The aria is in E.

phonic poems of the nineteenth century, roused the wrath of the critic of *Der Freimüthige*. He pointed out in the issue of September 11, 1806:

All impartial experts and music lovers have unanimously been of the opinion that never has such incoherent, shrill, confused, ear-shocking music been written. The most cutting dissonances follow each other in really horrible harmony. Some fussily insignificant ideas — among them the post-horn solo announcing the arrival of the governor — complete the disagreeably stunning impression. Only Beethoven's intimate friends admire and idolize such things, taking pains to thrust their opinion on others, desiring only to build an altar to Beethoven on the ruins of other composers. They want to include all that most definitely cannot be called beautiful in Beethoven's work under the wider sphere of the great and the sublime, as if real greatness and sublimity were not simple and unpretentious. The critic has often enough documented his esteem for Beethoven's genius and his love for many very beautiful instrumental works of Beethoven. Therefore he regrets the more that Beethoven obstinately travels this road of difficulty, shrillness, and oddity, which most surely leads away from real beauty. Clear beauty without sloppiness, the forceful and not overloaded use of all the instruments, full inner life without tension and overstrain, are all visible in a wonderful overture by Romberg [*sic!!*] which may serve as a perfect pendant for Beethoven's overture.

Thus the criticism which began with narrow-mindedness ends with being merely ridiculous. The historian of music criticism must preserve these examples, as medical men preserve freaks in bottles of alcohol, so that students may learn something about the strange behavior of nature and of man.

Chapter Eleven

MUSICAL MAGAZINES IN THE AGE OF THE CLASSICS

I. THE NEW LITERARY STYLE EXEMPLIFIED IN GERMANY

BETWEEN the years 1759 (in which Haydn wrote the first of his symphonies) and 1810 (in which E. T. A. Hoffmann wrote his first romantic essays on Beethoven's music) the style and manner of the musical magazines had changed. The language of criticism lost the pompous heaviness that had characterized the diction of the first influential critics of Hamburg, Leipzig, and Berlin, and shook off its scholarly slowness. It became more flexible, lighter, more natural. It took leave of the theoreticians and entered the homes of music lovers and amateurs; it knocked on the doors of coffeehouses and went to parties. This change in style was similar to the change that brought about the rise of the classical English prose — plain, clear, and efficient — of the eighteenth century. The change was early apparent in the magazines edited by Hiller: their language began to approach the daily life of the common reader.

The literary language of Germany gained in fluency when, under the influence of the great French writers of the eighteenth century, Wieland increased its mobility. He knew how to *badiner avec grâce*, as La Fontaine did in France. There was no other German poet who could deserve the praise that La Harpe bestowed upon La Fontaine: "He does not compose, he converses." In addition to the influence exercised by Wieland, literary German was inspired by the greatest of German writers: Lessing, Schiller, and Goethe. Lessing, the keenest journalist in Germany, wrote a clear, sunny prose, sharp as an arrow and

156

mobile as a bird. Schiller added glamour and heroic sound to the language, and Goethe contributed his pure humanism. In this manner writers, scholars, and critics were given a new language, more flexible, simpler, and more transparent than the language of the eighteenth century. The romanticism of the first three decades of the nineteenth century added new elements that had been almost unknown to the writers of the previous century: enthusiasm, poetical moods, and delight in feeling.

Thus musical criticism acquired a new and flexible instrument for praise and blame, for its enthusiasms, its malice, its benevolence, its prudence, and its narrowness. But a new danger arose when critical language grew close to the daily talk of the people. Everyone believed himself capable of handling the instrument. Whoever spoke the language of the street or of the middle class believed that he could discuss music as authoritatively as he discussed everyday events. Only an expert, a musician with humanistic training, theoretical knowledge, and practical experience could write in the manner of Mattheson and Marpurg. But now anyone could chatter about music, using everyday language. Critical language had, it is true, become fluent and pliable; it also ran the risk of becoming trivial. The great amount of commonplace criticism produced between 1760 and 1810 can be explained by the greater ease of writing. The average style had become everyone's style. There has never been so much dull, banal, and arrogant criticism of music as that produced by the writers of the latter half of the eighteenth century.

Progress is everywhere attended by mistakes and blunders, and the poularization of critical language was a form of progress. It was one of the means that connected the various strata of society so intimately in the age of classicisms Musical magazines ceased being reviews for experts only, and developed into reviews for the general public and for the amateurs, whose ranks swelled daily. These magazines contributed to the formation of a great critical society, and some of the editors, such as Reichardt and Rochlitz, became influential leaders of musical culture in Germany. The influence of musical magazines — the *Allegemeine musikalische Zeitung* of Leipzig, for instance — was great, for the critical voice of these magazines was the only one to be heard in public life.

II. REICHARDT AND HIS MUSICAL WRITINGS

The first editor of a musical magazine in this new era who gives the impression of a modern personality was Johann Friedrich Reichardt. The dignified writers of the Age of Reason are remote from the liveliness of modern times. Their lives and writings are too much a part of a bygone period. Hiller, in Leipzig, is closer to the present, but he had the traits of a philistine, though these traits were somewhat relieved by his charm. Reichardt was an artist, with all the virtues and weaknesses of the artistic temperament. His life did not progress along straight and well-defined paths. There was movement, adventure, and a fine contempt for conventional standards in his career. With him, one is far from the quiet dignity of the age of Bach, and closer to the complicated unrest of the age of Wagner.

Reichardt was born in 1752 in Königsberg, Prussia. He began to compose when only eight years old. He later became a student at the university in Königsberg, and was fortunate enough to hear the lectures of Kant, who spoke in his fine, high voice on nature, morals, and esthetics. But since Reichardt inherited his father's restless blood, he did not long remain in the town of "pure reason," whose people used to set their watches when Kant passed by their houses. The young man soon began to wander, and first stopped in Leipzig. There Hiller became his friend, but Reichardt's blood was boiling in his veins with the restlessness of youth, and even writing scores all day and drinking champagne all night could not exhaust his activity. Soon the desire to see strange towns and strange people set him moving again. Before he finally settled down, he had wandered through half of Germany.

When only twenty-four years old, he became court conductor for King Frederick II of Prussia. It was not easy to be court conductor for Frederick. When Reichardt asked the King to permit "his most submissive servant" to compose an opera, the King wrote on the margin of the petition: "He shall not compose operas. He does not understand how, and does not do the right things. He shall do only what I have ordered." What the King ordered was a great deal for any man to accomplish, for Frederick was accustomed to command his court musicians, librettists, singers, and composers in the intervals between battles, and sometimes even from the battlefield itself. And he was demanding. Once when the famous singer Mara interpolated an aria of Reichardt's in an opera, the King turned to his court composer Benda and said, "Have you ever heard such an infamous aria? The song sounds as if it came from a public house; only the ruffians in taverns play such things." Reichardt was to succeed in satisfying Goethe, whose poetry he anticipated Schubert in setting to music; but he could not satisfy the King of Prussia, who commanded his composers as he did his grenadiers. He ordered Benda to inform the court conductor that if he would not or could not compose better, he would send him to the Devil.

When the revolutionary ideas of 1789 spread like a forest fire through Germany, Reichardt incurred the royal displeasure by cutting off the head of a king in a pack of cards. For this revolutionary act he was punished by losing his position as court conductor. However, within a few years he got back his position, and displayed astonishing activity as a composer and writer in Berlin. His house there and his beautiful country seat at Giebichenstein became centers where artists and scholars gathered, among them Steffens, the great physicist; Raumer, the historian; Schleiermacher, the religious philosopher; and Tieck, poet and one of the leaders of the Romantic movement. The more romantic among the ladies also offered homage to the handsome and talented musician. Reichardt seems to have been a thorough man of the world, familiar with Paris and London, and friendly with Goethe, the greatest German poet of the age. There was nothing narrow or musty about Reichardt; he was one of the most vital men of his time.

The year 1791 saw the publication of Reichardt's first musical magazine, the *Musikalisches Wochenblatt* ("*Musical Weekly*"), issued with the collaboration of F. A. Kunzen. This was followed by the *Musikalische Monatsschrift* ("*Musical Monthly*") in 1792. In 1796 he became editor of the magazine *Deutschland*, a great part of which was devoted to music. Among the essays published in that journal were an article on Mozart's opera *The Clemency of Titus*, and a particularly interesting criticism of a performance of Gluck's *Alceste*. Reichardt's fourth magazine, the *Berlinische musikalische Zeitung* ("*Berlin Musical Times*") appeared in 1805.

We owe the book *Vertraute Briefe, geschrieben auf einer Reise nach Wien* ("*Intimate Letters, Written on a Journey to Vienna*") to Reichardt's brisk personality and his tendency to put himself in the center of the musical events of the day. The book gives us a lively picture of the Vienna of 1808 and 1809, as well as an admirable portrait of Beethoven. Our critic had already put himself on record as an admirer of the great composer in an article on the song *Adelaïde*, in which he had said that the composition was "not only very pleasant, but rich in the just expression of the melody and particularly important modulations." Now he stood face to face with Beethoven, and his descriptions have the breath of life in them. Reichardt was the first to look upon the trinity of Haydn, Mozart, and Beethoven and discover their essential unity. His characterization of the three composers is still valid today.

Haydn [he wrote] created [by] drawing from the clear, pure source of his charming original personality. He remains therefore always unique. . . . Mozart's more vigorous and richer fancy encompassed more, and in several pieces expressed the highest and deepest feeling of his inner self; moreover, he was more the virtuoso himself, and expected more from players; he attributed more significance to elaborate development, and thus built his palace upon Haydn's charming garden house of fancy. Beethoven early made himself at home in this palace, and so it was left to him to express his own personality in his own forms, the bold, defiant building of the tower to which no one could add without breaking his neck.

E. T. A. Hoffmann added his own variations on this theme when he discovered "the expression of a cheerful, childlike soul" in the instrumental compositions of Haydn. Mozart, he wrote, led one into "the depths of the realm of ghosts," while Beethoven entered the realm of "the monstrous and immeasurable." In his criticism of Beethoven's Fifth Symphony, Hoffmann said:

Haydn comprehends the humanity in human life romantically; it is easier for the majority to understand him. Mozart strives for the superhuman and the miraculous that dwell in the depths of the mind. Beethoven's music sets in motion the levers of fear, stirs shuddering, terror, and anguish, and rouses the infinite longing that forms the essence of romanticism.

III. OTHER GERMAN AND AUSTRIAN MUSICAL PERIODICALS

The *Berlinische musikalische Zeitung* ("*Berlin Musical Times*"), edited by Spazier in Berlin in 1794; the *Journal der Tonkunst* ("*Journal of Music*"), published in Braunschwieg and Erfurt; and the *Augsburger musikalische Merkur* ("*Augsburg Musical Mercury*"), 1795, were some of the less important musical magazines contemporary with those published by Reichardt. Vienna, the musical center of the German world, was poor in magazines. In this city, where everyone seemed to be a musician by nature, each person was his own music critic. Reichardt described the Vienna of 1783 as a city whose whole life was filled with music: "The court practiced music passionately; the nobility was the most musical that ever existed; the whole merry populace took part in the merry art. . . ." Vienna's first musical magazine began its life early in 1813, but in spite of every effort the *Wiener musikalische Zeitung* ("*Vienna Musical Magazine*") disappeared in the same year. Three years later, F. A. Kanne, an important critic whom Beethoven once asked for an opera libretto, made a second attempt to provide Vienna with a musical magazine with the publication of the *Allgemeine musikalische Zeitung* ("*General Musical Magazine*"). Kanne seems to have been a genius run wild. He was a real Bohemian who came to Vienna from Germany, lived as a parasite on Prince Josef Lobkowitz, and died with a bottle in his hand as testimony to the fact that his passion for drinking was equal to his enthusiasm for the music of Beethoven. In 1824 the magazine expired as miserably as its editor.

In Hamburg, Carl Friedrich Cramer edited his *Magazin der Musik* from 1783 to 1787. In 1789 Cramer's magazine was published under the title *Musik in Kopenhagen* ("*Music in Copenhagen*"). The issues of this last year contained valuable articles on the state of French music, on Slavic music, on tone-painting, and on other musical subjects. The musicologist Forkel, famous as Bach's first biographer, published his *Musikalisch-kritische Bibliothek* ("*Musico-critical Library*") in Gotha during 1778 and 1779. And from 1778 to 1781, Abbé Vogler, one of the most colorful musicians of the time and teacher of Weber and Meyerbeer, edited in Mannheim the monthly *Betrachtungen der Mannheimer Tonschule* ("*Considerations of the Mannheim School of Music*"). This periodical was well known for its many critical polemics. Likewise the *Journal des Luxus und der Moden*, which was edited in Weimar from 1786 to 1822 by Bertuch and Kraus, and the *Musikalische Realzeitung* ("*Technical Musical News*") of 1788 were important musical periodicals.

Berlin retained its rank as a center of musical criticism with the publication in 1824 of the *Berliner allgemeine musikalische Zeitung* ("*Berlin General Musical Magazine*"). The distinguished editor of this magazine was "the spirited Doctor Marx," as Beethoven called him. Adolph Bernhard Marx wrote a *Lehre von der Komposition* ("*Textbook of Composition*"), an authoritative guide in its time. Marx was one of the great theoretical teachers who grew up, like oaks, in German soil. He belongs to the tradition established by Marpurg, J. J. Fux, Kirnberger, and Simon Sechter. He was the first scholar to lecture on musical theory at the University of Berlin, and the first to write a biography of Beethoven. As a writer, he belonged to the imaginative class, for he was an enthusiastic man who contributed to the understanding of Bach, Handel, Gluck, and Beethoven. Many of his articles were published in musical magazines, particularly in the *Cäcilia*, which was published in Mainz from 1824 to 1848 and enjoyed great fame because of its valuable news and articles.

However, there was no musical magazine in Germany (one might also say, in the world) which could be compared with the *Allgemeine musikalische Zeitung* of Leipzig. From October 3, 1798, when its first issue was delivered, to 1834, when Robert Schumann began publication of his *Neue Zeitschrift für Musik* ("*New Journal of Music*") in the same city, it was the foremost and most respected musical authority in Germany.

Johann Friedrich Rochlitz was born in Leipzig in 1769. As a boy, he was a student at St. Thomas's School, and sang in the choir of St. Thomas's Church where Bach had played the organ. There were later recollections than that of Bach in the venerable school, for in 1789 Mozart came to Leipzig, and the choir of St. Thomas's School sang for him the Bach cantata *Singet dem Herrn ein neues Lied*, conducted by Doles, the cantor. Rochlitz saw the small, stylishly dressed composer, who played on the church organ, and in private houses on the viola. He heard Mozart praise Handel: "Handel knows best of us all what great effects mean. When he wants one, he strikes like a thunderstorm." No wonder that Rochlitz was enthusiastic about Mozart when he wrote in 1800 about the composer's two quartets for piano and strings, "In those compositions the composer's genius impresses one in a rare, strange manner, like an apparition from another world." But Rochlitz, unlike many critics of his time, was able to go beyond Mozart to Beethoven, whom he visited in 1822. It was he who suggested to Beethoven that he write music for Goethe's *Faust*. He described Beethoven's answer in an imaginative way: "'Aha,' he said, and raised his hand high. 'That would be a piece of work! That could be something!' He continued a while in this manner . . . and throwing back his head he stared at the ceiling." Meeting the great composers of his time, and touched by the spirit of the immortals, Rochlitz was well prepared to edit a musical magazine that was dedicated to the serious and sympathetic study of all new music.

Rochlitz was fortunate enough to find excellent collaborators.

In almost the same year (1809) Weber and E. T. A. Hoffmann, the two heralds of musical romanticism, published their first articles in the *Allgemeine musikalische Zeitung*. Thus, Rochlitz's magazine was in the vanguard of criticism, and the other critics followed in its path.

IV. EARLY MUSICAL MAGAZINES IN FRANCE AND ENGLAND

The first European country to follow the German lead in founding musical magazines was France. The earliest in date of the French musical magazines was *Sentiments d'un harmonophile sur differents ouvrages de musique* ("*Opinions of a lover of harmony on divers musical works*"), issued in 1756. This was followed by the *Journal de musique française et italienne* ("*Journal of French and Italian Music*"), 1764–68, and the *Journal de musique historique, théorique, et pratique* ("*Journal of historical, theoretical and practical music*"), 1770–71. *La correspondance des amateurs musiciens*, afterwards called *Correspondance des professeurs et amateurs de musique* ("*Correspondence of professional and amateur musicians*"), ran from 1802 to 1805 and was edited by one Cocatrix, whose first name is not known as, following the custom of the times, he signed himself "Citizen Cocatrix." The title of his magazine shows the increasing role played by amateurs in musical life, a characteristic of the period around 1800. The first French journal of international importance sas *La Revue musicale* ("*The Musical Review*") founded by Francois-Joseph Fétis in 1827. But this belongs rather to the period of Romanticism; so Fétis's activities are described in a later chapter. *Le Ménestrel* ("*The Minstrel*"), founded by the publisher Heugel in 1833, is still a faithful chronicler of musical life and contains many excellent and scholarly articles and reviews.

Among the men who produced this first generation of French musical magazines, the two editors of the short-lived *Tablettes de Polymnie* ("*Polyhymnia's Tablets*") (1800–01) have retained some slight fame. Giovanni Giuseppe Cambrini (1746–1825), an Italian adventurer-musician, was endowed with that extraordinary facility that characterizes many Italian musicians. Between dozens of operas, scores of symphonies, and hundreds of quartets, he managed to find time to edit the *Tablettes*. Alexis de Garaudé (1779–1852), the other editor, had, like most of his contemporaries, to change his skin with every new political regime, but he managed to retain his position in both the Imperial and Royal chapel choir, and ended his career as a professor of voice in the Conservatoire.

In England, the first journal of music to achieve a position of authority was *The Quarterly Musical Magazine and Review*, which flourished from 1818 to 1828. Edited by R. M. Bacon, it was unusually ambitious in its scope, for besides publishing musical reportage and criticisms of performances, it invited and instituted correspondence on all branches of musical knowledge, and reviewed compositions. The literary bent of the English was reflected in the *Quarterly's* publishing pieces of poetry which the editor deemed suitable for musical setting. The custom, still maintained by a number of musical periodicals, of printing a piece of music in every issue, began with the third volume of the *Quarterly*, and was adopted by *The Harmonicon* under the editorship of William Ayrton.

Although, like the *Quarterly*, it prospered for only ten years (1823–33), *The Harmonicon* was an ably run journal and dealt with a great variety of subjects. Ayrton (1777–1858), who also contributed musical and literary criticism to the *Morning Chronicle* and the *Examiner*, provides an interesting example of a situation rarely encountered in the annals of musical criticism: he performed his duties without pay. He was an active and influential promoter of music. One of the founders of the London Philharmonic Society and several times director of the King's Theater, he demonstrated his excellent musical taste by introducing to the British public Mozart's operas *Così fan tutte* and *The Magic Flute* in 1811 and *Don Giovanni* in 1817. Among other things, he wrote the chapters on music in Knight's *Pictorial History of England* and the notes on music for the *Pictorial Shakespeare*. He frequented Lamb's house, who wrote that he was "the last and steadiest left me of that little knot of whist-players, that used to assemble weekly, for so many years, at the Queen's Gate." Hazlitt called him "the Will Honeycomb of our set," and has left a pleasant, shadowy portrait of him in "Of Persons One Would Wish to Have Seen."

An earlier prototype of such excellent modern periodicals of musical criticism as *Music and Letters* was *The Musical World*, founded in 1836. While chiefly a musical journal, it was also concerned with letters and other matters not directly connected with music. The fifty-odd volumes of *The Musical World* disclose a range of interest in the humanities unparalleled in the highly developed German periodical literature devoted to music. *The Musical World* was just as much interested in current esthetic and dramaturgic theories as it was in the ideas of Aristotle and Lessing. In addition it published a great deal of original poetry, together with translations from languages ranging from Greek to Icelandic.

V. THE NEW BOURGEOIS MUSICAL SOCIETY

These many musical magazines, the greater number of which were published in Germany, demonstrate how greatly the interest in music had increased in the age of the classics. The new critical language shows that music had become the art of a much broader segment of the public. This new musical public had arisen during the seventeenth century. They had fought the political and religious battles of Protestantism in nearly all the countries of Europe. Their consciousness of personal worth, backed as it was by the insistence of Protestantism on the direct relationship between a man and his God, fomented democratic feelings. The new economic systems in France, England, and Austria promoted trade and new wealth, while the great wars of the eighteenth century produced a new type in the businessmen who had grown rich by war profiteering. This new group in society was augmented by the many high officials of the great states in the period of the Counter Reformation, which had everywhere strengthened the power of princes and created a new officialdom. Thus the feudal society of princes and aristocrats existed in the midst of a newly wealthy middle class, while below this upper middle class the bourgeoisie gathered strength, culture, and modest fortunes.

This new society built gorgeous palaces in eighteenth-century Vienna, Prague, and Budapest. Haydn wore the livery of the princes of Esterhazy: blue dress coat with silver lace and buttons, blue waistcoat, stitched frill, and white necktie. Beethoven, as a musician of the Elector of Cologne, was dressed in a green coat, green knee breeches with buckles, white silk stockings, three-cornered hat, and sword with a silver knot. They were the employees, if not the servants, of aristocrats. But there was also a group of wealthy middle-class men as a broad annex to aristocratic society. Haydn dedicated a number of his string quartets to Johann Trost, a rich trader. Mozart and Haydn were at home with Michael Puchberg, a manufacturer. The physician Genzinger was a friend of Haydn, while Mozart's acquaintances in Salzburg consisted of aristocratic officials of the archbishop and middle-class men like the merchant Hagenauer, Scharl, a professor, and Mayer, an official of St. Peter's Chapter.

It is apparent, then, that in the period of the classics there was already a large substructure of middle-class society in musical life. At the beginning of the eighteenth century musical societies sprang up in many German cities, their attendance at concerts marking the beginning of the first really public performances. Telemann inaugurated concert performances in Frankfurt in 1713, and in 1722 he began to arrange public concerts in Hamburg, the programs consisting of instrumental music, cantatas, and oratorios. These concerts took place every Monday and Thursday. The price of admittance was one gulden, eight groschen. In 1761 these concerts were transferred to a new, heated hall. Philidor performed a like office in Paris when, in 1725, he founded the Concerts spirituels ("Spiritual Concerts"). These took place in the Swiss hall of the Tuileries twenty-four times a year. Haydn composed six symphonies for them. In 1743 Doles arranged evening concerts in the Three Swans Restaurant in Leipzig, which later developed into the famous Gewandhauskonzerts. The Musikübende Gesellschaft ("Music Practising Society") began to perform orchestral music in Berlin in 1749. The year 1770 saw the formation of the Liebhaberkonzert ("Amateurs' Concert"), and 1787 the beginning of the Konzert für Kenner und Liebhaber ("Concert for Experts and Amateurs"). All these groups disappeared when Reichardt started his Concerts spirituels, which gave performances during Lent every Tuesday evening. In 1783 or 1784, the Liebhaberkonzerte began in Munich; and Vienna, not to be outdone, supported amateur concerts as well as those performed in the palaces of the aristocrats. The most noted were the concerts in the Mehlgrube and those in the Augarten park. The Mehlgrube concerts boasted gambling as an added attraction, card tables being set up in adjoining rooms. The Augarten concerts, on the other hand, offered the possibility of strolling in the park and flirting while Beethoven's symphonies were being played in the concert hall. A third amateur concert group was organized in 1807, first in the Mehlgrube and then in the great auditorium of the University. There, in 1807, Beethoven conducted his *Coriolan* overture and the *Eroica*. He conducted his Fourth Symphony there in 1808.

Choral societies formed by the men and women of the new middle classes also became important factors in the growing musical life. Fasch organized the Berliner Singakademie ("Berlin Singing Academy") in 1790, a group who dedicated their exertions to the performance of motets and madrigals as well as to the choruses of Bach and Handel. In 1809, Zelter founded the Berliner Liedertafel ("Berlin Singing Circle"). The first of these choral associations in Vienna gave its inaugural public performance in 1812. More than four hundred musicians were on the stage of the Redoutensaal to perform Handel's oratorio *The Power of Music*. Mosel, secretary of the court, conducted, Andreas Streicher, the noted manufacturer of pianos, was at the piano, and Haydn's friend Trost was concertmaster. The singers and instrumentalists were almost all members of the Viennese middle class.

Private associations of a similar character began to play a considerable part in Viennese musical life about the same time. In 1812 or 1813, the "Reunion" association was founded, which gave weekly concerts in a restaurant. This association arranged a performance of Beethoven's oratorio, *Christ on the Mount of Olives*, in 1813, conducted by the composer himself.

When the courts and the aristocrats began to diminish in importance, traveling musicians appeared at the concerts of these amateur associations. Others played in theaters between the acts of a drama. The marked increase in the number of these traveling virtuosos can be explained only in terms of the growth of the musical public after the middle of the eighteenth century. Complaints against the abuses and absurdities practiced by these virtuosos appear as early as 1793 in the columns of the Berlin *Allgemeine musikalische Zeitung*:

> Musical birds of passage, bustling violinists and players of wind instruments are to be seen in every town of the Holy Roman Empire. It looks as if all the swindlers from north and south had passed the word to cheat the German philistines and take their money for foolish tricks, which they pass off as artistic productions. Rarely is there a true artist among these travelers. More often bunglers and quacks come, who would do better to stay home and plant cabbage and beets than to go abroad and labor at music stands, clad in red trousers and silvery silk coats.

Each of these virtuosos played with an orchestral accompaniment, which was provided by the musical associations. The pianist Thalberg was the first virtuoso who dared to give a concert without an orchestra.

It was this evolution of musical life which was reflected in the musical magazines written for the public of the middle classes, now growing into a "Third Estate" of music lovers. As a matter of fact, all the great classical composers belonged to the middle classes. Plain citizens produced most of the spiritual energy of the eighteenth century. To this century of commoners belonged Rousseau, Voltaire, Diderot, Goethe, Schiller, Haydn, Mozart, Beethoven, Addison, Pope, Burke, and Goldsmith. The whole of musical life was influenced by this surging flood of in-

spiration. In a great, rich capital such as London, where trade
and industrial enterprises were concentrated, musical life began
to take on something of the character of a business. London was
the first great music market at which composers and singers gathered during the season and where managers made their entry into
musical life as the brokers of the new business.

The new musical journals spoke the language of the cultured
music lover. Their editors wished to disseminate musical enlightenment. Hence the critic became the leader of the society
of music-loving commoners, for he alone had the ability to discuss music in an acceptable literary form for readers who needed
instruction. Music had become part of daily life; as the interpreter of the art, the critic was important. He addressed his
analysis to readers of general culture. He became, in short, the
spokesman of the new musical parliaments, and, in the period of
romanticism, a literary personality as well. Thus the tone and
the character of musical criticism changed.

Chapter Twelve

THE FIRST MUSIC CRITICS IN DAILIES AND WEEKLIES

As INTEREST in music spread and became a part of public life, musical criticism, as was to be expected, began to appear in the daily papers. The first examples occurred in Germany.

The more the daily papers developed, the more difficult became the task of the music critics, for the tempo of writing became faster and faster as the great mass of dailies flowed ever more quickly from the printing presses. Life gained in speed as well. The earth grew smaller: news flew around the globe as fast as electricity could carry it. With the growing swiftness of modern life, critical judgment had also to become quicker. Other problems were set before the music critic by the fact that the daily papers were published for the general public. The music critics could no longer write, as in the days of the magazines, for an interested public, for they now had to include unmusical people among their readers. Hence they could no longer speak the language of the theoretician or of the technical expert. They had to discuss music as journalists, to display their knowledge in an interesting, spirited, personal form. The ship of musical criticism had to leave the barren shore of theory and sail on the wide, blue sea under the blaze of the sun.

These new tasks, then, demanded more from the critics than a knowledge of musical technique. Originality was required, acute thinking, imaginative writing, intelligence in fluid form, and, in addition to all these, an alive feeling for the intellectual and artistic trends of the day, nay, even of the hour. Zola defined the novel as "a slice of life seen through a temperament." Criticism became a judgment on contemporary music heard through a temperament. Some critics, like Hanslick in Vienna, Weissmann in Berlin, Huneker in New York, and Ernest Newman in London, accomplished the task — whose magnitude explains why so many critics fell so far short of the goal.

The beginnings of musical criticism in the dailies were very modest. Johann Karl Friedrich Rellstab of Berlin was the first critic to raise the standards of the criticism in the daily papers above the perfunctory dryness of the brief notices that had appeared in some dailies from the early eighteenth century on. Rellstab, who was born in Berlin in 1759, was a printer by profession. He studied music, however, with Agricola and Fasch, and began his musical activities by printing scores and by opening the first circulating library of music in Berlin. In 1787 he organized a concert group of experts and amateurs, which, with the help of visiting virtuosos, performed compositions of Bach, Hasse, and Gluck at his home. The rehearsals of the Berliner Singakademie also took place at his house. Rellstab arranged for the first performance of Haydn's *The Seasons*, and paid the production costs out of his own pocket.

Rellstab began to write criticisms for the *Vossische Zeitung*, the oldest daily in Berlin. When war broke out in 1806, he had to interrupt his activities as a critic, though he resumed them after some years. A series of articles in the *Vossische Zeitung* concerning the music and musical institutions of Italy and Vienna made a sensation on account of his keen wit. In addition to his musical criticism, Rellstab published some of his own compositions as well as some valuable books on music. The indefatigable man died in 1813.

All of his children became musicians. His daughter Caroline was one of the great singers of her age, but she unfortunately died when she was only twenty years old. Another daughter, Amalia, was a noted concert pianist, as was Henriette, his third daughter. His son, Heinrich Friedrich Ludwig Rellstab, became the first great music critic. His was a modern personality, and as a writer he was full of life, temperament, and energy. With him musical criticism stepped into the full light of the modern period.

Rellstab the younger began life as a soldier, and was promoted to the rank of second lieutenant in the Prussian army. He resigned, however, in 1821, and began to make his living as a writer. At first he wrote poetry and librettos for operas, later he wrote novels, short stories, books on musical topics, and a great many articles. His complete works fill twenty-four volumes. In Dresden he became a friend of Weber. He knew the world, having traveled much in Switzerland and in Italy. When he returned to Berlin, he acquired a reputation as a music critic by the articles published under his name in the Berlin *Allgemeine musikalische Zeitung*, edited by Marx.

His reputation was spread even faster by a pamphlet which he published in 1825. This was the year in which the famous coloratura singer Henriette Sontag sang for the first time in Berlin and made the sober Berliners crazy with joy. Her fame soon spread from Berlin to Paris and London. Only Malibran equaled her in the splendor of her virtuosity, and Paris went completely mad when Sontag and Catalani sang a duet from Rossini's *Semiramide* in concert, each singer trying to outshine the other. Sontag was one of the first great singers to conquer America. She traveled over the whole continent, filling theaters everywhere with her virtuosity and her brilliant coloratura. She graced the operatic stage for the last time in 1852 in a performance of *Lucrezia Borgia* in Mexico. Here she tasted the sweetness of enthusiastic applause for the last time, for she was presently stricken with cholera, and died in a foreign land.

This was the singer against whom Rellstab directed a pamphlet, entitled *Henrietta, or the Beautiful Singer. A Story of Our Days by Freimund Zuschauer*.[1] The author sneered at the enthusiasm roused by the beautiful singer. He ridiculed her noble admirers, who sent quantities of flowers to her dressing room and unharnessed the horses from her carriage. But in those days it

---

[1] Freimund Zuschauer may be translated as "Free-Mouth Spectator."

was dangerous to make fun of the high society of Berlin, and Rellstab was sentenced to three months' imprisonment in the fortress of Spandau. When he left his cell, he was a famous man.

He was engaged as editor of the *Vossische Zeitung* for politics, military affairs, and music. The initials with which he signed his musical criticisms — L. R. — were the trademark of a critic who wrote easily, wittily, charmingly, and delightfully for the readers of that influential journal. There is nothing old-fashioned about Rellstab's style. It is a living style and could be transferred just as it is to the columns of a present-day paper. Rellstab was a born journalist, temperamental, clear, and gay. His words still breathe, smile, and bite.

Like many other temperamental men, Rellstab was a writer who liked struggle. There are no good journalistic pens that would not serve equally well as swords or daggers. In 1827 he dared to attack Spontini in a criticism of the opera *Agnes von Hohenstaufen*. Spontini had become director general of music for the king of Prussia in 1820, and he impressed the public when he strode pompously into the orchestra pit with his ebony baton, which was as large as the baton of a field marshal, He was certainly the first of the modern operatic conductors, half artist and half showman. An unwearied worker, he often held eighty rehearsals for one performance, in order to work out details with the greatest possible care. And at the performances themselves he added more than a touch of vain showmanship: he adorned his chest with innumerable orders, he adopted a dictatorial mien, and was lavish with elaborately studied gestures.

Rellstab's journalistic talent made him able to hit Spontini's tender spots — his vanity, his theatricality, his pomposity, and his preoccupation with effects. He later gave a detailed account of his campaign in a pamphlet entitled *On My Relationship with Mr. Spontini as Composer and as Director General in Berlin, with an Amusing Supplement*. The pamphlet appeared in 1827. In it, like an honest man, Rellstab made a confession: "My respect for truth demands that I confess that I erred and did wrong, not in my judgment (that may be questionable), but in the form of my judgment, as I evidently lost the self-control that ought to be demanded from critics, and became too impetuous." Rellstab was as sympathetic in his sincerity as he was in his impetuosity. He is a living human being, not a statue with a pompous wig. When I once discussed the critical fault of aggressiveness with Ludwig Speidel, the greatest of Viennese music critics and my model, he answered slowly, looking through his glasses, "A sword would not be a sword if one could foresee-to the inch how deeply it would cut into flesh."

Rellstab's authority as a music critic remained unshaken until his death in 1860. The greatest days in his life were those he spent in the houses of Goethe and Beethoven. He was the guest of Goethe at Weimar in 1821, on the very day when the twelve-year-old Felix Mendelssohn-Bartholdy played Bach, Mozart, and Beethoven in the candle-lit room of the Olympian poet. Rellstab visited Beethoven three times in Vienna, and he described those great days in his own lively manner. He was present at the first performance of the string quartet in E-flat major, *opus* 127, and he describes it in these words:

About seven o'clock we were in a little place on the Graben which could not be called a private salon — at best it was only a big room where a great many listeners had gathered, among whom I met the first musicians of Vienna, whose acquaintance I had not made until then. There was not enough room to sit down, either in this room or in the adjacent anteroom. Only a few chairs could be set round. The four quartet players had hardly room for their desks and chairs. Everyone stood closely about them. They were some of the best younger virtuosos of Vienna. They had dedicated themselves to their difficult task with the whole enthusiasm of youth, and had held seventeen or more rehearsals before they dared to play the new, enigmatic work half-publicly before some experts. The difficulties and secrets of Beethoven's last quartets seemed at the time so insurmountable and so inscrutable that only the young, enthusiastic men dared to play the new music, while the older and more famous players thought it impossible to perform. . . . As the players had had to study and work before they climbed to this steep height, so the listeners were not permitted to take their task easily — it was therefore decided that the work should be played twice, one performance after the other.

This lively introduction was followed by an enthusiastic description of the new music. Rellstab was connected with Schubert too. No less than ten of Rellstab's poems inspired Schubert to music. The most popular among them is the *Serenade*, with its guitar accompaniment tinkling through the fragrant night.

At the same time that Rellstab was writing his criticisms in Berlin, the Parisian *Journal des débats* opened its columns to discussions of music. Paris was on the eve of the great musical epoch in which she became the musical center of the world, and the great opera houses of Paris — the Opéra, the Opéra Comique, and the Théâtre Italien — were attracting great audiences. Rossini, whose melodies excited the world, had settled in Paris and had become director of the Théâtre Italien. He had been preparing new triumphs for Paris since his arrival in October, 1823, feeding meanwhile on goose-liver pies, inventing fine sauces, and drinking champagne. Meyerbeer came to Paris in 1827, already famous as the composer of *The Crusader*, which was invading all the opera houses of Europe after its triumph in Venice. The operas of Bellini and Donizetti were providing new, sensuous melodies. And there were new French composers as well, who exchanged the pompous solemnity of Spontini for wit and charm, French grace and spirited repartee. Auber had his first success in 1820 with *The Shepherdess becomes a Lady*, and had begun to work with Scribe as his librettist. This combination delighted the Parisians with the spirit of French comedy. The year 1828 saw the first realistic opera, Auber's *Masaniello*, which moved its audiences with its full life and the revolutionary mood of its choruses. Only a year later, Rossini's *Guillaume Tell* made history with the greatness of a new and colorful operatic style. In the same year, Halévy's successes began in the Théâtre Italien and in the Opéra Comique. He, too, enchanted the public with French grace and cheerfulness in the realm of musical comedy. The atmosphere of Paris echoed with operatic melodies.

The editor of the *Journal des débats* wanted the musical life of

Paris reflected in his paper, and engaged François-Henri-Joseph Castil-Blaze (1784–1857) as editor of its music section. This spirited, amusing, yet somewhat superficial writer had come to Paris to study law, but had been more attracted by music. His father was a learned notary who composed during his leisure hours. The son did not like dividing his time between dry law books and music, so he turned entirely to music. Like those of most Frenchmen of his time, his musical interests centered around the lyric stage, of which he became a noted chronicler (*De l'Opéra en France*, 1820). Other books of his were a dictionary of contemporary music, a work with the ambitious title *Dancing and the Ballet from Bacchus to Mlle Taglioni* (1832), and a history of the Parisian lyric theaters (1855–56). Castil-Blaze was a curious figure. A man of considerable learning and industry, he often furnished the raw material for other — notably German — writers. In fact, H. M. Schletterer, a distinguished Prussian Hofkapellmeister, honorary doctor of philosophy of the University of Tübingen, and bearer of many titles and honors, thought so highly of Castil-Blaze's *Chapelle-musique des Rois de France* ("*Chapel Music of the Kings of France*") that he plagiarized it *in toto* in a ponderous three-volume work entitled *Studien zur Geschichte der Französischen Musik* ("*Studies in the History of French Music*"). Now, this worthy has his reputation besmirched in every biographical reference work. There is, however, another side to Castil-Blaze's character: he had rather poor taste and a leaning for irresponsible tinkering, which resulted in abominable translations and arrangements of Mozart's and Weber's operas, as well as of Rossini's *Barber*. He bequeathed his literary talent to his son, Henri Blaze de Bury, a friend of Meyerbeer, who wrote articles on music for the *Revue des deux mondes* and the *Revue de Paris*, as well as publishing books on Rossini and Meyerbeer.

The French tradition of choosing critics from the ranks of composers — for example, Hector Berlioz, Ernest Reyer, Alfred Bruneau, and Florent Schmitt — began with Adolphe-Charles Adam (1803–56), the composer of the opera *The Postilion of*

Longjumeau. The articles that Adam wrote for the *Constitution-nel*, the *Assemblée nationale*, and the *Gazette musicale* are as charming as his melodies. Adam was a kind critic, totally lacking in bitterness. A choice of his articles, showing his amiable mind and his graceful style, was published in 1857 as *Souvenirs d'un musicien* ("*Recollections of a Musician*"). This was later followed by a second volume, *Derniers souvenirs d'un musicien* ("*Last Recollections of a Musician*"). They can still be read today with pleasure, and remind one of a quiet old room with antique chests and embroidered curtains. We look upon Adam as upon a good, simple, friendly old grandfather of musical criticism.

In England, aside from the dailies, the especial popularity of weekly reviews — *Examiner* (1808), *Atlas* (1826), *Spectator* and *Athenaeum* (1828) — also provided a field for musical criticism. *The Atlas*, whose name was derived from the size of its format, owed its celebrity in the musical field largely to the efforts of Edward Holmes, its music critic. Holmes (1799–1859) was a friend and fellow student of Keats. He was one of those English writers on music whose knowledge and interest in Continental music resulted in publications that antedate the better known works of his German colleagues. These things are seldom known and rarely acknowledged by more recent writers. But Jahn, the "first" biographer of Mozart, was a more gentlemanly scholar than most of his later confreres, for in the second edition of his *Mozart* (1867) he expressly states that Edward Holmes's *Life of Mozart* (1845) was the most useful, complete, and trustworthy biography then in existence. Holmes also wrote a life of Purcell, which marks one of the earlier stages in the rehabilitation of that great and long-neglected composer. In 1849 Holmes settled in America as a critic and teacher.

Chapter Thirteen

THE DEVELOPMENT OF ROMANTICISM
IN GERMANY

At the beginning of the nineteenth century a new spiritual movement arose in England and Germany which changed music, musicians, and musical criticism. This was the Romantic movement. It spread from England and Germany to the neighboring European countries, and around 1830 the younger generation of painters, poets, and musicians in France were fired with similar ideas, the glow of which was reflected to Italy. The Scandinavian countries, too, were overcome by the spell of new colors and fanciful imagination. Even vast Russia was shaken, and passionate emotion awakened great poets and novelists like Pushkin and Turgenev as well as musicians like Glinka. The new ideas converged on Bohemia from east, west, north, and south, and there Smetana conjured up romanticism in musical stories about the peasants of his country and tales of long-dead princes and kings. Romantic feeling and romantic fancy marched throughout Europe like the armies of Napoleon, everywhere awakening dreams, fairy tales, legends, together with the history, songs, and dances of the people which rose out of the soil of the nations.

Romanticism was the countermovement against the rationalism of the eighteenth century. The Age of Reason had used its powers of thought and clear reason to destroy the last remaining traces of the Middle Ages, and to create a new social order, a new science, and a new art. It was the shining day after a long night of fantastic clouds. Romanticism, however, was a new return to twilight, where the play of imagination was not re-

stricted by reasonable thinking, and dreams appeared more colorful than the clear light of day.

The German romantic writers, August Wilhelm Schlegel,
Friedrich Schlegel, Friedrich Tieck, Novalis, E. T. A. Hoffmann,
Richter, and the rest, were all dreamers, passionately fond of the
dark hours in which forms lose their clear contours, when mystic
ideas flutter like moths through the darkness, when noises become louder in the silence of the night, and when the rustling of
leaves, the dripping of water, and the movement of the wind
sound like the voices of ghosts. In those days Richter wrote,
"The plastic sun shines monotonously like one awake; the romantic moon gleams changeably like one dreaming." And another Romantic, Novalis, wrote wonderful *Hymns of the Night*,
which praise "the miraculous realm of night" in words that
Richard Wagner used in the night scene of the second act of
Tristan and Isolde.

The legends of the past and its poetry are akin to dreams.
Both are remote from reality: they are the fruit of the imagination. The Romantics were all attracted by these old histories,
these legends, and this old poetry. Following the example set
by the Englishmen Percy and Ritson, Arnim and Brentano published their collection of old German poems, *Des Knaben Wunder-
horn* ("*The Boy's Magic Horn*"), in 1806. Arnim also published
tales and plays dating between the fifteenth and the seventeenth
centuries. Görres produced his *Deutsche Volksbücher* ("*German
Folk Legends*") in 1807. The Brothers Grimm looked for old
people who could tell old fairy tales, and they published what
they heard from toothless women and wrinkled old men in the
Kinder und Hausmärchen ("*Children's Stories and Domestic Tales*"),
which came out between 1812 and 1815. Their *Deutsche Sagen*
("*German Legends*") were published a few years later, between
1816 and 1818. The same impulse prompted the Brothers Boisserée to collect paintings of the fifteenth century. In 1804 Friedrich Schlegel wrote his essay on the works of the old masters of
Cologne; and about the same time Romantics discovered the
mystic beauty of Cologne Cathedral, the magic of high Gothic

buttresses, Gothic pillars. As a result Boisserée published his
proclamation demanding the completion of its steeple. Romantics began to discover the beauty of the Gothic German city as
well. Tieck and Wackenroder were the first to wander through
the streets, admiring Gothic houses, with their bull's-eye windows and pointed arches. They looked, too, at the churches,
and in the semidarkness of their arched naves they saw the dusty
works of Dürer and Peter Vischer. They saw the towers and
walls behind which the burghers of Nuremberg defended their
city. Through these same streets some thirty years later walked
Richard Wagner, gathering inspiration for the poetic imaginings
that shine through the *Meistersinger of Nuremberg.*

The predilection of the romantic poets for Gothic mysticism
was not confined to legend and to architecture, it also made
them susceptible to the attraction of Catholicism. In 1808 Friedrich Schlegel and his wife Dorothea were converted, and were
baptized in the Cathedral of Cologne. Nine years earlier Tieck
had edited the *Leben und Tod der Heiligen Genovefa* ("*Life and Death
of St. Genevieve*"), and had been won over by the mystical ideas
of Catholicism. Friedrich Schlegel went on to publish his *Ideen
über Religion* ("*Thoughts on Religion*"), which praised Catholicism, and Novalis wrote a similar book *Christenheit oder Europa*
("*Christendom or Europe*"). At the same time, Châteaubriand was
writing his *Génie du Christianisme* ("*Genius of Christianity*") in
Paris. By 1802 the Catholic movement was a part of the Romantic movement in all countries, a trend that culminated in
Richard Wagner when he wrote the Supper Scene in his *Parsifal.*
Every kind of mystical exultation exercised an invincible appeal
on the minds of the Romantics. They were early attracted by
hysterical symptoms. Clemens Brentano sat at the bedside of
the nun Catherina Emerich, who was blessed with the stigmata,
and as a result of his experience wrote a book called *The Bitter
Grief of Our Lord Jesus Christ According to the Meditations of the God-
blessed Anna Katherina Emerich.*

The several arts began to lose their clarity of outline in this
twilight realm of romantic fancy. The sharp contours so char-

acteristic of classic art were softened, and the very distinctions between the arts were felt to be false. Statues, the Romantics felt, might perhaps come alive or be transformed into paintings, paintings into poems, and poems into music. The same romantic feeling is expressed by Tieck when he writes: "What? Is it not possible to think in tones and to make music with words and thoughts? Oh, in what a plight would the arts be if it were not so! How poor the language! How poor the music!" The whole world of nature lost reality for these poetical dreamers and seemed to exhale music. We find in Tieck's *Zerbino*, for instance, "Flowers and sounds kiss, while roses, tulips, birds, the heaven's blue, brooks, streams, rivers, and ghosts sing in the garden of poetry."

August Wilhelm Schlegel was the first to speak the sentence that was to become the motto of the Romantic movement: "Antique art and poetry strove for the separation of what is heterogeneous; romantic art is fond of mixtures. It expresses the mysterious trend toward the chaos that is struggling for new and wonderful births and which lurks in the background of all regular creations." Thus, poetry, painting, and music ought to fuse together: "Color rings, form sounds. Each has a tongue and a language fitting its form and color. . . . Color, fragrance, and song call themselves brothers and sisters." So proclaims a poem by Tieck. The central idea of Richard Wagner's "Universal Artwork" stems from Schlegel, Tieck, Novalis, and the other Romantics.

Thus poetry began to fuse with music, and music with the other arts in the Romantic era. A. W. Schlegel, who called architecture "frozen music," came back again and again to the idea of fusing all the arts together. It was no mere chance, then, that led the Romantics to imagine musicians as the principal characters of their works. Again E. T. A. Hoffmann took the lead when he created the imaginary picture of a musician in the likeness of his own fantastic personality, and it was this picture that will live on in the immortality of Schumann's *Kreisleriana*.

In Kapellmeister Johannes Kreisler, E. T. A. Hoffmann created the figure of a romantic musician wrapped in his own enthusiasm and living in a higher world. The prosaic world of everyday life seems a caricature to Kreisler. The superficial music-making of society is ridiculous to a man of his stamp. How absurd it is to think of music in terms of a middle-class home "where father, tired from the serious business of the day, in dressing gown and slippers, cheerfully and amicably smokes his pipe while his son plays his favorite pieces on the piano."

When we read the essays of Kapellmeister Kreisler, published by Hoffmann in his *Phantasiestücke* (Schumann transformed these, too, into poetic piano music), we have the impression that we are being led into a world revolving in the shining atmosphere high above the earth, where all phenomena become notes and chords. Hoffmann, in one story from the collection, indulges his fancy about the keys. He begins with A-flat minor. "Alas! Chords carry me into the country of eternal longing! But when they lay hold on me, pains awaken that will fly out of my bosom, tearing it forcibly." He improvises in the same poetic manner on all the keys — continually fortissimo — until he comes to C-flat minor. "Don't you know him? Don't you know him? Look! He grasps my heart with glowing claws! Do you see the bleak ghost with red sparkling eyes stretching the clutch of his bony fists out of his torn mantle, and shaking his straw crown on his bald, smooth skull? It is madness! Johannes, be brave!"

Gustav Mahler, who was not unlike Johannes Kreisler in character, wrote the "Devil's music" of his Fourth Symphony under the influence of such passages; and Anton Bruckner's symphony in E flat, whose bugling horns justify the title *Romantic Symphony*, seems to parallel the following passage from Kreisler's interpretation of E-flat major: "Follow the chord! Follow it! . . . Its longing is the sweet sound of horns. Do you hear it rustling behind the bushes? Do you hear its sounding? The sound of horns full of joy and sweetness? It is they! Up! Let us go to meet them." The chapter in *Kreisleriana* called "*Johannes Kreisler's Indenture*" contains the essence of Hoffmann's ideas about music, in words as solemn as those of a testament:

Our realm is not of this world. Where could we find, like the painters and sculptors, models of our art in nature? Sound is everywhere,
but tones — that is, melodies speaking the higher language of the
world of spirits — rest only in the breast of man. . . . The musician
— that is, he who develops music to clear, distinct consciousness —
is everywhere surrounded by melody and harmony. It is not an empty
simile and not an allegory when musicians say that colors, scents, and
beams appear to them as tones, and that musicians are aware of their
intermingling as in a wonderful concert. In the same sense in which
. . . hearing is a seeing from within, so the musician may call seeing a
hearing from within. . . . Thus the sudden inspirations of musicians
and the formation of melodies within the soul would be the conscious
apperception and understanding of the secret music of nature as the
principle of life and its activities. The sounds of nature, the rushing
of wind, the bubbling of springs, and so on, are first of all sustained
chords to the musician, and later melodies with the accompaniment of
harmonies.

The romantic creed, as formulated by Hoffmann, turns out to be
musical pantheism.

A new concept of music rose out of these feelings, dreams, and
fantasies of the romantic poets. Music in the eighteenth century
was the handicraft of a guild. Musicians worked at their compositions as artisans worked at their trade. Their technique was
delivered from master to journeyman in the same way that the
great painters of the Renaissance bequeathed their technique to
the pupils who mixed paints and ground colors for them. There
was everywhere the same foundation of technical experience on
which new forms could be built. Seen from the outside, musicians were middle-class men living in a middle-class world.
They were neither above nor below their fellow craftsmen.
They did solid work with the tools of an inherited technique,
and they wrote their scores with the conscientiousness and the
guild spirit of their craft, without dramatizing their personalities or their work. The literary and artistic culture of the great
eighteenth-century musician was not conspicuously different
from the culture of other middle-class professional men.

All this was changed by Romanticism, which looked upon Beethoven as upon the new Prometheus who formed men out of clay, and brought them fire from heaven. As music was the language of the beyond and the essence of all things, the musician became the brother of the prophets who proclaimed the secrets of the infinite and of the future in sublime raptures. Novalis pointed out, "Poetical sense is related to the sense of prophecy, to religious feeling, to madness." Thus the artist lived on another plane from the commoners, and his personality developed new and peculiar traits. The series of musicians and composers whose lives begin to be irregular is coeval with the rise of Romanticism. Virtuosos like the pale, devilish Paganini appear. The great violinist even looked like a character from Hoffmann's tales, and his violin seemed to generate hellish sparks. Chopin, sick and melancholy, sat at the piano playing music from which blood seemed to drip. Liszt looked like a mixture of priest and actor, with his hair streaming from his majestic head. These virtuosos began to have romantic relationships with women: the story of Chopin and George Sand, the liaisons between Liszt and the Countess d'Agoult and the Countess Wittgenstein, Berlioz's love for Miss Smithson, the red-haired Irish actress, Schumann's love for Clara Wieck — all these bear witness to the truth of the statement.

The lives of artists became adventurous, like the life of Byron, who sailed to southern shores, and traveled, restless and uneasy, until his death in the blue mountains of Missolonghi overlooking the blue sea. Richard Wagner summarized the whole content of Romanticism in his dramatically restless life. He had adventures with women, surprising turns in fortune, a weird acquaintance with the mad King Ludwig of Bavaria, who sailed at night on the Bavarian lakes clad in the gleaming armor of Lohengrin. And not content with romantic lives, a great many artists of the period had romantic deaths: so it was with Shelley, with Chopin, and with Schumann. About 1870, however, the Romantic movement became commercialized, and demoniac pianists and violinists appeared on the stage, to be accompanied by conductors whose melancholy locks rippled, as they gestured with the air of a sorcerer who had a fixed rate of enchantment on the musical stock exchange. This was the clearance sale of Romanticism.

The cultural standards of musicians in the Romantic era had changed. Music had drawn closer to the other arts, and poetical notions fused with musical patterns. Schumann composed short stories and wrote descriptions of his *Davidsbündlertänze* with the facility of a novelist. Liszt was inspired by sources as diverse as *Faust*, *The Divine Comedy*, and the poetry of Lamartine and Lenau. Richard Strauss drew inspiration from Cervantes and Nietzche. The forms and colors of paintings were translated into sounds. Other picturesque ideas were suggested by the colors of landscapes. Mendelssohn was praised by Wagner as a painter of landscapes, and his *Hebrides* overture excited Wagner's admiration as a masterpiece of this art. From Mendelssohn's *Italian* and *Scottish* symphonies to the symphonic poem *From Italy* by Richard Strauss, the sun and shade of foreign countries, their life and their moods, have been reproduced by means of sound. The glowing sun and the burning colors of the Orient, the hot Spanish nights, the shadows of northern countries, the stormy seas, and the snow-covered Alps have all been rendered in sound. Music left its artistic isolation and dipped into all the moods of nature. Never before had music shown so great a wealth of colors.

Color broke loose from its musical bonds and reveled in independent magic. Out of the *Midsummer Night's Dream* music of Mendelssohn flashed sparks, shining points, and spots of color — a development which was to lead to Berlioz, Liszt, Wagner, Strauss, and Debussy. The sonata form began to melt into colors. Harmonies became fluid when chromaticism dissolved the chords.

Musicians were poets, magicians, men of the spirit, connected with the literary and philosophical movements of the day. Some of the composers — Franz Liszt, for example — were among the most cultivated men of their age. Some combined musical and literary culture: E. T. A. Hoffmann was both poet and composer. Schumann, Berlioz, Weber, Liszt, Bülow, and Hugo Wolf wielded the pen like writers born and bred. The time when a musician was only a musician and nothing else was over.

It had become unfashionable to write on music only from the standpoint of a theoretician, for music had enlarged its range to extend over all fields of knowledge. The spiritual forces of music had grown along with its purely musical forces. Romantic mysticism had enlarged the technique of music, its power of expression, its poetical feeling, and its color. Musicians had become part of an enchanted land. This new world of art was high above the everyday world of business and entertainment, and a rift began to grow between real life and art. Thus the music critic's task of bridging the gap from one side to the other became more complex and more difficult.

The Romantics instantly perceived the need of a new type of criticism. They felt, justly enough, that the dogmatic rationalism of the Age of Reason was not capable of adequately judging a music that had outgrown rational boundaries and was striving after irrational values — among them, poetical and picturesque feeling, dreams, adventures, ecstasies, and the expression of subjective personality. It was part of the greatness and originality of Romanticism that it approached the task of creating a new type of musical criticism.

Chapter Fourteen

THE NEW BEETHOVEN CRITICISM

IN THE CENTER of romantic musical esthetics and romantic musical criticism stands the altar on which the new enthusiasm for Beethoven burned its offerings. Beethoven was regarded by romantic musicians, writers, and critics as the prototype of the romantic musician; consequently, it was Romanticism that built the temple in which Beethoven was adored throughout the nineteenth century as the greatest of all musicians. It was not until the end of that century that Bach and Mozart took the place they now occupy in our esteem as the ideal musicians. The writings of Berlioz, Schumann, Liszt, and Wagner, as well as the music of Brahms and Bruckner, bear witness to this worship of Beethoven. In the eyes of the Romantics Beethoven's life was the epitome of Romanticism. The tragic destiny of the deaf musician, his heroic struggle against misfortune, his adoration of women, his spiritual raptures, his storming through field and wood — all these seemed to the critics to be Romanticism in its purest form. The flights and ecstasies of his music, its passionate melancholy, the pensive spirituality of his last quartets, and the moving choruses of the Ninth Symphony and the *Missa Solemnis* were the highest pinnacles of romantic art. He was fighter, prophet, and apostle, proclaiming the higher world of love, humanity, and God, "freeing the forms of classical music," and expanding sonata and fugue, variation and chorus with the force of a giant who snaps iron chains.

When the Romantics began this new interpretation of Beethoven, his last and greatest works were hardly understood. As late as 1852 Johann Christian Lobe, one of the most celebrated of German theoreticians, could write about Beethoven, "He completed the building begun by Haydn and developed by Mozart, but it was he also who later began the destruction of that building." And one can read, even in Hanslick, "The first of Beethoven's compositions *are* music; in his last compositions Beethoven *makes* music." The Beethoven enthusiasm of the Romantics was indeed a bold and far-sighted performance of intelligence and imagination. It was one-sided, in so far as it had more visionary insight into the irrational elements of Beethoven's music than understanding of the logical power of his thought; but it was a contribution of great consequence.

The romantic Beethoven legend lasted as long as Romanticism lasted. Not until the beginning of the twentieth century and the outbreak of the first World War did Romanticism lose the last vestiges of its spiritual power, and not until then did Beethoven's immense figure begin to move farther away from the life of the new and revolutionary age, characterized by discontent, disillusion, and social upheaval. Beethoven's music — the music of a great Romantic — was not spared in this revaluation. A new period of criticism of Beethoven began with Debussy, who called the composer a "genius without taste," and said, "In Beethoven's symphonies, the exciting climax of a period ends with a noisy solution of quiet banality." The new generation, thirsting in a shocked, unhappy, unquiet world for harmony and freedom of mind and soul, preferred the harmonic beauties of Bach and Mozart to the struggles of Beethoven. This was the difference between the twentieth century and the nineteenth, which had found in Beethoven its god. All nineteenth-century music is closely connected with that of the master: the work of Schumann, Weber, Mendelssohn, Berlioz, Wagner, Brahms, and Bruckner is all saturated with the influence of Beethoven. Only Michelangelo in the world of the visual arts can be compared with Beethoven in creative force that impressed its seal on an age.

I. E. T. A. HOFFMANN (1776–1822)

The first to recognize Beethoven's greatness was E. T. A. Hoffmann, the musician-poet, whose influence was felt by the whole generation of writers in the first half of the nineteenth century. As a matter of fact this influence can easily be traced as far as the writings of Richard Wagner, whose *Beethoven* grew out of the fertile soil of Hoffmann's ideas.

Hoffmann is best known as the writer of fantastic stories that impressed the imagination of men like Edgar Allan Poe and Barbey d'Aurevilly. One might add that he looked like a character in one of his stories. When he walked the streets of Berlin in his capacity of Prussian Councillor of Justice, he resembled a goatlike being, with his small head, soft little hands, burning dark eyes, and fine lips that never smiled. In the daytime he was a stiff, formal magistrate. At night he sat with friends in wine houses, smoking his long pipe and drinking his glass of punch. It was the custom in those days to ignite punch, and in its blue flames one could imagine grotesque apparitions, the devil, automatons, cats, and the faces of pale girls. When he began his career in Poland, he was writer, painter, and musician all at the same time. "A motley world of magical apparitions glitters and flares around me," he wrote in those days. "It is as if something great may soon happen — some work of art must come out of this chaos — it may be a book, an opera, a painting — God knows." After the French occupation of Warsaw, where he was a Prussian government official, Hoffmann went to Bamberg. This was one of the romantic German cities. Seventeenth-century palaces clustered around the thirteenth-century cathedral. Hoffmann lived close to the town in an old castle, covering its walls with fantastic murals, and conducting opera performances in the Bamberg theater. At night he seemed to see demoniac characters lurking in the shadowy old corners of the streets, among them Kreisler, his *Kapellmeister*.

At Bamberg he met Tieck and Weber. Here he began his opera *Undine*, which was performed in 1816 in the Berlin opera house.

"This evening," wrote Weber to his bride, "they gave *Undine*. I attended with intense expectation. The music is very characteristic, indeed often striking, and always effectively written. So I felt great joy and delight." Much in this opera foreshadows Wagner's declamation, orchestra, and use of leitmotives. Beethoven, Gluck, and Mozart all inspired Hoffmann's music; the two latter also inspired two of his best stories. Hoffmann said of Gluck's *Iphigenia in Aulis*, "Gluck's opera is the true musical drama, in which action irresistibly progresses from instant to instant." About Mozart he wrote, "Mozart opened new roads and became the inimitable creator of the romantic opera."

It was in Bamberg in 1810 that Hoffmann wrote the article on Beethoven that was to become the classic document of the new Beethoven enthusiasm, "On Beethoven's Instrumental Music." Friedrich Rochlitz, editor of the *Allgemeine musikalische Zeitung* in Leipzig, had invited Hoffmann to write for it. He enclosed the score of Beethoven's Fifth Symphony, asking for an article on the new composition: "Let it be a real criticism or only a sketch, a fantasia on the fantasia, an art work on the art work." Rochlitz received in return a real criticism, a thorough analysis, beginning with an enthusiastic hymn on Beethoven's Romanticism which praised the composer as the master of instrumental music. Hoffmann adduces this as a reason why Beethoven was less successful in vocal music, for vocal music does not "express indefinite longing, but only moods clearly defined by means of words . . ." Consequently Beethoven's music rarely pleases the crowd, because the crowd does not grasp the depth of the composer's thought. It looks upon his music chiefly as "the product of a genius who does not care for form and the choice of ideas, but delivers himself to his impulses and the creations of his imagination." Hoffmann adds that superficial observers complain about the lack of organic unity in Shakespeare's plays, just as they do about the lack of coherence in Beethoven's music, but more thorough critics see under the surface to "the inner structure of Beethoven's music," and perceive that it "exhibits the great self-control of the master . . . nourished by a continuous study of his art. Beethoven fosters deep in his soul the Romanticism of his music. . . ." This Romanticism is expressed in his music with great "mastery and consciousness." Hoffmann's analysis, the work of a man who was himself a great writer and a great musician, is an example of thorough study of a work of art. It is also a foundation stone of the new romantic criticism. It leaves far behind the rationalistic criticism that makes use of fixed theoretical principles and regards art as a sort of handicraft that can be judged by rules, regulations, and recipes:

The lyre of Orpheus opens the door of the underworld. Music opens the entrance of an unknown world to men, a world with nothing in common with the material world that surrounds them, a world where all the feelings expressed by means of distinct ideas are left behind. There men are able to give themselves up to the ineffable. . . . Haydn and Mozart, creating the instrumental music of today, produce art shining in full glory. The man who approached music in entire love and penetrated its inmost being was Beethoven. . . . The instrumental music of all three masters exhales the same romantic spirit, which has been produced by the same intimate penetration into the peculiar essence of art. . . .

Hoffmann's analysis of the Fifth Symphony remains the best that has been written. Equally penetrating is his article for the same journal on the three trios, *opus* 70. "These wonderful trios," he writes, "prove again how Beethoven carries the romantic spirit of music in the depths of his soul, and how his keen genius and his great clarity animate his works with that spirit." A third article deals with the *Egmont* music. In this paper Hoffmann says, "Among many composers, Beethoven was the one who grasped delicate and powerful poetry with the profundity of his feelings. Every note touched by the poet sounded in his soul."

Another detailed criticism deals with the Mass in C major. Hoffmann surveys the whole development of church music from the early Italian period to his own time. His comparison between the old and the new is striking, for he speaks of them as reminding him of "the contrast between St. Peter's and the

Strasbourg Cathedral." The proportions of St. Peter's, he admits, are grand, but they are comprehensible by reason. How different the reaction produced by the Strasbourg Cathedral, a Gothic church that "rises loftily into the air with bold windings and with the strangest entanglement of variegated fantastic forms and ornaments. This unrest, of course, stirs the soul, which anticipates the unknown, the mysterious; and the mind abandons itself to dreams that reveal the supernatural and the infinite to it. This is the impression made by the pure romanticism that lives in the fanciful compositions of Mozart and Haydn." Contrary to his expectations, however, Hoffmann found that Beethoven's Mass was not filled with the musical expression of the terrors of the soul, but was, instead, "the expression of a childlike cheerful heart, which believes in its own purity, and confides in God." Hoffmann did not live to hear the *Missa Solemnis* performed. Otherwise he would have seen his expectation fulfilled.

Beethoven's influence on Hoffmann extended not only to his criticism but also to his creative writing. In his *Serapions Brüder* the critic described an ideal association of friends — which later gave Schumann the inspiration for his Davidsbündler group — who met to discuss art and to read their writings. Fruitful musical ideas were disseminated at each meeting. An idea dear to Hoffmann appears here for the first time: "Is not the stupidity and the one-sided education of most composers the reason why they need the help of others in their work? Can there be perfect unity of text and music if the poet and the composer are not one and the same person?" In all of these discussions, Beethoven is praised as the ruler of all music. He speaks in divine language of "the wonderful miracles of the distant, romantic country in which, seized by ineffable longing, we live."

An essay in the *Phantasiestücke* is dedicated to "Beethoven's Instrumental Music," and describes "the realm of the immense and immeasurable" in words that are almost music. Speaking of the "Ghost" Trio in D major, *opus* 70, Hoffmann characterizes Beethoven's genius as "grave and solemn. . . . It is, as the master would say, that one cannot speak of profound, mysterious things in common words, but only in sublime, magnificent ones, even when the spirit, intimately familiar with them, feels joyfully and happily elevated. The dancing music of a priest of Isis cannot but be a loudly jubilant hymn."

When Beethoven read Hoffmann's articles in the *Allgemeine musikalische Zeitung*, he was more than delighted. He often spoke (as we know from his conversation books) about Hoffmann, and on one occasion he sent his friend a letter: "I make use of this opportunity to approach so intelligent a man as you are. You have written about my humble self, and Mr. N. N. has showed me some lines in his album which you wrote about me. Well, as I must believe you take some interest in me, permit me to tell you that I enjoy this very much from a man gifted with such excellent virtues."

Most of Hoffmann's articles and criticisms appeared in the Leipzig journal, but some were published in other periodicals. All bear witness to his vision. He had the most precious talent of a real critic — that of recognizing genius in men of his own time. When Weber's opera *Der Freischütz* was performed for the first time in Berlin, Hoffmann wrote criticisms that appeared in the *Vossische Zeitung* on July 21, 26, and 28, 1821. In these reviews he said that Weber "in this latest of his great works set up a monument that will mark a new epoch in the history of opera," and expressed his opinion that *Der Freischütz* and *Fidelio* were the two greatest operas since the time of Mozart.

Hoffmann also wrote an interesting article in behalf of the young Meyerbeer. The daily *Der Freimüthige* had the dubious honor of being the first German newspaper to season its criticism of the young composer with the antisemitism which, unfortunately, was later to become so widespread. The occasion for the criticism was the performance of Meyerbeer's opera *Emma di Resburgo*, a work which had already been successful in Venice. The newspaper critic scented, he said, Judaism in the melodies of this Italian opera. Hoffmann's answer, published in the same paper, proves his sense of justice and his honesty.

He boldly defended the young composer. "Criticism may be keen," he said, "but never biased. I would not deny that in the form of many melodies, especially in the embellishments that appear in some places, a certain peculiarity comes through, which reminds one of the church songs of the people to whom the composer belongs. They are reminiscent of the highly impressive songs that the so-called synagogal singers intone. This proves that the soulful composer bases his composition on these church songs, and it is praiseworthy that he keeps to the tunes of his fathers, honors them, and displays what he carries in the depths of his soul." Hoffmann goes on to blame the critic for his "want of knowledge of those peculiar songs," and says, "The composer used such tunes and melodies only rarely . . . preferring to promulgate the glory of great masters, especially the glory of . . . Rossini, and to follow the suggestions of such masters, as pious pupils heed the advice of wise teachers."

Hoffmann's influence also reached France. One of his musical stories, *Don Juan*, inspired Alfred de Musset to some magnificent verses in his poem *Namouna*, which appeared in 1833. Baudelaire was also an admirer of Hoffmann and gave him much praise in his *Curiosités esthétiques*, remarking that "dreamy Germany has given us some excellent examples of humor," and going on to quote from some of Hoffmann's stories. The writings of the poet-musician were translated into French and published as early as 1829. They left their mark on the esthetics of French Romanticism, and in 1851 his stories and some of his fantastic characters were popularized by Offenbach's opera, *Tales of Hoffmann*.

Deep and lasting evidence of Hoffmann's enthusiasm for Beethoven are to be met in all contemporary musical criticism. His imagination, his passionate warmth, and his perception of music as the language of the beyond impressed all writers on music. He communicated his fantastic spirit and his romantic feeling to musical criticism. After a century of rationalistic criticism, the readers of his tales and articles must have had the impression that a magician had transported them to a remote country where exotic climbing plants wove themselves around tropical trees and brightly colored birds sang strange songs. Thus Hoffmann's enthusiasm for Beethoven thrilled all the romantic writers. It was a new spiritual element in the world.

II. ADOLF BERNHARD MARX

Dr. Marx, the editor of the Berlin *Allgemeine musikalische Zeitung*, was not immune to Hoffmann's enthusiasm. He appears to have been exceptionally fond of Hoffmann's *Don Juan*, for he praised the story highly: "Hoffmann has drawn a picture of Don Juan about which one can truly say: it is Mozart's *Don Giovanni* as a poem." Marx also criticized operatic singers because, in their impersonations of the character, they did not show that they had read Hoffmann's story. In like manner Hoffmann's admiration for Beethoven set Marx's imagination on fire. When he wrote his biography of Beethoven, he reprinted Hoffmann's analysis of the "Ghost" Trio,[1] saying, "We want to hear what E. T. A. Hoffmann said about this trio, as he was the first to speak about Beethoven with an understanding heart."

When Marx began to edit his musical magazine, he dedicated it wholly to the new Beethoven enthusiasm. He published Rellstab's dithyrambs on Beethoven's genius, and outdid them with his own. In 1824, he published an article on the *Meeresstille und glückliche Fahrt* overture, *opus* 112. "An immortal grips the hand of another immortal," he wrote. "Who would not be moved by this greeting from Beethoven to Goethe? It is always a festive day when this journal is permitted to speak of Beethoven, the living among so many who are living-dead." And it was Marx who induced A. M. Schlesinger, the Berlin publisher, to buy the *Scottish Songs*, *opus* 108, and the last three piano sonatas, *opus* 109, 110, 111. In one of his letters to Schlesinger Beethoven asks him to give his regards to Marx, and includes a musical joke — a little composition on the words, "*Si non per portas, per muros, per muros, per muros.*" [2]

---

[1] *Vide supra*, pages 193–4.
[2] "If not through the doors, then through the walls, etc."

Marx was a forceful writer. We quote in evidence a part of his description of a concert by Paganini:

One must await him in an overcrowded opera house among thousands of visitors and hear the strange rumors running from row to row. And now, after a long pause, see the odd, sickly, wornout man sliding through the orchestra, the face fleshless and bloodless in its entanglement of dark locks and beard, the boldest of noses with an expression of contemptuous scorn, eyes that shine like black jewels out of bluish-white. And now, instantly, the hasty beginning of the *ritornelli*, and then the tenderest and boldest song ever heard on the violin.

Such a description could hardly be surpassed in vividness and intuitive power: the method was invented by Hoffmann and bequeathed by him to music critics.

It was a great day in Marx's life when, on November 15, 1826, Beethoven's Ninth Symphony was performed in Berlin for the first time. We may read the description of the music in the Berlin *Allgemeine musikalische Zeitung*:

Beethoven's symphony is too great, too rich and deep, to be comprehended in its totality and its full magnificence when heard for the first time. Every hearer will feel . . . some doubts. Besides infinite beauty there will remain some passages that have not been understood and some that are even repugnant. But do not forget that the symphony is the profoundest and most mature instrumental composition of the greatest genius and the most conscientious among living composers. Therefore, such passages as have not been understood will, in themselves, promote the wish to repeat the feast of art, and we shall become worthy and able to march forward on the road of artistic culture, led by the hand of Beethoven.

When the composer died, Marx dedicated a special issue of his magazine to Beethoven. In a black frame on the cover could be read these words: "Beethoven has died. Do not mourn for the departed. Remain close to him in your thinking."

III. J. F. REICHARDT

Reichardt and Rellstab, the other important Berlin music critics of the early nineteenth century, were not less influenced by Hoffmann's enthusiasm for Beethoven than was Marx. With them, as with the lesser Romantics in general, enthusiasm often degenerated into sentimentality, simplicity into childishness. Yet there is real sincerity under the swooning superlatives that had become the *lingua franca* of the minor writers of the day.

Reichardt had recognized Beethoven's greatness as early as 1805, and in 1808 he met him face to face. When he first visited the composer, he saw him "in a great, lonely, dark apartment. At first he looked as gloomy as his apartment, but soon he was exhilarating. He is a forceful personality, looking like a Cyclops, but very hearty, cordial, and good." Reichardt also had the good fortune to hear Beethoven improvising on the piano in the house of the Countess Erdödy. He described the event later:

He improvised for about an hour with craftsmanship and skill, revealing the inmost depths of his artistic feeling, and climbing from the deepest depths to the highest heights. Ten times I felt hottest tears streaming, and at the end I was unable to find words to express my fervent delight. I clung to his neck like a deeply moved, happy child.

On December 10, 1808, Reichardt describes another musical party at the house of the Countess. This time, however, the emphasis is on the Countess:

The dear, sickly, and yet so touchingly cheerful Countess and some of her friends, a Hungarian lady among them, enjoyed every bold, beautiful passage, every fortunate, free turn so deeply and enthusiastically that I was as happy to see their faces as I was happy about Beethoven's masterful work and performance. How fortunate the artist who may be sure of such hearers!

He describes a Liebhaberkonzert in the same letter. The

overpowering, gigantic overture to *Coriolanus* was performed in a small room. Brains and heart almost burst open at the powerful strokes. . . . I was happy to see Beethoven present and enthusiastically honored, the more so since he has in his head and his heart the unfortunate hypochondriac whim that all the people in Vienna persecute and despise him. His outward obstinate manners may, of course, frighten away some good-natured, merry Viennese, and some of those who recognize his great talent and merit may not employ enough humanity and delicacy. . . . I often feel sorry when I see this good, excellent man brooding and suffering, although I am sure that his best and most original compositions were produced in just such obstinate, deeply discontented moods.

Reichardt saw Beethoven again at a concert that the composer gave in the Kärthnerthor Theater on December 22, 1808. Beethoven played his new piano concerto in G major. The critic wrote: "I heard a new piano concerto, full of immense difficulties, played astonishingly well by Beethoven in the fastest tempo. He really sang the adagio, a masterpiece of beautiful, stretched-out song, on his instrument, with deep, melancholy feeling, which also poured through my soul."

IV. LUDWIG RELLSTAB

Rellstab also intoned enthusiastic poems on Beethoven in the Berlin *Allgemeine musikalische Zeitung*. Here he published his report on the first performance of the string quartet in E-flat major, *opus* 127. He was, of course, present at the concert, which took place in Vienna, and he described his experience in poetic language:

Solemn feeling animated everyone who was present. Deep, expectant, and thoughtful quiet prevailed. Only friends and admirers of the master were in the room. Indeed, it was deeply moving to me that his brother and others of his relatives were present and felt happy to bear his name. They were, so to speak, the deputies of the poet, who was excluded by his sublimely great misfortune from the paradise into which he led us.

Then follows the description of the quartet; finally Rellstab summarized the whole impression made by the new composition in one sentence: "Everyone had the same feeling, even though impressed in a different way, that he had met something greater than himself, greater than his mental capacity, and altogether greater than his creative power."

Rellstab was twenty-six years old when he went to Vienna to meet Beethoven. He naturally looked forward to the event with the enthusiasm of youth. Finally the long-expected hour arrived; and, he says:

I was sitting at the side of the sick, melancholy sufferer. The hair, almost perfectly gray, rose shaggily and wildly on his head. It was not smooth, not curly, not stiff, but a mixture of all. When first seen, his features looked but little imposing — the face was much smaller than I had imagined it from pictures, which showed it forced to the vehement wildness of genius. There was nothing to express the roughness and storming unrestraint which have been given to his features in order to make them conform to his music. Why . . . should Beethoven's face look like his scores? His complexion was brown, but not such a healthy, strong brown as is acquired by hunters, but mixed with a yellow, sickly coloring. His nose is narrow, sharp, his mouth benevolent, his eyes small, pale, gray and expressive. Sadness, unhappiness, and kindness I read in his face; but, I repeat, I did not see one trait of severity, and not even one transitory trait of the mighty boldness that characterizes the flight of his imagination. . . . In spite of this, he did not lack the mysterious, attractive power that is supposed to rivet us irresistibly to the exterior of great men. For the suffering, the silent, heavy pain was the result of all his unique destiny, which united the greatest wealth of creative power with the most cruel denial. As long as we do not have to tell of a Raphael grown blind in the vigor of his life, Beethoven will not meet with his equal in happiness and misfortune, either in art or in the history of the world.

When Rellstab took leave of Beethoven, on May 3, 1825, the composer took both of his visitor's hands, drew him to his breast and kissed him.

It was like a dream to me, and yet real, warm, humanly true, and divinely elevating at the same time. The great, the immortal Beethoven upon my breast! I felt his lips touching mine, and his face was moistened by my warm, irresistibly flowing tears. And so I left him. There was no thought, only glowing feeling pouring through my inmost heart: Beethoven has embraced me! . . . I did not go to Vienna the following year. On March 26, 1827, he breathed out his generous, heavily weighted soul, weary of life.

Reichardt and Rellstab made the sober Prussian capital a center of Beethoven enthusiasm. When *Fidelio* was performed in

Berlin for the first time, this enthusiasm broke all bounds of romantic extravagance. Anna Milder-Hauptmann, who sang the part of Fidelio, was Beethoven's favorite singer, his "beloved friend" as he had called her in one of his letters. It was for her voice that he wrote the high notes in the prison scene. She was twenty years old when she sang in the first performances of the opera in Vienna in 1805, and it was she who sang the aria *Ah, perfido* in Beethoven's concert of 1808. The proudly titanic Beethoven was very humble with this singer. When he wanted her to sing in his concert, he wrote, "Tomorrow I am coming myself to kiss the hem of your skirt." After she came to Berlin in 1815, Rellstab praised her" quiet dignity," her "queenlike deportment," and her "pure, sonorous voice." Reichardt joined in the chorus of praise, speaking of her voice as "one of the greatest and most beautiful voices I have ever heard." He added, "her figure was noble, and her facial expression imposing and expressive." Marx contributed his bit of eulogy, and even Goethe and Napoleon came under her spell. For her, Cherubini composed his opera *Lodoiska* and Schubert wrote his song *Der Hirt auf dem Felsen.*

Among her best friends were the poet Uhland and the writer Varnhagen van Ense. It was in Varnhagen's drawing room that Madame Milder used to sing the songs of Beethoven and Schubert. "Madame Milder," wrote Varnhagen, describing one of these scenes, "had approached the piano in the meantime and prepared to sing. Soon all were silent and waited for the mighty sound of silver bells. They began with the tenderest purity and sweetness, and swelled to the greatest fullness without hesitation. A magical simplicity operated in these sounds, moving the inmost heart, and the soul felt touched and elevated."

V. BETTINA BRENTANO (1785–1859)

It remained for Bettina Brentano to fan the flames of this enthusiasm to their greatest intensity. With her mobile, fanciful face, she possessed a magic that fascinated men like Goethe and Beethoven — a magic spun out of sensuousness and spirituality, fancy and intelligence. Bettina was one of the most attractive women of the Romantic age, and she seems to have understood Beethoven better than any of his contemporaries.

Bettina met Beethoven in Vienna in the same year — 1810 — that Hoffmann's analysis of the Fifth Symphony began the new age of Beethoven enthusiasm. Beethoven was sitting at the piano in her brother's apartment when Bettina entered the room, glided over to Beethoven, bent close to his ear, and whispered, "I am Brentano." The novellike story of Bettina and Beethoven began with this first meeting. In her *Correspondence of Goethe with a Child* (in which reality and imagination are strangely mixed) Bettina described the impression Beethoven made on her:

Seeing that man of whom I wish to speak to you now, I forgot the whole world. The world vanishes when memory takes hold of me. Yes, it vanishes. . . . It is Beethoven of whom I wish to speak to you, and with whom I forgot world and you. I am but a child, but I am not mistaken when I say (what perhaps no one understands and believes) that he is far in advance of the whole culture of mankind, and I wonder if we will overtake him. I doubt it. I hope he may live until the great and sublime enigma that is in his mind ripens to its fullest perfection. Nay, may he reach his highest goal. Then he will certainly leave the key to heavenly wisdom in our hands, so that we may come one step closer to true happiness. I can confess to you that I believe in divine magic, which is the essence of spiritual nature. This magic Beethoven practices in his art. All that he can teach you is real magic. Every stage serves the organization of a higher existence, and therefore Beethoven feels himself the founder of a new sensuous basis of spiritual life.

Bettina, the sister of a romantic poet, Clemens von Brentano, and the wife of another romantic poet, Achim von Arnim, created her Beethoven myth independently. Words spoken by Beethoven she transposed into her own romantic idiom. There was Italian blood in her veins; perhaps that was the reason why she saw colors that were far brighter than the colors of the real world, and why she heard words more pregnant with meaning than any mortals spoke. It is doubtful if Beethoven ever spoke precisely the words that Bettina put into his mouth:

What I see is against my religion. I must despise a world that has not the slightest notion that music is a higher revelation than all wisdom and religion. Music is the wine that fills people with enthusiasm for new creation; and I am Bacchus, who presses that wonderful wine for men and makes their spirits drunk. When they are sober again, they have caught something that they can take with them back to dry land. [Or, again:] When you speak to Goethe about me, tell him he may hear my symphonies. Then he will agree that music is the only spiritual door to a higher world of knowledge, which comprehends mankind without mankind being able to comprehend it. [And, finally:] A thousand people are associated with music without having its revelation. . . . All real invention is moral progress. In this way, art always represents the deity, and the human relationship to it is religion.

The voice may be the voice of Beethoven, but the words are the words of Bettina.

Bettina created a legend, a new religion. Never before had anything of this sort been written about musicians. Beethoven was the first composer to be received with philosophers and scholars as one of the spiritual leaders of mankind. There Bettina's imagination saw him, high in the clouds.

VI. RICHARD WAGNER

Romantic enthusiasm for Beethoven, however, reached its climax in the pamphlet written by Richard Wagner on the occasion of the Beethoven centenary in 1870. From the days of his youth, when the eighteen-year-old Wagner copied the score of the Ninth Symphony amidst ecstatic tears, until his old age, when he listened to the playing of the C-sharp minor string quartet while the score of *Parsifal* lay on the table of the study of his Bayreuth house, Wagner was accompanied on his fantastic way by the music of Beethoven. He wept when he heard the Ninth Symphony in Paris. He conducted the same work with fanatical energy at Dresden, and he compared it with Goethe's *Faust*, suggesting that the poem dramatized the tragic sounds of the symphony. He opened his festival theater in Bayreuth with the Ninth Symphony, thus establishing a bond between his own

music and Beethoven's.   His pamphlet on Beethoven celebrates
the master, in long, involved sentences seething with romantic
exuberance, as a prophet, the brother of the blind seer Tiresias.
The ideas of E. T. A. Hoffmann, Novalis, and Schlegel shine
through the haze of words: Music, as the inmost language of the
world, comes to us as a revelation from the beyond.   The artist
is an interpreter of nature who "understands forests, brooks,
meadows, the blue ether, the cheerful crowd, loving couples,
the songs of birds, the flight of clouds, the blowing of the storm,
and the delight of blissful rest."   All these ideas, of course, are
to be met in the mysticism of the romantic poets as well as in
Wagner's book.   Like all other Romantics, he conceives of music
as reaching up to religion: "What our thinkers and poets expressed only with difficulty and touched upon obscurely . . .
Beethoven's symphony stirred to its depths — the new religion,
the world-redeeming redemption."   Beethoven, Wagner describes as "truly demoniac," a man who "speaks the highest
wisdom in a language that cannot be understood by his reason."
It would not be difficult to trace all these concepts of music,
musicians, and Beethoven in particular, to the ideas of Wagner's
romantic predecessors, beginning with Hoffmann, who glorified
music as "the most romantic of all arts, as its subject is the infinite," and closing with Novalis, who praised music as the interpretation of the mysteries of the universe.

This romantic conception of Beethoven ruled the musical life
of the nineteenth century.   This new enthusiasm transformed
critical writing on music.   Compared with the dry sobriety of
musical criticism as it had prevailed until this time, the new
Beethoven criticism was poetical, excessive, and colorful.   It
was emotional criticism, instead of the rational criticism that
had preceded it.   There can be no doubt about the connection
between romantic musical criticism and the ecstatic transports
of Beethoven himself.   The criticism is a kind of echo answering
the passion of the music.   It is a music of its own, couched in
words instead of notes, and making use of bold similes, poetical
images, and rhythmical phrases.

The new critics wanted to approach creative power at its fountainhead and to fill their vessels with the heavenly drink. In this sense it may be said that Beethoven was the creator of modern musical criticism in the Romantic age, just as he was the creator of the modern orchestra, the modern conductor, the new piano, the new virtuosity, and the modern relation between music and the people. His energetic spirit inspired the critics to let their battered pens grow wings.

Enthusiasm, poetical feeling, increased sense of the spiritual values in music, and greater subjective emotion were new intellectual qualities that the public now demanded of music critics. Schumann and Berlioz may properly be said to begin this latter age of criticism. Of course, in both great and small cities, there were any number of everyday critics, insignificant, dry, and prosaic. Eduard Hanslick, too, was something of an exception in his rationalistic approach to the problem. But, on the whole, musical criticism had achieved higher standards, greater goals, and finer methods. Literary life in the nineteenth century would have been less rich and less colorful, without the romantic critics in whom literary art, personality, and enthusiasm were combined.

Chapter Fifteen

PARIS, 1830

I. THE NEW SOCIETY AND ITS MUSICIANS

ROMANTICISM in Germany was the fancy of quiet dreamers. Romanticism in France grew in revolutionary soil. After the epoch of the Napoleonic wars, all the political, intellectual, and social movements of the new century met, between 1813 and 1848, in Paris. And the battle between old and new ideas was fought on ground that was itself shaking. Two revolutions — that of July, 1830, and that of March, 1848 — filled the streets of Paris with the noise of shots and the groans of the wounded and dying. Amid such upheavals a new society rose to power.

It was a society of great industrialists and wealthy bankers, the victorious leaders of the new age of industry and speculation, the knights of the stock exchange, by whom the former aristocratic society was superseded. The Greek columns of the Paris Bourse echoed to the shouting of stock quotations. The wealth of the public flew into the strongboxes of the companies that built railways, factories, gas works, and ships, or was transformed into government funds. The new money of the speculators built houses, dressed elegant demimondaines, rented boxes at the opera, inundated parties in champagne, bribed, founded newspapers that became the handmaidens of business and speculation or blackmailers or tale-bearers. The new society is portrayed in the plays of Augier: the headstrong speculators, the venial journalists, the demimondaines, the sceptical old aristocrats, the idealistic sons who hate their money-making fathers. Certainly, anyone who had listened could have heard, beneath the surface, the distant roar of coming earthquakes: Fourier and

Saint-Simon were living in Paris and preaching a new, just society. But no one feared them, and the rulers of the day kept on buying stocks, houses, women, theaters, newspapers, and politicians.

For the men and women of this society, Meyerbeer and Halévy wrote their luxurious operas, in which the imagination of musical genius was combined with the taste of snobs. The director of the Paris Opera, Véron (and, later, his successor, Duponchel), delighted in splendid pageants, magnificent spectacles, and lavish ballets, and competed with Franconi's circus. "The paradise of the hard of hearing," said Heine of the Paris Opera. There was the Italian Opera, too, to delight the ears of men who sat in their boxes thinking of new business ventures, of the women who sat before them thinking of their next affairs. The Odéon Theater was "a nest of nightingales." There the great Italian tenors and prima donnas sang: Rubini, Tamburini, Grisi, Lablache. Rossini became its director in 1824; in the same year Donizetti wrote his *The Favorite* for it. In one year — 1835 — three famous Italian opera composers contended for victory at the Odéon — each with a new opera: Donizetti with *Marino Falieri*, Mercadante with *The Brigands*, and Bellini with *I Puritani* In the concert halls the great virtuosos played for the rich. Paganini came to Paris for the first time in 1831, pale as a ghost, black as the devil himself, sparks of hellish fire flashing from his eyes, stamping the measure with his right foot, and magically producing harmonics and double stops like exploding pinwheels. From 1830 on, Chopin played in drawing rooms and concert halls, wailing in the darkness of night, sad, fantastic, wrapped in a mourning veil. Lizt and Thalberg, Bériot and Vieuxtemps were giving concerts at the same period. La Taglioni danced to Meyerbeer's music. In the new dance called the "*cancan*," the dancers kicked off the hats of the apoplectic gentlemen who surrounded them.

II. HEINE AND WAGNER AS CRITICS

The most vivid picture of the musical life of Paris in those years is to be found in the series of articles Heinrich Heine (1797–1856) wrote for the Augsburg *Allgemeine Zeitung.* In a history of musical criticism Heine cannot be overlooked. He was the first to write about music and musicians not as an expert but as a journalist. As a reporter, he was spirited, witty, and brilliant — a "one-man fireworks display of the mind." His writing is personal, of course, but in the highest degree graceful, it is amusing and malicious and always lucid and bright. Heine created the easy, conversational style of writing on music that was used by hundreds of imitators. He taught them to write personally, wittily, and amusingly. But there were dullards among his pupils, who went no further than using cheap jokes, puns, and mean witticisms as tools of musical criticism. The worst of them all was M. G. Saphir; for twenty years (1827–47) he tyrannized over the musical life of Vienna with his paper *The Humorist,* using vile puns and low jokes as a whip.

In Heine's articles, the musical Paris of 1830–40 lives again. The principal figure is Meyerbeer. Heine describes him as a "timid genius," who pesters the singers at rehearsals of new operas.

He is never satisfied. A single note from the orchestra wounds him like a dagger; he hardly expects to survive. . . . God himself can't do the right thing for him on the days when his operas are performed: if it is cold and rainy, he fears that Mademoiselle Falcon will catch cold; if the evening is warm and clear, he fears that the lovely weather will tempt people outdoors and that the theater will be empty. He is forever altering his scores. Only Meyerbeer, who is not only musical director of all the royal musical institutions in Prussia but also the kapellmeister of the fame of Meyerbeer, can conduct the vast orchestra of that very fame. He nods his head, and all the trombones of the great newspapers sound *unisono*; he blinks his eyes, and all the violins of praise try to outfiddle one another; he moves his left nostril, and all the feuilleton-flageolets flute their sweetest notes of flattery. In this orchestra there are also unheard-of antediluvian wind instruments, trumpets of Jericho, and yet undiscovered Aeolian harps, stringed instruments of the Future, whose use betokens his unusual gift for orchestration. Yes, no composer has ever had as deep an understanding of [this kind of] orchestration as our Meyerbeer. . . . Whereas Mozart's and Rossini's finest operas failed at their first performances and years passed before they were appreciated at their true value, our dear Meyerbeer's masterpieces are an unqualified success the first time they are given and the next morning every newspaper contains an article of praise and thanksgiving.

Besides this sort of witty malice, Heine's criticism contains a very fine analysis of Meyerbeer, whom he contrasts with Rossini, the composer of the Restoration period "in which, after great struggles and disappointments, men became blasé and the sense of common interests was pushed into the background." Meyerbeer is "the man of his time, and Time, which always knows the man to choose, raised him tumultuously on its shield, and proclaimed his lordship, and together they made a solemn and joyful entry."

Heine is discussing *The Huguenots* in detail. He praises the balance it achieves between "enthusiasm and artistic perfection": "In this work the man and the artist vied with each other, and when the former tolls the alarum bell of wildest feeling, the latter knows how to transform nature's raw sounds into strangely sweet harmonies. While the crowd is impressed by the inner energy and the passion of *The Huguenots*, the connoisseur admires the craftsmanship displayed in its forms." He describes the choruses, "which speak like individuals. . . . Since *Don Giovanni*, certainly nothing greater has appeared in the realm of music than this fourth act of *The Huguenots*, where the terrible, shattering scene of the benediction of the poignards — the very consecration of blood lust — is followed by a duet that even surpasses it in effect." He calls the second act "a rich idyl that in its charm and grace suggests the romantic comedies of Shakespeare and perhaps even more the *Aminta* of Tasso. Indeed, beneath its roses of joy there lurks a gentle melancholy that evokes the unfortunate court poet of Ferrara."

An equally detailed criticism is devoted to Rossini's *Stabat Mater*. With this composition Rossini has left

the worldliness of opera music . . . and dreamed himself back into the

Catholic memories of his boyhood, to the time when he sang in the
choir of the cathedral in Pesaro or served at Mass as an acolyte. . . .
Now, with the old music of the organ thundering in his memory —
now, taking up his pen to write a *Stabat*, he was under no necessity to
make a learned reconstruction of the spirit of Christianity, still less to
copy Handel or Sebastian Bach slavishly; he had but to call to mind the
earliest notes of his childhood and — wonder of wonders! — as
gravely, as painfully and deeply as this music sounded, as powerfully
as it sighed out and bled out the most moving of stories, through it all
it retained something childish. . . . The sublime and terrible martyr-
dom was represented, but in the most naïve of childish notes; the terrible lamentations of the Mater Dolorosa rang out, but as if they pro-
ceeded from the throat of an innocent little girl; against the veils of
blackest mourning rustled the wings of a thousand graceful cupids; the
horrors of the Cross were softened as by a playful pastoral; and the
sense of infinity flowed round and enclosed the whole like a blue sky.
. . . The hall of the Italian Opera looked like the vestibule of heaven;
there holy nightingales sang, and there the most fashionable tears
were shed.

Great artists were appearing in the concert halls: Chopin,
"who is rather a composer than a virtuoso. Hearing Chopin, I
quite forget his mastery as a performer on the keyboard and sink
into the sweet abyss of his music, into the hurting loveliness of
his creations, as deep as they are tender. Chopin is the great
composer of genius, who should only be named together with
Mozart, or Beethoven, or Rossini." He is the "Raphael of the
piano." Skillfully Heine portrays the personality of Liszt, his
bent toward speculative thinking, his interest in social questions.

All praise is due to this ceaseless striving after light and Godhead;
it bears witness to his sense of sanctity, of religion. That such a restless mind, which . . . feels it its business to look into all the business
of mankind, and sticks its nose into all the pots in which God is cook-
ing up the future — that Franz Liszt is no quiet pianist for peaceful
citizens and respectable sleepy-heads stands to reason. When he sits
down at the piano and pushes his hair back from his brow again and
again and begins to improvise, he often storms all too wildly over the
ivory keys and a chaos of heaven-high thoughts sounds out.

Thalberg passes by next, Liszt's rival at the time: "the musical *gentleman* who, even without his piano-playing would be welcomed everywhere as a fascinating man, and who, in fact, seems to regard his talent as a royal grant."

Witty phrases are scattered over these articles like spices over dishes. Heine speaks of Mendelssohn's fine "lizard-ear," of "Donizetti's fertility — not inferior to a rabbit's." There are humorous sketches, like that of the composer Dessauer, who wrote an opera and succeeded, by "noble perseverance," in getting it performed; as to his face, "some people say it is an emetic, others a laxative." There is the half-moving, half-humorous picture of Donizetti in the lunatic asylum:

While his magical tunes bring joy to the world, while everyone sings them and trills them, he himself sits, a terrible picture of insanity, in a lunatic asylum near Paris. Until some time ago, he had kept a childish consciousness of clothes: he had to be attired carefully every day in full dress, his tail coat decorated with all his orders; and so, from early in the morning until late at night, he sat motionless, his hat in his hand. But even that is over with; he now recognizes no one. Such is the destiny of man.

Another grotesque portrait is that of Spontini, "a terrifying, wasted figure with pale face and coal-black hair, . . . whose appearance always foretells musical disasters," torn by envy and hatred of Meyerbeer; "a withered specter . . . offended by the life of the living." There is a brief glimpse of Wagner, who, after a series of sad experiences, "finally heeding the voices of his reason and his stomach, sensibly gave up his dangerous project of setting foot on the stage of Paris and flitted back to his German potato country."

Across the orbits of these fixed stars, the erratic comet of Hector Berlioz flamed from time to time. Heine recognized his genius: "He is without doubt the greatest and most original musician France has produced in a long time." After one of Berlioz's concerts Heine wrote:

Even the dullest minds were carried along by the force of the genius that is manifest in all the great master's works. Here is a wing-beat that reveals no ordinary songbird, it is a colossal nightingale, a lark as big as an eagle, such as must have existed in the primeval world. Yes, for me Berlioz's music in general has something primeval about it, if not something antediluvian; it reminds me of extinct species of animals, of fabulous kingdoms and fabulous sins, of sky-storming impossibilities, of the hanging gardens of Semiramis, of Nineveh, of the wonderful constructions of Mizraim. [And in another article:] His bent is the fantastic, not connected with feeling but with sentimentality; he bears a strong resemblance to Callot, Gozzi, and Hoffmann. To this, even his outward appearance points. It is a shame that he let his huge, antediluvian locks, the bristling hairs that rose from his forehead like a forest from a steep cliff, be cut. So, six years ago, I saw him for the first time; and so he will forever remain in my memory. It was at the Conservatory of Music; a great symphony [1] of his was being performed, a fantastic night-piece, which is only occasionally lighted up by the sentimental white of a woman's dress, which now and again flutters through it, or by a sulphur-yellow flash of irony. The best thing in it is a Witches' Sabbath, where the Devil says Mass and Catholic church music is parodied with the utmost in ghastly and bloody ludicrousness.

With Heine, musical criticism became as entertaining as a good comedy. The ponderous scholarship, the dogmatism of the earlier criticism has vanished without leaving a trace; gone too are the cloudy raptures of the Romantics. One is plunged into the real life of a modern age, carried to the boulevards of Paris where elegant strollers take the air, to drawing rooms where well-turned epigrams flourish. A living man speaks, intelligently, ironically, charmingly, now enthusiastically, now maliciously. It was Bernard Shaw who, at the end of the century, revived Heine's personal and witty writing on music.

About the time that Heine was writing his articles on Parisian life for the Augsburg *Allgemeine Zeitung*, another German artist came to Paris, with a wife, a big dog, and a big score of an opera in the style of Meyerbeer. He spent two and a half years there — 1839 to 1842. It was Richard Wagner (1813–83), who had

---

[1] The *Symphonie fantastique*.

come with letters of introduction to Meyerbeer and borrowed the story of his *Flying Dutchman* from Heine. During his stay in Paris he wrote articles on musical events, operatic first nights, singers, and Parisian life for the *Gazette musicale*, the Dresden *Abendzeitung*, and Lewald's *Europe*. His model was Heine. "Any of our young men who picks up a pen," he wrote in one of his articles, "tries to imitate Heine." So, though his original style was heavy, insensitive, and unbalanced, he attempted to write in Heine's easy, gracious, witty way. Of all Germany's great men, Wagner certainly wrote the worst German, with his over-loaded and tortuous sentences, which the reader must make a violent effort to unravel. Among Wagner's articles that on a performance of Weber's *Freischütz* at the Paris Opera and that on the first night of Halévy's *The Queen of Cyprus* are the most valu-able. In the latter he praises Halévy as a "real dramatic com-poser," his talent being "pathetic and highly tragic." He re-grets that "our young French composer did not follow in the footsteps of the creator of *The Jewess*." In the same article he praises Mendelssohn, who "most characteristically represents the basic German tendency. The spiritual, imaginative inner life that expresses itself in his carefully worked-out instrumental compositions and the poetical, unimpassioned longing for purity which penetrates his church music are as close as possible to German feeling." In short, the twenty-nine-year-old Wagner, admirer of Meyerbeer, Mendelssohn, and Heine (whom he called "my friend Heine" in one of his articles), had not yet reached the spiritual height of his later Jew-baiting. Further, he writes musical criticism quite like an ordinary journalist, and shows no reluctance to belong to a guild which he later reproached with "heedlessness and dishonesty" [1] and of which, in his "Project for organizing a National Theater" (1848), he wrote, "The im-moral profession of musical criticism must be abolished."

III. MUSICAL CRITICISM IN THE DAILIES: THE FEUILLETON

The increasing importance of the Parisian money market, the

[1] "On Musical Criticism," *Neue Zeitschrift für Musik*, 1852.

growth of industrialism, big business and worldwide speculation, favored the development of the daily newspaper in Paris.
Cheap journalism began there in 1836, when Girardon founded
his daily, *La Presse* (*"The Press"*), and Dutacq followed his example with *Le Siècle* (*"The Century"*). The circulation of these
papers grew from day to day. *Le Siècle* had a circulation of
thirty-eight thousand, unrivaled at that period. Under Louis
Philippe in 1828 twenty-eight million newspaper-stamps were
sold; ten years later the figure had risen to forty-two million.
After July, 1830, booming business enriched the fertile field of
advertising. The struggles between political parties, clericals
and liberals, democrats and conservatives, Republicans, Bour-
bonists, and Bonapartists, the social life of Paris, the theater,
music, art exhibits, the exchange, the races — all were reflected
in the more or less clean mirror of the daily press.

The great Parisian theater critics created the literary form
which to this day remains the special form of French criticism:
the "*feuilleton*." The *feuilleton* is as light as a leaf falling from a
tree, but in the garden of the classical writers of *feuilletons* the
tree had a big trunk of science and wisdom. Julian Louis Geof-
froy (1743–1814), who in his dramatic criticisms written for the
Journal des débats was the first to adopt the charming, chatty,
spirited form of the *feuilleton*, was a great scholar, and so was his
great successor, Jules Janin, who became dramatic critic of the
same journal in 1830 and whose history of French literature is
still an esteemed work. This charming writer's *feuilletons* were
published in six volumes in 1833. They were masterpieces of
French, and Sainte-Beuve, the greatest among these great critics,
praises their style; "which, on its good days and when the sun
smiles, is vivid, charming, sublime, made from nothing, as light
and transparent as silk-gauze. . . . No one ever talked better of
the fugitive, momentary things, which, though they were the
event of only a day or an hour, were for the time, alive." Geof-
froy himself, who created the form, once answered an attack on
his graceful essays, written for a single day: "It is no trifle to
amuse readers three or four times a week, to have wit ready

every day and for every kind of subject, to treat the most serious subjects humorously and always to put something serious into the lightest; to refurbish used material over and over, to make something out of nothing."

During this period the musical *feuilleton* took its place beside the literary *feuilleton* in the Paris dailies — a place which, in the more serious papers, it has held down to our own times. I have already mentioned Castil-Blaze as musical editor of the *Journal des débats*. He was succeeded by Joseph-Louis d'Ortigue (1802–66), a scholar who was especially interested in church and medieval music. His taste placed him in opposition to the current enthusiasm for Rossini, against which he brought out a pamphlet entitled, "On the War of the Amateurs, or the Revolution in French Opera brought about by Rossini" (1829). In 1833 he published a selection of his *feuilletons* under the title, "The Balcony of the Opera." A serious-minded musician, he admired Beethoven and was enthusiastic over Berlioz and Liszt. When Liszt was attacked by other critics, he stood up for the great pianist valiantly:

His rendition is his language and his soul. It is the most poetical, the most perfect condensation of all the impressions he has received and of all that has captivated his thought. . . . It reproduces these impressions, which he obviously could not render through language or transform into clear and distinct ideas, with a degree of sensitivity, with a magical charm that can never be equaled. Now his art weakens, an instrument, an echo. It copies, it translates. Now it recovers: it speaks, it is the instrument he uses to reveal his ideas. That is why Liszt's rendition is no mechanical, material exercise, but rather, and in the literal sense of the word, a composition, a real work of art.

IV. LISZT: PERFORMER AND CRITIC. FÉTIS

This criticism led to the battle of the music critics over Liszt, which took place in 1835 when, after an absence of three years, Liszt again began to give concerts in Paris. Meanwhile, a new pianist, Thalberg, had played for the first time there and had had a great success with the public and the critics. He was a noble pianist who showed (I quote once more from Heine):

innate tact in his art as in his life. His performance is so gentlemanly, so opulent, so decorous, so entirely without grimaces, so entirely without any forced acting the genius, so entirely without that well-known brashness that makes a poor covering for inner insecurity. Healthy women love him. So do sickly women, even though he does not engage their sympathy by epileptic seizures at the piano, even though he does not play on their overstrung, delicate nerves, even though he neither electrifies them nor galvanizes them.

This elegant pianist — the illegitimate son of an Austrian aristocrat — specialized in melodies swathed in passage work, using his thumb to bring out the melody.

When Liszt learned of Thalberg's success in his retirement in Switzerland, he immediately returned to Paris. He was anxious to hear his rival, who, however, had already left for Vienna. To prove to the world that he was still alive, he invited musicians to two private concerts in the Salle Pleyel. He was heard by an audience of four or five hundred, among whom was Berlioz, who wrote that Liszt had proved that he was "the pianist of the future." In the same year, Liszt also gave four chamber-music concerts, devoted almost entirely to the music of Beethoven. The angry lion was shaking his mane and roaring.

Liszt's enemies among the critics were not frightened, and continued to snap at him. Apparently Liszt, irritated by the yapping pack of hounds, lost his temper; at any rate he did the worst thing possible: on January 2, 1837, he published an article in the *Revue critique* ("*Critical Review*") gibing at Thalberg: "M. Thalberg's Grande Fantaisie, *opus* 1 and 2. Caprices, *opus* 15 and 19." This article aroused the wrath of the pontiff of Parisian musical criticism: François-Joseph Fétis (1784–1871).

Fétis was a great historian of music, and one of the pioneers of modern musicology. He was the first to organize concerts at which works of ancient music were revived and the first to give public lectures on musical history and esthetics. As professor of theory at the Paris Conservatory (a position he had held since 1821) he was one of the grandees of Parisian musical life. In

1826 he founded the *Revue musicale* ("*Musical Review*"), the first journal devoted to musicology, and for the first five years of its life he wrote it entirely himself. In the *Temps* and the *Nationale* Fétis looked at modern music through the spectacles of history; in a period which was about to create new musical principles of its own, he was one of those dogmatic critics who judge scientifically. The history of music was being written daily in the Paris of that time, and new laws of esthetics, of which Fétis had never read in his old parchments, were being formulated by Liszt, Chopin, and Berlioz. Heine made fun of the old scholar, who could not see the beauty of the new, leafy woods, though he could well understand the beauty of old bare trees:

I know of nothing more uninspiring than a criticism by M. Fétis, or by his son M. Fœtus,[1] in which the value of a piece of music is reasoned into it or reasoned out of it a priori, from first principles. Critical writing of this sort, composed in a particular slang and sprinkled with technical terms of which the ordinary educated reader is ignorant and which are known only to the practicing musician, gives these empty growths a certain authority with the general public.

Fétis, sitting down to write about Liszt, poured gall into his ink:

You thought you had brought forward something new, something strong, something decisive, against an artist who troubles your sleep; but you are mistaken. You are a great artist. Your talents are prodigious, your skill in conquering difficulties is incomparable. You have carried a system, which you derived from your predecessors, as far as it is possible to go; but you have remained inside it, only modifying it in details. No new thought has given the miracle of your playing a creative and original character! You have remained the product of a school that has come to an end and has nothing more to do. But you are not the man of a new school. That man is Thalberg! There lies the whole difference between you.

Liszt replied to this attack in an open letter to Fétis, to which Fétis made a polite rejoinder in a letter to the editor. After all this snapping and barking, Liszt did a noble thing: he appeared

[1] Fétis's son, Eduard, wrote on music for the *Revue des deux mondes*.

on the concert platform with Thalberg, and was enthusiastically received by the audience. At this concert six great pianists played their variations on the March from Bellini's *Puritani*: Liszt, Thalberg, Chopin, Herz, Pixis, and Czerny.

V. MUSICAL CRITICISM IN THE MAGAZINES

The chorus of musical criticism that rose from the dailies around the doings of the great composers and virtuosos who displayed their art on the lavishly lit stage of Paris was reinforced by the articles published in the *Gazette musicale de Paris* ("*Parisian Musical Gazette*"), which was founded by Meyerbeer's publisher, Schlesinger, in 1834, and, soon united with the *Revue musicale*, continued in existence until 1880. Heine, in one of his articles, described satirically how "the most celebrated artists lay submissively at Schlesinger's feet, crawling and wagging their tails, to get good criticisms in his magazine. One might say that, on the laurel crowns of our most famous virtuosos, who receive homage in all the capitals of Europe, the dust of Moritz Schlesinger's shoes can still be seen."

Liszt, Berlioz, Chopin, and Jules Janin had joined in persuading Schlesinger to publish a magazine in which composers and artists could express their opinions. Liszt himself led the procession of famous contributors with an article: "On the Position of the Artist." He nobly advances that the artist, who had been degraded to the position of a servant, must climb the heights of culture and develop as a human being. He criticizes the current musical life of conservatories, concert halls, and theaters. He criticizes musical criticism too, which may have contributed to the hostile attitude of the Parisian music critics toward him. He says frankly that conditions in the realm of musical criticism are bad. He attacks the current condition of musical criticism, not with any hope of improving the critics, which he regards as impossible, but to open the eyes of the public to the shallowness of their work. He insists that music critics should be subjected to knowledge and ability tests. He asks that artists should themselves become critics, acquiring the highest culture in order to fit themselves for the work of criticism.

When he became director of the opera house in Weimar, Liszt repeated these demands. In the "Dramaturgic Papers" published in connection with his work in Weimar he wrote that "criticism must itself become creative," and approach artists with loving understanding. Liszt had the right to make such a demand: no one has ever had a more sensitive appreciation of others' work than he. His essay on Wagner's work, published in the same series of papers on the occasion of the first performance of *Lohengrin*, is a beautiful example of this sensitivity. After reading it, Wagner wrote to Liszt: "For the first and only time you give me the joy of being understood. See, in you I have unfolded completely. Not a tiny fiber, not a smallest heartbeat remains which you have not felt with me." In an article on Schumann published in the *Gazette musicale de Paris* Liszt returned to the subject of musical criticism. Composers had come of age, and dared to criticize their "superiors," as Mahler used ironically to call the Viennese critics.

The *Gazette musicale de Paris*, adhering to its policy of providing a place in which the composer could express his opinion, published articles by Berlioz and Wagner, as well as others by Liszt. The Berlin critics Marx and Rellstab were also among its contributors.

VI. THE YOUNG ROMANTICS

Far removed from the world of new wealth that filled the boxes at the opening nights of operas by Meyerbeer, Halévy, Donizetti, and Auber, or at concerts by Paganini, Liszt, Thalberg, and Chopin, there was another world: the world of the young men. Many of them had pale cheeks and melancholy countenances. Others wore wild beards and streaming hair. Others dressed in extravagant costumes of all possible colors. There were many poets and painters among them, and one ecstatic young musician with flaming red hair who wrote Masses for hundreds of performers and symphonies for giant orchestras: Hector Berlioz. They were the Romantics: nursed on the mouth-filling lines of Shakespeare, on Byron's poems, on Beethoven's titanic music, or — the painters among them — daubing at their canvases with "drunken brush."

There were first nights at which the two generations clashed. So it befell on the evening of February 25, 1830, at the first performance of Hugo's *Ernani*. The galleries were full that evening: the young "Shakespearean barbarians" had invaded the sacred Théâtre Français, dressed in silk and in velvet, singing ballads by Hugo or street songs, or mimicking the cries of animals. The boxes were full too: the rich sat in them, and every beautiful woman who had entered a box had been received with applause. And now they were all laughing — men and women — at a young man who stood in the orchestra wearing a vest of vermilion Chinese satin, which shone aggressively like the *muleta* of a bullfighter, the young poet Théophile Gautier. Two generations had met, two enemy armies. All that evening the excitement of a great battle filled the theater. It was the same on the first night of Alfred de Vigny's *Chatterton*, when, on the stage, a romantic poet strove against the world and committed suicide by drinking laudanum. The new speculators, the financiers and brokers and merchants of the Parisian bourgeoisie, clashed with the pale younger generation again when Alexandre Dumas's *Antony* was performed for the first time at the Théâtre Porte Saint-Martin in 1831: the audience — or rather, the two audiences — roared and shouted and even sobbed deliriously.

The young Romantics hated the new society, which had emerged from nowhere after the Napoleonic wars and was filling the world with business and speculation. They could find no room for their dreams and their feelings. Impassioned, imaginative, flinging themselves onto life with full hearts and ardent desires, they found themselves in a sober world of factories, offices, shops, in which the stock exchange figured as a kind of modern Acropolis. They were discontented and unhappy; their imaginations took refuge in dreams, in words fuller and stronger than any words that were ever spoken, in colors more intense

than the colors of daily life. Poets and painters traveled to the
East, Châteaubriand sailed for the primeval forests and the endless prairies of America. They longed for space and air, for vivid
colors and a burning sun, for fantastic happenings and passionate
emotions.

No classical art of clarity and measure could satisfy such longings. They were jubilant when Hugo proclaimed in the Preface
to his *Cromwell*: "Let us bring down the hammer on theories and
arts of poetry and systems. Let us tear down the old plaster that
hides the façade of art. There are no more rules — or, rather,
there are only the general rules of nature." Such sentences
sounded like a trumpet call to battle. The restless, tumultuous
genius of the time was in the verses of Hugo, De Musset, Gautier, in the melancholy moods of Châteaubriand's *René*, in the
canvases that Delacroix brought back from Morocco, in the
flaming waters of Géricault's *Raft of the Medusa*, in Berlioz's
delirious and gigantic symphonies.

Unlike their German brothers, who dreamed away their lives
in quiet old towns that were not to know the touch of modern
industrialism for almost another fifty years, the young French
Romantics, flocking to the greatest capital in Europe, had
plunged into all the struggles with which the epoch and the
city seethed. Their romanticism was a different romanticism.
It had the rhythm and the mentality of a capital. It was excited, passionate, and it wore a red cap on its head. Drunk with
Shakespeare, Byron, Goethe, the East, emotional and restless,
Romanticism in Paris fought from a barricade.

Writers and painters bivouacked in the same tent and exchanged ideas. Delacroix illustrated *Hamlet* and made litho-
graphs for *Faust*. Gautier felt uncertain whether to become a
painter or a poet. The painter Deveria wrote poetry. Ary
Scheffer's paintings were inspired by Dante, Goethe, Bürger.
Liszt was an intimate friend of Lamartine's and was enthusiastic
over the socialism of Saint-Simon and the religious ideas of
Lammenais. All alike were captivated by Shakespeare, whose
Othello was performed, in De Vigny's translation, at the Théâtre

Français in 1829. All alike worshipped Beethoven, whom the Paris of that day called "a wild, raving savage, impossible to perform."

VII. HECTOR BERLIOZ (1803–69)

The representative composer of this overheated epoch was Hector Berlioz. He whirled into the musical life of Paris like a firebrand thrown onto a wooden roof. Of all the passionate, ecstatic, and excited young artists in Paris, he was the most passionate, the most ecstatic, the most excited, always on the verge of rapture, of hysterics, or of tears. When he first saw a play of Shakespeare's (it was *Hamlet*, performed at the Odeon by an English company), he was "struck, as by a thunderbolt. His lightning opened the heaven of art for me with a sublime crash and lighted up its furthest depths." When, in *Romeo and Juliet*, he saw Romeo bear Juliet off in his arms, he "gave a shriek and ran away," wringing his hands. When he first heard a symphony of Beethoven's, his enthusiasm reached the pitch of delirium. When he was present in the opera house at a performance of Gluck or Weber or Mozart, he shouted at every cut or every alteration in the score, exhorting the orchestra and cursing the conductor. He yelled and screamed, wept and fainted, at bad performances; like a religious soap-box orator, he was always ready to preach — in theaters, cafes, or the street.

His fury over the disfigurement of classical compositions made him a critic. He could not bear the cuts Kreutzer made in Beethoven's music when he conducted those sacred works at the Opera. He raged when Habeneck omitted instruments in performances of works by the same master. He thought that the end of all art had come when he saw works like Mozart's *Magic Flute* or Weber's *Freischütz* stuffed with ballets and interpolated music, till they looked like descendants of Meyerbeer's *Robert the Devil*. "Shall we not," he thundered, "denounce the culprit whenever we see them wronged, and pursue him, and cry out with the whole strength of our wrath: Your crime is idiotic — Despair ! ! Your stupidity is criminal — Die ! ! Be scorned and spat upon and cursed ! Despair and die ! !"

When, in the papers that supported Rossini, he read attacks on Spontini and Gluck, he seized his pen as if it were a club and battered at the "rambling discourse of one of those idiots" like a madman. He himself admitted that the article was "badly ordered and badly written and overstepped all the bounds of polemics." Michaud, the editor of the *Quotidien* ("*Daily*"), to whom he offered his insults, would not print them, saying, "It is all true enough, but you are just breaking windows." Afterward, when his anger had cooled, he wrote several enthusiastic articles on Gluck, Spontini, and Beethoven, which were published in the *Revue européenne* ("*European Review*") in 1827.

For several years after that eruption the volcano ceased to belch out critical fire. Once there was an outpouring of smoke. It was when he composed his *Lélio*, the continuation of his *Symphonie fantastique*. In one of the monologues of this work he attacked Fétis for having presumed to correct Beethoven's harmonies.

In 1835 Berlioz began to write musical criticism and articles on music regularly for the *Rénovateur* ("*Renovator*"), the *Monde dramatique* ("*Dramatic World*"), the *Gazette musicale*, and the dignified *Journal des débats*. The editor of the latter, Bertin, a great Parisian journalist, put the wild horse to his heavy wagon and succeeded in making him go slowly, as befitted the *Journal's* academic style. Berlioz was a slow worker; writing made him sweat: "I have to make eight or ten bites of it," he confessed, "before I can finish an article for the *Journal des débats*. It usually takes me two days to write one, even when the subject I am writing on pleases me, amuses me, or even excites me. And what erasures! What blots! You should see my first draft!"

In his *Memoirs* he describes his labor pains vividly:

Once I stayed shut up in my room for three whole days, trying to write a *feuilleton* on the Opéra Comique and not able to begin. Sometimes I sat with my elbows on the table, holding my head in my hands. Sometimes I paced up and down, like a soldier on guard with the temperature twenty-five below. I went to the window and looked out on the near-by gardens, the heights of Montmartre, the setting sun, and immediately my thoughts carried me a thousand miles from that accursed Opéra Comique. And when I turned around and my eyes fell on the accursed title inscribed at the head of the accursed sheet of paper, so blank and so obstinately waiting to be covered with more words, I felt simply overwhelmed by despair. At last, like a schoolboy who cannot do his lesson, I tore my hair and sobbed with furious indignation.

Berlioz, as this paragraph shows, was a great writer. Like an organist sitting at his royal instrument, he uses all the stops. He knows how to tell a story, he is a master of irony, of wit, he can employ the full volume of his instrument, the exciting chords, the roaring pedals. His ardor makes him one-sided both in what he admires and what he hates. Handel is "a barrel of pork and beer." Palestrina has "no spark of genius." But when he writes of Beethoven, he lets the notes of his organ swell like a stream in flood. Beethoven is "a Titan, an Archangel, a Throne, a Domination"; in his adagios his genius "soars aloft, immense and solitary, like the colossal bird above the snowy summit of Chimborazo." A sober critic like Ernest Newman asks: "Did Berlioz ever see a colossal bird above the snowy summit of Chimborazo?" Of course he did — when he was hearing Beethoven's music! He was a Romantic and could see colossal birds even in Paris.

After Beethoven, Weber and Gluck were his highest gods. His essays on the operas of Beethoven, Gluck, and Weber belong among the masterpieces of musical criticism, which needs the flames of enthusiasm more than it does the cold rain of carping rationality. Romanticism produced that enthusiasm in musical criticism in Paris as well as in Germany.

Chapter Sixteen

ROBERT SCHUMANN AND CARL MARIA VON WEBER AS MUSIC CRITICS. THE UNDERWORLD

1. ROBERT SCHUMANN (1810–56)

THE YEAR that saw the birth of the *Gazette musicale de Paris* also saw that of a new musical magazine in Leipzig — the *Neue Zeitschrift für Musik* ("*New Journal of Music*"), edited by Robert Schumann. The first issue of the new journal, in which one of the greatest of German romantic composers was to discuss composers and compositions in articles that belong among the masterpieces of musical criticism, appeared on April 3, 1834. Schumann, like Liszt and Berlioz, was an example of the high artistic and literary culture of the romantic composers. Schubert, the simple schoolmaster of the Viennese suburbs, was the last composer who, despite his sensitive appreciation of the finest poetry, felt no urge to express himself through any medium but music. The Romantic period inaugurates the series of composers who were also writers, mastering that finest and sharpest tool of expression, the pen. Mendelssohn's letters are as gracefully composed as his scores. And at the time that Schumann wrote his first article, he was admonishing himself in his diary: "Write simply and naturally. Goethe will always remain a beautiful model."

Schumann had shown a talent for writing even before the talent for musical composition had been awakened in him. He grew up among books, for his father kept a book shop and was a publisher and a writer. From him Schumann inherited his literary gift, as he inherited his musical gift from his mother. Even as a schoolboy, he began to write, both poetry and prose;

at fifteen, he was regarded by his friends as a poet. He made translations from the Greek poets at this period, and gave himself up to the delight of rhythm. "What I really am," he confessed in his diary, "I do not yet clearly know. Imagination, I believe I possess, and no one has denied it to me. I am not a profound thinker; I can never logically follow up the lines of thought on which I may have made a good start. Whether I am a poet — for one can never *become* a poet — posterity must decide."

Richter's exuberant novels were his models at this time. They were full of a romantic extravagance of feeling that appealed to the musician-poet and did not lose its hold on his imagination until long afterward. He clothed his first dreams of love in Richter's exuberant language in a story, *June Evenings and July Days*, and the garlands of tone that often hang about his melodies like ivy on a summerhouse are woven of flowers from Richter's romantic gardens. As a young man, he put Richter above Schiller. Hoffmann, as well as Richter, fed his imagination, and the two together stood godfather to his "David's League." The model for his league of artists passionately discussing works of art, he found in Hoffmann, and the principal speakers of the League — Florestan, the stormy, fanatical enthusiast, and Eusebius, the dreamer — were suggested by a novel of Richter's.

They are already present in the first article that Schumann wrote, published in the Leipzig *Allgemeine musikalische Zeitung* in 1831, under the title "An *Opus* II" — Florestan and Eusebius and Master Raro, the mild, wise old chairman of the League. The article begins like a novel:

Eusebius walked quietly in at the door the other day. You know his pale face, and the ironical smile with which he tries to arouse attention. I was sitting at the piano with Florestan. Florestan, as you know, is one of those rare musicians who as it were divine things to come, the new, the unexpected, long in advance. But that day he was to have a surprise. With the words, "Hat's off, gentlemen, a genius!" Eusebius laid a piece of music on the piano. He would not let us see the title. I turned the pages over carelessly; there is something fascinating in this partaking of music without sound. Besides, it seems to me that each composer's music has a look of its own, simply to the eye: Beethoven looks different on the page from Mozart, rather as Jean Paul's prose looks different from Goethe's. But in this case I felt as if nothing but strange eyes — eyes of flowers, eyes of basilisks, eyes of peacocks, eyes of girls — were miraculously looking at me. In some places there was more light — I thought I saw Mozart's *Là ci darem la mano* winding through a hundred chords. Leporello seemed quite to wink at me, and Don Juan flew past me in his white cloak. "Now play it," Florestan said. Eusebius agreed. We listened, sitting close together in a window-niche. Eusebius played as if inspired, and countless figures, alive with the utmost intensity of life, passed by. . . ."

What follows is a poetical description of Chopin's *opus* 2, *Pianoforte Variations on Mozart's Là ci darem la mano*, which had been cooly received by the German critics. Rellstab had devoted a sober article to it. Chopin's new style, with its romantic play of colors, its harmonic sensitiveness, was troublesome to indolent minds.[1]

In this his first article Schumann showed his sense of new artistic values and his ability to recognize genius. His lyrical description of the variations ends with the words, "I bow my head before such genius, such ambition, such mastery." The editor of the *Allgemeine musikalische Zeitung*, wanting to pacify such of his readers as had complained of this praise of revolutionary music, published another article on the same subject, intended to please his more conservative subscribers. The anonymous writer of the second article found nothing in Chopin's music but "virtuoso passages." The subscribers were not given another opportunity to complain of Schumann's audacity; his connection with the magazine ceased. He had been happy at beginning a career as a writer on music and had written to his mother: "If only you knew what joys a writer's first joys are — even being engaged can hardly equal them!"

[1] Chopin made Schumann a polite return for his article by dedicating his *Ballade*, *opus* 38, to him. But he did not like Schumann's music — not even *Kreisleriana*, which Schumann had dedicated to him. Speaking to the publisher Schlesinger, he said, "Schumann's *Carnaval* is not music at all."

He had more success with other journals, such as the *Komet* ("*Comet*") and the *Leipziger Tageblatt* ("*Leipzig Daily*"), in which he published articles from 1832 to 1835. He contributed sixty-three biographical articles to the *Damen-Konversationslexicon* ("*Ladies' Encyclopedia*") and his fame as a writer on music spread. When he founded his own magazine in 1834, he was already a well-known composer; in some circles he was even regarded as a flag-waving revolutionary. Fink, the editor of the *Allgemeine musikalische Zeitung*, in which Schumann's unsuccessful start had been made, was aghast at the "red" musician's journal; but Schumann found adherents among young writers for other periodicals, who attacked Fink. "David's Leaguers to the left, David's Leaguers to the right, Figaro here. . . ." Fink answered in his magazine; "but so far we are still on deck, and we intend to speak, and that fairly." Fink, however, found few friends among the younger musicians. Mendelssohn characterized him most aptly, saying, "Fink had the art of showing up a weak place in a fine work and of finding merit in a botched job." And Schumann magnanimously wrote to his mother: "I am sorry that an otherwise honorable old man lowers himself so meanly. At all events there will be a fight, dignified as our language will remain."

Schumann represented a new generation of artists, who fought for originality in music under the banner of Bach, Beethoven, and Schubert. He fought for Mendelssohn, whose nobility and aristocratic attitude he loved and whose mastery of form he recognized. He fought for Berlioz, whose *Symphonie fantastique* frightened its audiences, and for Chopin. He fought for poetry, and against superficial elegance and mediocrity. There was no music critic in Germany who wrote more clearly and charmingly about music than Schumann. Schumann knew what bad critics were. He once wrote wittily: "Music sets nightingales to singing of love, it sets pugdogs to yapping." He was himself a nightingale who sang of love. There is no more loving essay on Schubert's symphony in C major than Schumann's. It was he who discovered the forgotten score, which had been gathering dust in a drawer in the house of Schubert's brother in Vienna, and introduced it to the musical world ten years after Schubert's death. The article he wrote on it is one of the masterpieces of musical criticism; it would suffice by itself to make the fame of a writer. At the same time it is a most penetrating analysis of a composition and a perfect presentation of its musical and poetic values, set before the reader with the utmost lucidity and employing all the resources of language; it is delicate, tender, light, colorful, at the writer's will. Schubert's music sounds through this essay; it exhales the fragrance of Schubert's landscape. The full magic of romanticism is there to enchant the reader. But it is a romanticism without Hoffmann's exuberance and luxuriousness; it is romanticism being cheerful, like a sunny garden beside a pleasant house where girls are singing.

Schumann wrote two more sentences on bad musical criticism which deserve to be quoted: "They [the bad music critics] ply their saws, and timber and proud oaks are reduced to sawdust." And, "Like the Athenians, when they want to declare war, they send out a sheep." But though he could make magnificent fun of his opponents, he was incapable of hatred. He had courage, and he attacked mediocrity wherever he found it, but he was happier when he could admire and praise. No music critic has done so much constructive work as Schumann. His last essay, like his first, was devoted to the discovery of a great composer; it was a glorification of Brahms, published, under the title "New Paths," in 1853:

Sitting at the piano, he began to reveal wonderful landscapes. We were drawn into more and more magical circles. The impression was heightened by his masterly playing, which transformed the piano into an orchestra of mourning or rejoicing voices. There were sonatas, or rather, veiled symphonies — songs, whose poetry could be understood without the words being known, although a deep singing melody pervades all his music — separate piano pieces, partly demonic in nature under their very attractive form — then sonatas for violin and piano — string quartets — and each work so different from the others that each seemed to flow from a different source. And then it seemed as if, roaring on like a torrent, he gathered them all together into one cascade, that bore a quiet rainbow over furious waves, falling between banks where butterflies played and nightingale voices sang.

Schumann sent the manuscript of this article to Brahms's father with a letter in which he wrote: "To make his first entrance into the world easier, I have given my private opinion of him public expression."

In 1854 Schumann arranged his articles for publication in book form; they were to appear in four volumes under the imprint of the Leipzig publisher G. Wigand. He found that he had to make hardly any changes; he wrote to a friend: "As long as I wrote for the public, I thought it was my sacred duty to scrutinize every word I wrote for publication. I now have the happy satisfaction of being able to leave almost everything unchanged in the new edition of my writings." A few days after writing this letter, Schumann, driven by an insane terror, tried to drown himself in the Rhine. In the sanitarium to which he was sent he had the joy of seeing the collected edition of his writings. It was the last joy of his life.

Schumann's work is the model for creative musical criticism. From his first essay to his last, he worked like a gardener, rooting up weeds and fostering the growth of new plants. As a composer, he himself was still under attack by the conservative critics of the time. H. F. Chorley, music critic of the London *Athenaeum* from 1830 to 1868, described Schumann's music as a "display of unattractive cacophony," and added, "Not many more experiments with this composer's works — bad ones, because generally ugly and essentially meager — will be ventured in England." In Germany Schumann's music was put in the same pot in which, with Wagner's and Liszt's, the critical cooks were stewing up the "Music of the Future." When his symphony in B flat and his piano concerto in A minor were played in Vienna for the first time in 1847, the performance was followed by an icy silence.[1] But these things, which usually transform unsuccessful composers into critical poisoners, had no effect on

[1] As late as 1853 the theorist and critic Christian Lobe wrote of Schumann: "In his

Schumann's warmth, his idealistic devotion to art, and his objectivity. All his criticism shows the same lucidity, the same poetic imagination, the same almost feminine sensitivity. He is kind to every talent, enthusiastic about every genius, and courageous whenever indolence or impotence tries to stem the progress of music. His style is rich and varied, unsurpassed in fineness, warmth, imagination, integrity, and humor. There is nothing extravagant in his writing, there is no cloudy excitement — only a grace that is like the smile on a kind and thoughtful face.

During the first half of the nineteenth century musical criticism had become a a rich and living thing. Hoffmann's enthusiasm, Heine's wit and malice, Schumann's warmth, Berlioz's passion, Liszt's noble rhetoric were new spiritual elements in the musical world, which lesser critics could use like spices in their watery soups. Another valuable ingredient in the critical kitchen was afforded by the rise of musicology, which, with the work of Burney, Hawkins, and Forkel, had added a new province to learning toward the end of the eighteenth century, and offered new outlooks, new knowledge, and new formulas. Romanticism, with affection for the past, helped to forward this historical study of music; but its greatest contribution remained the enthusiasm, the warmth, and the imagination with which the Romantic critics and composers approached music itself. Schumann's musical criticism, in which Romantic writing on music reached classical perfection, bears witness to the creative power of these spiritual forces.

II. CARL MARIA VON WEBER (1786–1826)

Beside Schumann's wonderful intuition and mastery of form, the musical criticism of another leader of the Romantic move-

---

later work there is hardly a trace of expressive melody." He maintained that Schumann's fame was a product of "coterie spirit"; in his two symphonies he had "departed from the right road"; and "his harmonies and modulations are sometimes interesting, piquant, and surprising, sometimes harsh and painful to the ear." (*Musikalische Briefe eines Wohlbekannten*, 1852) ment in music, Carl Maria von Weber, looks pale. Weber, who in his opera *Der Freischütz* had combined the thrill of the world of spirits with the simple middle-class world of the *Singspiel*, was a cultivated man who had read Kant and Schelling, Schiller and Hoffmann. He wrote in a clear and natural style, but he lacked Schumann's imagination and Schumann's sense of new values in art. Schumann was a born music critic; Weber became one more by chance. At times his judgment even failed him completely, as in his criticism on Beethoven's Fourth Symphony:

There is no longer any question of clarity and intelligibility, of a display of feeling, as the old composers, Handel and Mozart, supposed. No! Listen to the recipe for the latest symphony, which I have just received from Vienna, and judge for yourself. First we have a slow tempo full of short, abrupt ideas, of which not one is allowed to have any connection with another! Every quarter of an hour, three or four notes — that produces tension! Then a hollow roll on the kettle-drums and mysterious viola passages, all embellished with an adequate quantity of complete silences and rests; finally, after the listener, in utter suspense, has given up the allegro, comes a furious tempo, in which the principal object is to prevent any leading idea from making an appearance, so that the listener is left even more in confusion; modulations from one key to another must not be omitted; but they are nothing to worry over, all that is necessary is . . . to run through the half-tones and stop on the tonic of the key you want — that ends the modulation. Above all, shun all rules, for rules only fetter genius.

Weber's punishment for this kind of criticism was what the poet Grillparzer wrote in his diary after the first performance in Vienna of Weber's *Euryanthe*:

This music is horrible. In the great days of Greece this subversion of all melody, this rape of beauty, would have been punished by the state. Such music is a criminal offense. It would bring forth monsters if it were gradually to achieve universal acceptance. This work can please only fools or idiots or scholars or highway robbers or murderers.

The criticism of hate knows no bounds.

No composer clashed with his critics earlier than Weber. He was a boy of fourteen when his opera *The Forest Maid* was staged in the small Saxon town of Freiberg. The music critic there was an old organist and composer of church music, J. G. Fischer, who wrote for the little town paper a criticism that annoyed Weber, although it was not a very harsh criticism (February, 1801). The young composer — helped, I suppose, by his father — wrote a letter of protest to the editor, which was published; and when the critic and the conductor of the new opera answered, he wrote further argumentative letters, which appeared in the following issues. The sleepy streets of the little town grew noisy with the three-cornered battle between composer, critic, and conductor. Weber was in a fighting mood. He was not polite, he lashed out at his critic:

I was indeed astonished by the extraordinary insolence with which Cantor Fischer attempted to disparage my opera. . . . Were I to discuss his article in detail, it would arouse a very impolite echo — but this my temperament and the education I have received both forbid. . . . I am very willing to be criticized and I am very grateful to anyone who undertakes to teach me in a becoming manner, but not to anyone who comes charging in full of pride and rudeness. Furthermore, Herr Cantor, you are by no means my competent judge, and I no more intend to learn anything from you than I intend to harbor the criminal thought of teaching you anything.

Weber concluded his article with a derisive poem in which he says that he regards his detractors as he does a shower of rain, which soon streams away. The boy-composer undertakes to play the critic the score of his opera, in order to convince him that he had not heard it properly. Then he promises to forget the whole matter, in which case he will remain "with real esteem, the devoted servant" of his critic. When the critic finally found a partisan in Chemnitz, who defended him in the paper, Weber answered curtly: "The proper answer for the unknown gentleman from Chemnitz is that I pay no attention to the barking of puppies." After which the little streets of Freiberg returned to their usual sleep.

Weber's activities as a music critic fall into two periods: the period around 1810 and the period from 1815 on.

From 1809 to 1813 Weber wrote for many magazines and newspapers on concerts, operas, singers, new compositions, and composers. He was correspondent for papers in Leipzig, Munich,
Weimar, Berlin, Stuttgart, and Dresden, signing his articles
"Maria" or "Carl Maria" or "M" or "Melos" or "Simon-
knaster" [1] or "B. f. z. Z." [2] In 1809 he joined the ranks of the
correspondents for the *Allgemeine musikalische Zeitung*, whose
editor, Rochlitz, wanted him to devote himself entirely to musical criticism. One of his articles for this journal deals with *God
and Nature*, an oratorio composed by Meyerbeer, who had been
a fellow pupil of Weber's in Darmstadt, where they studied with
Abbé Vogler. After this work of Meyerbeer's youth had been
performed in Berlin in 1811, Weber wrote:

Intense life, winning charm, and, above all, the true power of rising
genius are unmistakably present in [the work]. . . . The instrumentation is well considered throughout, often original and new. All the
melodies, even the most winning, remain within the bounds of the
serious style. If Herr Meyerbeer continues to follow the road of art
with the same perseverance, industry, and discretion for which he has
been valued until now, we can promise the art rich fruit from him.

When this criticism was written, Meyerbeer was twenty.

The most famous publishers of the time — among them the
celebrated Cotta — now asked Weber to contribute to their periodicals. But Weber stopped writing, and did not resume his
activities as a critic until he became director of the Prague opera
in 1815. Seeking a way to dispel the indifference with which
the public usually received new operas, he began to publish articles before first nights in the *Prager Zeitung* ("*Prague Times*").
In these articles he analyzed new works, explained the principles
upon which he directed the opera house, and set forth general
considerations on operas and the world of opera. His first such
introduction to a new opera was written to precede the first performance of Meyerbeer's *Abimelek*. On this work of his friend's

[1] "Knaster" was a popular cheap pipe tobacco.
[2] An abbreviation for "Beharrlichkeit führt zum Ziel" ("Perseverance leads to the
goal.")

he published another article in the *Allgemeine musikalische Zeitung*, enclosing with the manuscript a letter to the editor, Rochlitz: "The only pleasure and reward that I derive from my position comes when it is possible to bring some unappreciated good thing into honor. The success of Meyerbeer's opera has given me endless pleasure."

Not long afterward, Weber found himself in Dresden, in the midst of the struggle between the enthusiasts for Italian and for German opera. Dresden was a city with old Italian musical traditions. In Dresden, as throughout Germany, Italian opera had been the opera of the court and the aristocracy in the seventeenth century. Fortunes were squandered on performances of Italian operas. The Dresden performance of Bontempi's *Paride* had cost the equivalent of three hundred thousand dollars. Even now, when Weber had been engaged to direct the German opera in Dresden, the Italian opera was still the real opera of the court. The German opera was only a poor annex to the Italian, and Weber's position was subordinate to that of Morlacchi, the director of the Italian opera at court.

The conflict between the Italian and German parties broke out in 1820 on the occasion of the performance of Meyerbeer's *Emma di Resburgo*, which the young composer had written for Venice at the time of the most intense enthusiasm for Rossini's sweet melodies. Weber, in the Dresden *Abendzeitung* (*"Evening News"*), published an article in which, notwithstanding his great esteem for Meyerbeer, he expressed the wish that Meyerbeer might dedicate his genius to German opera:

"My heart bleeds to see a German artist, endowed with original creative talent, degrading himself to become an imitator for the sake of the miserable applause of the crowd." Weber concludes by expressing the wish that Meyerbeer, now that he has studied the various national styles and demonstrated the flexibility of his talent, may "return to his German fatherland and help the few, those who truly reverence art, to raise the building of a German national opera, which is willing to learn from foreign sources, but which gives back what it has learned, with the lineaments of truth and of its own uniqueness."

The partisans of Italian opera were roused to fury. They mounted their cannons in the *Literarischer Merkur* ("*Literary Mercury*") and fired at Meyerbeer, accusing him of stealing Rossini's happiest ideas, mixing them with bright and lovely ideas from the masters, old and new, and giving out the "unquestionably clever mixture as a new discovery. . . . In the music of *Emma* the only original thing is the claim with which the composer thinks he can deceive the public." So Meyerbeer was no representative of Italian music at all. As for Weber, "The old classical composers educated the taste of their countrymen through works, not words. May Herr C. M. von W. do likewise! Let him make himself dear to his country as well as to foreign countries as an opera composer, let him win the ears and the hearts of the public, let him guide their taste through works. . . ." Weber published a long reply, in which he remarked that it was extremely painful for a German artist to see his efforts so wilfully misunderstood, even to the point of being personally lampooned. He closed by saying that he intended to continue on his own path, respecting honest criticism and despising vicious attacks. A year later his *Freischütz* was given its first performance in Berlin, whence it traveled to every opera house in Germany and to Paris — the first great popular opera in Germany since Mozart's *Magic Flute*.

Weber, publishing articles in the Dresden *Abendzeitung* regularly from 1817 on, not only did battle for great issues like the question of Italian against German opera but for more personal matters too. He was particularly angry at the criticisms written for the *Abendzeitung* by a lady named Therese aus dem Winkel. This lady, who was harpist, writer, and painter at once, signed her critical effusions with the letter C. Weber honored her with a little poem, which opened the hostilities:

> Swim, courageous little letter,
> Swim on the surface of the glowing stream.
> You are empty, and light enough — and crooked,
> Only you can't hold your ink.[1]

[1] Weber used to say, "She has a serious disease: she can't hold her ink."

So, more or less, runs the second stanza of his tribute to the lady critic.

When "C" wrote a certainly insignificant criticism on a performance of Spontini's *Vestal*, Weber angrily asked: "It is an old convention that one should have some understanding of matters upon which one passes judgment. Is this properly so in the case of the letter C?" In the same tone he answered the letter C's critical chattering against his new arrangement of the orchestra and her florid enthusiasm for Italian music. The editor of the *Abendzeitung* could not put up with so much amiability, and dismissed the ink-stained lady critic.

Weber remained victorious on the field. But a more dangerous battle was in store for him. The whole phalanx of the Dresden music critics drew up against him when he attacked the musical wise men in the *Allgemeine musikalische Zeitung* in 1818. Weber did not lose courage. He wrote to Professor Gubitz in Berlin: "When my opponents go entirely mad, I often just march in among them, and then as often as not one of them is left lying on the field." In another letter, to J. P. Schmidt, he wrote, "I am returning to criticisms again. In that field we are badly off. There is absolutely no one here who will take up the matter with warmth. Those who could, are unwilling to be truthful; so I am obliged to stop them in their careers, one after the other."

These letters were written to explain an article which he had just published in the *Allgemeine musikalische Zeitung*:

"Every town has its supreme judges in matters of art, who rule more or less openly. As a rule, the artists — or I should rather say, the art-makers — who live there are dissatisfied with them; and this is natural when one considers that artists are, and are bound to be, an irritable race. . . . Dresden too has its judges and its discontented artists." Weber hints at the music critics' private interests, which sometimes stand in the way of objectivity. Cleverly, truth is never directly assaulted, but "simply hushed up at the right moment, or forgotten." The critical fraternity must help to build a German opera.

How uplifting it would be for all concerned if criticism, equipped with these great powers, would walk the straight path of simple truth, remembering that it can but bring what it unjustly praises to bitterness and exposure; otherwise, its praise and its blame will alike end in smoke, in short its chief object will be defeated, when all that it has raised so high collapses of itself, once it goes out into the world!

These words have the power of a moral personality. They are still effective today, for morals are eternal.

Weber's article, which courageously pointed out the dirty spots and the rents in Dresden's critical garments, was given a dignified answer by the united critics in the same magazine. They respectfully inform Weber that they do not permit anyone to dictate to them in matters of criticism and express the hope that there will be no more battles; controversies are of no interest to readers; except for the few people concerned, they afford nothing but amusement. Signed: "The correspondents A. C. H." [1]

The magazine published Weber's final answer: ". . . I do not intend to *prescribe* to the gentlemen — truth will do that — but I shall certainly write *postscripts* to them whenever I consider it necessary. I too hope that we shall not come to blows again, and that the case will hereby be regarded as closed." (Feb. 17, 1819.)

Among the articles that Weber contributed to the Dresden *Abendzeitung*, his essays on Méhul's *Joseph and his Brethren*, Boieldieu's *Jean de Paris*, Cherubini's *Lodoiska*, and Mozart's *Elopement from the Seraglio* are important contributions to musical criticism. There is wisdom in Weber's words on Mozart's opera: "I make bold to say that I believe that, in the *Elopement*, Mozart's artistic experience had reached ripeness and that thereafter his experience of the world continued to create his work. The world was justified in expecting several more operas like *Figaro* and *Don Giovanni* from him; even had he wished to, he could never write an *Elopement* again."

In 1817 he published an article in the *Allgemeine musikalische*

---

[1] August Boettiger, Therese, and T. Hell.

Zeitung in praise of E. T. A. Hoffmann's opera *Undine*: The opera is after the German taste,

an art work complete in itself, in which all the parts and elements of the related and contributing arts are fused together and vanish, and, in a sense destroyed, build a new world. . . . The entire work is one of the most ingenious that the new age has given us. It is the beautiful result of the most perfect familiarity with and understanding of the subject, brought to accomplishment by deeply meditated consideration and calculation of the effects of all the materials of art, and hallmarked as a work of fine art by its lovely and heart-felt melodies.

We have already seen Hoffmann bowing to Weber's *Freischütz*. Now we see Weber bowing to Hoffmann's *Undine*. It was not only two music critics who thus greeted each other, but two great artists.

III. THE UNDERWORLD

At the feet of the great artist-critics — Hoffmann, Schumann, Weber — more and more diminutive criticasters plied their pens as musical activities increased and interest in music became more general in Germany, where the daily papers were beginning to play an important role as mouthpieces of public opinion. This aspect of the musical world in nineteenth century Germany is admirably reflected in the chapter on musical criticism in Johann Christian Lobe's *Musical Letters of a Well-known Man*. Lobe (1797–1881), a composer and theoretician, was from 1846 to 1848 editor of the Leipzig *Allgemeine musikalische Zeitung*. He complains that there is too much writing on music (to this he himself, however, contributed richly)!

Everyone who wants to assert himself, chooses from the journalists a band of retainers to precede and surround him on his artistic path, to announce his coming with trumpets, to extol at the top of their voices the wonders he is going to perform. . . . Even when he sneezes, the whole band cries out: "Listen to the great man! Only a genius can sneeze like that!"

Lobe divides the music critics into four classes: the "art-enthusiasts," who merely, so to speak, "enthuse"; the "art-chatter-ers," without knowledge and without judgment; the "art-hypocrites," who think one thing and say another, for fear of being thought ignorant; and the "art-liars," who form coteries. He praises Rochlitz and Hoffmann as critics, but says: "The number of people now writing about music who are competent to do so is very small."

Written in the year 1851, Lobe's descriptions may, at some times and in some places, still be applicable today. Not only intelligence, but stupidity too, has a sort of eternal life.

Especially bad were the conditions in Vienna after Beethoven's death and before the Revolution of 1848, which cleared the pestiferous air. Absolutism tried to suppress all serious and independent thinking, which was regarded as breeding revolutions. The Emperor Ferdinand was a good-natured idiot, the police were almighty, and the populace were regimented and left free only to eat, drink, and love. Certain popular periodicals, like the corrupt and superficially witty Saphier's *Humorist* and Bäuerle's *Theaterzeitung* ("*Theater News*"), indiscriminately praised all mediocrity and catered to the public with puns, quibbles, and buffoonery. Even venal critics were not lacking, as we learn from a letter by Lortzing, a composer of delightful and successful musical comedies, dated February, 1848:

Here in Vienna anyone who offers anything to the public has a fellow at hand who writes for him, and whom in return he pays, dines, dresses, and so on. Among all these regularly salaried or occasionally tipped scoundrelly dogs, Herr Saphier stands first and foremost. Since I never stood drinks for critics, never paid them, and never subscribed to their papers, it is perfectly natural that — in this city at least — I remain entirely unnoticed.

The pestilent air of the period — which historians call the "Pre-March Epoch" (i.e., the epoch before the March Revolution of 1848) — was not easy to drive from the gay city. It was one of the virtues of the young Eduard Hanslick that he tried to educate the Viennese public to a more serious understanding of music. But as late as 1860 Hans von Bülow could still write:

"The Orchestra and the Opera in Vienna are wonderful — aside from them, there is nothing but filth, idiocy, and incredible meanness."

Having thus waded through the sewers of criticism in rubber boots, we may return to the heights and breathe freely again, not forgetting that, as in all other human affairs, in musical criticism too there are both greatness and baseness. But fortunately only greatness tells.

Chapter Seventeen

THE FIGHT AGAINST WAGNER. EDUARD HANSLICK. THE BIRTH OF MODERN MUSICAL CRITICISM IN EUROPE

I. THE CRITICS AND WAGNER

ROMANTICISM had been excavating so deep a chasm between the artist and society that, as the nineteenth century wore on, the two were widely separated. That harmony between creative artists and the general public which characterizes all great artistic periods was destroyed. On one side of the chasm were the artists, living in a spiritual world. On the other side were the people, the public, the cities, living in a material world, which since the beginning of the century had known an almost miraculous expansion through factories, steamships, railways, electricity, and trade. Where were the music critics — the born interpreters and intermediaries between the artists and the public — when the earth began to rock and crumble under their feet?

We have already seen that the Romantic music critics sided with the artists. However, since the middle of the century, more and more music critics had gone over to the side of the public and become mouthpieces for all the public's ideas, all its likes and dislikes, especially in the daily papers, whose circulation and influence depended on the general public. The Romantic music critics had been enthusiastic Apostles of great composers. The music critics of the new industrial age sided with the readers of the papers — who looked for entertainment in theaters and concert halls of an evening — and in general opposed the independent artists and fought with all their intelligence and all their wit — and often with all their narrowness — against the great composers of the time.

A witty French *feuilletoniste*, Clément Vautel, even went so far as to justify those critics whose aim it is to become the mouthpieces of the indolence and narrow-mindedness of the public. In an article entitled "Praise of the Public," he tells the public that had hissed Wagner, Brahms, Bruckner, Debussy, Strauss, Mahler, Stravinsky: "The public is not so stupid after all; left to itself, it has more intelligence than Voltaire."

Such was the condition of things when Richard Wagner turned his colorful imagination upon myths and legends, gods and heroes, and put them on the stage of the opera house. The more imagination Wagner displayed, the more impassioned became the fight against his work and his ideas. The more victoriously his dramatic work overcame what Goethe called "the resistance of the lazy world," the more heated the battle grew. There is no doubt that in Wagner's time the majority of music critics, and especially the influential music critics of the great dailies, fought against him. Their attitude expressed the taste of the elder generation of the new industrial epoch, of the businessmen and entrepreneurs, the rulers of the new middle-class society, who relaxed over the melodiousness of the Italian opera and the luxurious pomp of Meyerbeer. The young men and the women were enthusiastic over Wagner's poetic imagination and sensual music. And when the younger generation had grown up, the whole world turned Wagnerian. But before that, the battle against Wagner moved from town to town, from country to country, from continent to continent. The same arguments for and against him were to be read in papers all over the world. It was the same tune that the music critics whistled — whether Hanslick in Vienna called Wagner "a fanatic of absence of melody," or Chorley in London confessed that he had never been "so blanked, pained, wearied, insulted" as by *Tannhäuser*, or Fétis in Paris discovered that "Wagner suppresses melody and rhythm," or the *New York Times* wrote in 1856 that *Lohengrin* contained "from the beginning to the end not a dozen bars that can be called real melody."

II. EDUARD HANSLICK (1825–1904)

The Berlin music critic Tappert has collected all the insults and stupidities that were heaped on Wagner by the critics of those days of fury, insensitivity, and glory in a book entitled *Wagner Dictionary*, and it is not my intention to retail its ill-savored contents. Only one music critic is important in this connection, since he was the greatest writer among his contemporaries and the most outstanding personality, and represents modern musical criticism with all its virtues and all its faults. That critic is Eduard Hanslick, whose work appeared in Vienna, in the *Presse* ("*Press*") from 1855 to 1864 and in the *Neue Freie Presse* ("*New Free Press*") from 1864 to the time of his death in 1904. Hanslick's fascinating articles were read not only in Vienna, but all over Germany, as well as in all the great musical capitals throughout the world. His essays and articles have been published in twelve volumes, in which his intelligence, charm, clarity, and wit are preserved, like drugs and poisons in cut-glass vessels on the shelves of a pharmacy.

I can write of Hanslick from personal experience. When I attended the University of Vienna, he was Professor of the History and Esthetics of Music, and I had registered for his lectures on "the Opera in France and Italy." Not without some trepidation I succeeded in finding the room where he lectured. It was a small room in the magnificent building on the Ringstrassse Beside the reading desk was an old upright piano, on which Hanslick used to play examples to illustrate his lectures, with short, round fingers in a somewhat old-fashioned way. He was already an old man — short, with a bent back and white hair and white pointed beard. With his sharp nose under his bushy eyebrows, he looked like an elderly hawk.

I was disappointed when he spread his manuscript on the desk and began to read it in a feminine, falsetto voice, without looking up. So witty on other occasions, he was boring as a lecturer, and I did not often go to hear him. I received a more pleasant impression when, as a young music critic, I began to attend concerts and would meet him there every evening. Personally, he was a charming old man. His vanity was remarkable. He never entered the hall without making a long pause before the looking glass in the anteroom and carefully combing his hair and beard. Then he was ready to enter the hall, passing by deeply bowing auditors and taking his corner seat in one of the first rows; there his colleagues gathered around him, and he offered them his silver snuffbox in greeting. He himself took a pinch of the black powder and then drew an old-fashioned blue handkerchief out of the tail pocket of his coat. After sneezing thoroughly, he was ready to retail the newest anecdote or pun or malicious bon mot about some musician. He was perfectly kind and amiable as long as his vanity was not aroused. I could easily understand his becoming angry when Wagner read the libretto of the *Meistersinger* aloud in his presence at Dr. Standhartner's house in Vienna and Hanslick recognized himself in the character of Beckmesser.

Hanslick loved life and the good things of life — parties, beautiful women, conversation, melodious music. He lived and wrote in a Vienna that was being transformed into a modern capital. The old walls of the fortress were dismantled and the festive Ringstrasse took their place, decorated with splendid palaces, charming gardens, the new University, the new Stock Exchange, and the Renaissance palace of the Opera. As in Paris, the new society of manufacturers, bankers, speculators, and businessmen took possession of the shining city and made it the scene of their festivals. In the fall the rich aristocrats came to Vienna from their castles in Bohemia, Hungary, Poland, and Croatia, and enjoyed life in the great city, which was becoming more glamourous every day. They drove to the restaurants in the Prater in elegant *fiacres*, sat in the boxes of the great theaters, danced to the new waltzes of Johann Strauss. Life was easy, gay, and voluptuous even for the lower middle classes, who drank

cheap wine and sang popular songs in the courtyards of the
taverns in the suburbs. "There is only one Emperor's city,
there is only one Vienna," so ran the popular song.

Hanslick's criticism must be read with this atmosphere in
mind. His clarity and ease and wit are as much a product of
that period as his sensuous musical taste. Hanslick represented
the charming and superficial Viennese taste to perfection. The
perfect harmony between Hanslick and the musical taste of
Viennese society explains the hold he had upon his Viennese
readers. After reading the stock-exchange quotations, the most
unmusical banker turned to Hanslick's latest critique, enjoying
his elegant style, his wit, and his poisoned remarks on the music
of Wagner or Liszt, which the banker disliked just as violently
as Hanslick did. Hanslick, then, represents the type of critic
who is his readers' mouthpiece. He is the man who finds the
finest formulas — even scientific ones — to express his readers'
likes and dislikes, who transforms their most undistinguished
opinions into intelligence, grace, and wit.

The *Neue Freie Presse*, for which Hanslick wrote for so many
years, was the authoritative daily not only for Vienna and Austria, but for Germany and other countries too, between 1866 and
1900. On the front page, under the editorial that made political
weather, appeared Hanslick's *feuilleton*, signed "Ed. H." Every
day *feuilletons*, chatting on cultural and social topics, fascinated
the readers of the great paper. Ludwig Speidel, the *Neue Freie
Presse* theater critic, Hanslick himself, Nordau, Herzl and the
causeur Hugo Wittmann — all of whom were contributors —
were among the first journalists in Europe, real masters of the
art of treating serious subjects gracefully. They had all come
to Vienna from abroad — Hanslick from Bohemia, Speidel and
Wittmann from Swabia, Herzl and Nordau from Hungary —
but the charm and cheerfulness of Vienna made them all real
Viennese writers. Despite his Slavic descent, Hanslick was
Viennese to the core. He loved the facile sensuousness of Italian
arias, the wit of the French *opéra comique*, the melodious stream
of Strauss's waltzes and Offenbach's operettas, just as the care-

less, pleasure-seeking, brilliant, and elegant society of Vienna did. From the viewpoint of Viennese optimism he regarded Wagner, Liszt, and Bruckner as rude intruders into a world of pleasure, sensuality, and easy wit. One must have met the little old gentleman at parties, have seen him joking, paying compliments to the lovely Viennese ladies, retailing the latest witticisms, and finally, after a good meal, to which he did justice like a connoisseur, sitting down at the piano and playing Strauss waltzes; then one could realize that he belonged to Viennese society in heart and mind and soul. Brahms dedicated to him, not one of his weighty works, but his *Liebeslieder* waltzes, as if he meant to say, "Waltzes — that is your music, my friend!" The great composer was malicious even in his dedications.

Hanslick's admiration for Brahms seems to contradict his inborn love of light, gracious, and melodious music. Brahms was weighty and brooding, with no bright colors. He was the typical Protestant from northern Germany, attracted by the sensuousness and ease of Vienna, like a serious man falling in love with a light-minded and perpetually smiling woman. Vienna, like Paris, was a gay city; and when Brahms produced his earliest works there, the Viennese public would have none of their dark and passionate romanticism. And Hanslick, as the representative of Viennese taste, did likewise. But before long Professor Billroth, a famous surgeon who was Brahms's friend, succeeded in changing Hanslick's mind. Billroth was an excellent musician himself; coming home from his hospital, he would sit down at the piano and play for hours. Or he would sit down at his desk and write Hanslick long letters about Brahms's latest compositions, analyzing every detail with care. No one understood Brahms's music better than Billroth — to whom Brahms was to dedicate two of his profound string quartets. Billroth, who loathed Wagner's music, recognized that Brahms carried on the classical tradition and was therefore Wagner's opposite. This discovery he communicated to Hanslick, who was clever enough to raise the banner of Brahms as the banner of counter-revolution. He worked hard to understand Brahms and finally confessed, "I do not like all of Brahms, but I have learned to like *almost* all of it." Even the *Requiem* did not meet with his approval; when he first heard it he found that the mighty double fugue, *Denn die Gerechten sind in Gottes Hand*, "aroused uneasy feelings, like driving through a tunnel." He laid hold of the heavy timber of Brahms's music to save himself from the flood of Wagner's, the waves of which were rising every day.

Hanslick's musical taste was like a bright and sharply cut lens of crystal, which collected all the beams radiated by intelligent and melodious music. It was not a large lens, and through it one could not see truly great music — not even the last great compositions of Beethoven. But music that fell within its focus was never analyzed so masterfully as it was in Hanslick's criticism. Hanslick, indeed, had the clear intelligence of the great French writers of the eighteenth century, and his style is related to La Fontaine's and even to Voltaire's. He was the offspring of a long line of French rationalists.

He certainly was the last of the great dogmatic critics. Like them, he deduced his judgments from general ideas, which he set forth in his brilliant way in his book *Vom Musikalisch-Schönen* ("*On the Beautiful in Music*") (1854), which has been translated into French, Spanish, Italian, English (1891), and Russian. The central idea of the book, that "musical beauty derives from the play of sounding moving forms," was not Hanslick's own; he was indebted for it to his colleague Zimmermann, professor of philosophy at the University of Vienna, who expounded it in scholarly terms in his *Ästhetik*. But Hanslick — great writer that he was — set it forth with so much lucidity and grace that his book can be read today with pleasure. It is clear that Hanslick's general principles emanated from his personal approach to life and his gay sensuousness. Lemaître, the great French theatrical critic, wrote of the Parisian *feuilletoniste* J. J. Weiss: "When Weiss took up his pen, it was clear that his 'principles' were only his most passionately favored predilections, expressed in general maxims. What predilections? Those of his temperament." So it was, no doubt, with Hanslick. His taste, his doctrines, his style, his convictions formed a whole that centered in his happy personality.

All his talents would not suffice to explain his great influence, had not his connection with Viennese society been the most intimate possible for a writer. He and he alone was the real representative of the taste of Viennese society. His position can be compared only with that of the dramatic critic Francisque Sarcey in Paris during the same epoch. There were other interesting critics in Paris besides the middle-class man who sat in a theater every evening, his face, with the glasses and the gray beard, turned to the stage, his hand resting on the silver knob of his cane. But no other critic was as close to the limited taste of the average theatergoer as Sarcey. He expressed what the average theatergoer thought, in the cultivated style of a writer who knew the French classics by heart. He rejected all the plays that the ordinary man disliked — Tolstoi and Ibsen, Strindberg and Maeterlinck — and proved, by detailed quotations from Racine and Corneille, that those plays were bad plays. He could be counted upon to feel just like the little shopkeeper at the next corner. He never disappointed his readers by praising a play that they had disliked. Jules Lemaître, his fellow critic, who was more flexible, more sceptical, and less pontifical than Sarcey, wrote of him: "M. Sarcey said to himself: 'I will be one of the crowd.' And he was right. It is with the crowd that the critic must side." Hanslick sided with the crowd too, using his intelligence, his mastery of writing, his art of analysis, and his wit, to justify the taste of the crowd, an elegant crowd, of course, clad in tails and evening dresses made by expensive tailors and *couturières* on the Graben, Vienna's Fifth Avenue — but still a crowd.

Thus Hanslick's power in Vienna was great, and where there is power, there is abuse of power. Hanslick did not avoid the temptation to hold back the progress of modern music not only by his fascinating writings but by personal intervention as well. I do not want to repeat superannuated Viennese gossip — an unworthy thing to do in respect to so fine a writer. I shall only

quote from the letters of Anton Bruckner, whom Hanslick
fought against not only because of the Wagnerian sound of his
symphonies but because the unfortunate man was given the
modest position of Instructor in Theory at the University of
Vienna, contrary to Hanslick's wishes. "It is the old story,"
the sixty-two-year-old Bruckner wrote to the conductor Hermann Levi in Munich. "Without Hanslick, all is lost in Vienna.
Ever since 1876 I have been outlawed, because I accepted the
position of instructor at the University" (November 16, 1886).

Bruckner was an old man when Arthur Nikisch conducted his
Seventh Symphony in Leipzig (1885) and the composer, derided
and sneered at in Hanslick's Vienna, had his first success. Afterwards, the Vienna Philharmonic wanted to perform the symphony, but Bruckner wrote to the committee: "May I be permitted to beg that the committee may desist for this year from
its project of performing my symphony in E-flat major, honored
and delighted though I am. The reasons have to do solely with
the unfortunate local situation in regard to that influential criticism which could only impede my nascent reputation in Germany." In a similar vein Bruckner wrote to a friend in Hamburg in 1886: "I have been told such dishonorable stories concerning Hanslick and Brahms, that I would rather not mention
the subject at all. Hanslick commands two more critics [1] to
abuse me; indeed, every effort is being made to alienate Hans
Richter, who is enthusiastic about me, for Richter's fear of the
press is well known." The same year, Bruckner had his first
success in Vienna — and it was at the Philharmonic concerts.
His Seventh Symphony was finally performed, and was received
with enthusiastic applause. Bruckner was presented with a
laurel wreath, and his success was celebrated at a festive dinner.
He closed the letter in which he reported his success to Baron
Wolzogen, with the following sentence: "But the five hostile
journalists will destroy this success, obedient to Hanslick's
wish." Again, "Herr Richter told me," he wrote to Franz
Schalk, "that he intends to perform the *Te Deum*. But he will

[1] One of these critics was Max Kalbeck, Brahms's friend and biographer.

not get the Seventh Symphony — Hanslick!!! I told Herr Richter that when he wants to perform one of my symphonies he can take one that Hanslick has already ruined — one of those, he can do no more harm to" (Sept. 7, 1885). And so, when Richter wanted to perform the Seventh Symphony in London, Bruckner wrote to Hermann Levi: "Hanslick — I have been trustworthily informed — has repeated to Hans Richter the request, which had already been conveyed to him by Brahms, that he should not perform the Seventh Symphony in London" (April 29, 1885).

The great light of Eduard Hanslick — which, like all great lights, cast dark shadows — shone far over the world and still shines brightly, while so many hundreds of critical candles have gone out. Hanslick was a journalist of genius, who made the position of the music critic for a daily paper one of importance. Today every great daily wants to have a music critic who can interest the average reader in music; Eduard Hanslick, by his peculiar talents, contributed largely to this development. He lost the battle against Wagner, Liszt, Berlioz, Bruckner, Hugo Wolf, and Verdi, because every productive artist is greater than the most intelligent journalist; but he was victorious in his effort to give daily criticism more weight, more brilliance, and more literary intelligence. If we measure the talent of a journalist-critic according to his ability to amuse the public and to capture readers, Hanslick was certainly one of the greatest. First of all his profession, he consciously took his stand beside the public — or better, in the midst of the public — on which the circulation of every great newspaper depends. Thus he widened and deepened the calamitous chasm between creative composers, critics, and the public, turning away from the living springs of his time and trying to stop their flow, using his wit as a plug.

III. OTHER OPPONENTS AND DEFENDERS OF WAGNER

As the battle against Wagner was not merely an art fight, interesting only to experts, but filled first Germany and then the whole world with its excitement, its noise, and its abuse, the daily papers, as the voices of public opinion, were obliged to give more and more space and prominence to articles on musical subjects. Thus Wagner, the greatest enemy of musical criticism in his time, increased the importance of criticism in the dailies. His curse was transformed into a blessing. Hundreds of music critics lived on Wagner. Every daily wanted to have its own Hanslick, and in every town in Germany — even the smallest — some little Hanslick was sharpening his pen and spluttering ink in the name of the classics against the musical revolutionary from Leipzig. The practice of invoking so-called laws of musical beauty against their violation by Wagner became general — as if the classics had not been revolutionaries in their own days, and as if Brahms had not used to say that Beethoven could as well have become a great criminal. All these critics professed to know the deepest laws and rules of music — mysterious as the laws of nature, to which they are related — and, like Hanslick, demonstrated that Wagner tried to destroy the sacred laws of beauty in art, whose guardians they undertook to be. Nobody inquired into the legal title of all these judges to condemn artists, and few of them could have pointed to such knowledge and intelligence and personality as Hanslick's.

And, since real talent in writing is as rare as real talent in art or music, there was plenty of mediocrity among the critics who welcomed Wagner too. The Wagnerians lacked a great critical leader such as the Anti-Wagnerians possessed in Hanslick. The best pages on Wagner were written, not by professional music critics, but by poets and philosophers.

The poets were Baudelaire, who wrote his magnificent essay on *Tannhäuser* in 1861, when Wagner's work was produced at the opera house in Paris, and D'Annunzio, who closed his novel *The Triumph of Death* with a wonderful description of *Tristan and Isolde*. The philosopher was Nietzsche. I cannot refrain from quoting Nietzsche's paragraph in *Beyond Good and Evil* on the Prelude to the *Meistersinger of Nuremberg*, as this poetical description may demonstrate the difference between productive and unproductive discussions of works of art:

Once again I have heard Richard Wagner's Overture to *The Meistersinger* anew — it is magnificent, overladen, difficult, and late art that arrogantly expects a living knowledge of two centuries of music in order to be understood — it is an honor to Germans that the expectation has not been disappointed! What essences and what forces, what seasons and what points of the compass are not mingled here! Now it appears archaic, now unfamiliar and overnew; it is as arbitrary as it is pompously conventional; it is not infrequently roguish, and still more frequently coarse and crude; it has fire and force and at the same time the flaccid, sallow skin of fruits that ripen late. It streams on broad and full; and suddenly [there is] a moment of inexplicable pause, like a hiatus between cause and effect . . . but presently the old stream of pleasure sweeps and broadens out again — the stream of manifold pleasures, of old and new delight, a very large factor in which is the artist's delight in himself, which he refuses to conceal, his surprised, happy discovery of the masterfulness of the devices he is employing, his new, newly acquired, untried artistic devices, as he seems to be trying to tell us. On the whole, no beauty, no southernness, nothing of the delicate clarity of the southern sky, no grace, no dancing, hardly any desire for logic; even a certain clumsiness, that is actually emphasized, as if the artist wished to tell us, "it is part of my intention"; a cumbersome costume, something wilfully barbaric and ostentatious, a scintillation of pedantic and venerable trinkets and tags; something German, something many-sided, formless, and inexhaustible in the German manner; a certain German strength and exuberance of soul that is not afraid to hide itself under the refinements of decadence, that perhaps first feels thoroughly at home among the refinements of decadence.

After this mirroring of the poetic content and the poetic moods of Wagner's festive music, I open Hanslick's criticism on the same work:

The Overture is not at all calculated to produce a favorable state of mind in the audience. One after another, it crumbles the leitmotives of the work into a flood of chromatic passages and sequences, finally to fling them in inextricable confusion into a veritable ocean of sound. A composition painfully mannered and positively brutal in its effect.

If the distance that separates Nietzche's paragraph from Hanslick's could be measured, it would be possible to measure Wagner's genius in inches and feet.

IV. THE END OF ROMANTICISM. ISOLATION OF ARTISTS AND CRITICS

Wagner's genius was so powerful that it continued to dominate even after his death in 1883 and was still appreciable at the beginning of the first World War in 1914. After Wagner was gone, the younger generation of composers continued to write their scores in Wagner's style. The music critics were Wagnerians. The directors of the great opera houses — as, for example, Mahler in Vienna — shaped repertoire and style of performance in Wagner's spirit. The disturbance Wagner had set up continued to act long after his death, as the ocean keeps dashing its surf on the shore after a marine earthquake.

Even before the middle of the nineteenth century Romanticism had, as we have seen, come into conflict with the mentality of the epoch, an epoch of natural science and technical accomplishment, which was growing more and more materialistic. Artists tried to adjust themselves to modern life. As early as 1856 Taine wrote a proclamation against Hugo and Lamartine, the leaders of French Romanticism: "They are apart from the younger generation — relics of an age that was once great." About the same time Sarcey, in the Paris *Figaro*, published an essay entitled, "Forward, Friends! Down with Romanticism!" Dumas the younger had begun to ridicule Romanticism in 1850. Realism invaded literature and painting. Flaubert published his *Madame Bovary* in 1856. Edmond and Jules de Goncourt were at work between 1864 and 1879 on their *Germinie Lacerteux*, *Elsa*, and *The Zemganno Brothers*, studying the material for these novels in the spirit of naturalists. Flaubert read innumerable books and historical documents for his *Salammbô*, working like an archaeologist who intended to write a scholarly study of ancient Carthage. It is said that he studied one hundred and seven books in order to write thirty lines about agriculture in his *Bouvard and Pécuchet*. Zola published his *Thérèse Raquin* in 1867, the first of his naturalistic novels.

The same turn against Romanticism and toward Naturalism

gave a new impulse to painting. Lavoron had already published an attack on Delacroix in 1833, proclaiming, "The real art, the art of the future, is Naturalism." In 1851 Courbet, who called himself a "pupil of nature," sternly and soberly painted his great "Stone-cutter." The year 1859 saw the birth of Millet's "Angelus," 1863 that of Manet's "Breakfast Outdoors" and "Olympia" — canvases filled with the atmosphere of the period. The dramas of Ibsen and Strindberg moved over Europe, and under the influence of the great Russian novelists Dostoevski and Tolstoi, Gerhart Hauptmann wrote his *Before Sunrise*, *The Weavers*, and *Hannele* — plays that filled the stage with the dismal life of the poorest and most hard-working people. Great as was the art that Naturalism produced, the movement did not last long; and, with the coming of Maeterlinck, Huysmans, and Claudel, Romanticism — a late, refined, and nervous Romanticism — again exercised its seductive power over artists and audiences.

The separation between art and reality became more and more profound. There was no artistic movement in the nineteenth century which did not encounter the hostility of the public. Performances of Ibsen's plays were invariably followed by laughter and jeers, and I remember, with some ironical pleasure, how at the first performance of the *Wild Duck* in Vienna the last act was drowned in laughter and how old Ibsen stood up in his box, watching the hissing audience and laughing and waving his hat to the jeering crowd. I also remember how at the first performance of Maeterlinck's *The Intruder* in Vienna the audience laughed as if they had been present at a joke. At the first performance of Hauptmann's first play, *Before Sunrise*, in Berlin, during the scene where, on the stage, a woman gives birth to a child in a hovel, a famous obstetrician stood up on his seat in the orchestra and waved his forceps as an officer waves his saber. All Paris flocked to the wooden hut on the Champs Elysées where Manet exhibited his paintings after the official expositions had refused them, and all Paris shook with laughter at what they saw. It was the same when the impressionistic painters — Monet, Pissarro, Sisley, Cézanne, and Renoir — who are today the pride of the Salle Caillebotte in the Luxembourg Museum — exhibited their sun-filled canvases at 35 Boulevard des Capucines. There were laughter and booing at performances of Richard Strauss and Mahler, and if hissing could kill, neither Stravinsky nor Schœnberg would be alive today. In all these cases most of the critics sided with the public — those of the important papers almost unanimously, those of the smaller papers somewhat less so. Everywhere there were some critics whose feeling for new artistic values could not be stifled by prejudice. When Manet's paintings were sneered at, no less a person than Zola wrote a series of articles in his defense. Romain Rolland proclaimed the greatness of Richard Strauss and Mahler in French magazines. Neither Berlin nor Vienna was without some judicious critics. But everywhere the critical bigwigs admitted the justice of everyman's opinion, and saved the sheep from recognizing the modern geniuses who represented sometimes the greatness, sometimes the harshness and restlessness, of their epoch. The fact is beyond doubt: the connection that should have existed between the public on the one hand and great writers, great painters, and great musicians on the other, did not exist; common ground was lacking, and a common atmosphere. Imagine the Italian Renaissance painters without the court and city society that surrounded them, respectful and responsive — artists and public sharing a common background of ideas and feelings! Or imagine Haydn and Mozart and Beethoven without the society of Vienna, without the men who were accustomed to hearing music and to appreciating it as connoisseurs, without the women who admired Mozart's *galant* playing and Beethoven's brilliant improvising! The art life of sixteenth-century Rome and Florence, of eighteenth-century Vienna, would be utterly changed — with the artists isolated on one side, the public on the other, and the critics leaping the abyss, mostly to the side of the public, a few only to the lonely spot where the artists labored. The complete isolation of Arnold Schœnberg, his brooding over abstractions and his writing of skeleton music after so much music of the greatest tonal beauty, proves the loneliness of independent artistic minds in our age, when the artist is severed from the public. One can admire Schœnberg's noble attitude; Schœnberg's epoch one cannot admire.

There are other causes that contributed to the isolation of artistic life and made the music critic's task extremely difficult. The growth of the leading cities during the nineteenth century, particularly the capitals, the crowding of the masses into them, the increasing separation between rich and poor in the countries of Europe, the political, cultural, and social rise of the working class, the separation of the lower from the upper middle class,[1] brought about a cleavage in social, cultural, and political interests in European society, which destroyed the unity of ideas that had given eighteenth-century criticism its strength and its dignity. The eighteenth-century critics may look antiquated, but they represented the progressive ideas of the Europe of their time, and all of them, even when speaking ex cathedra, claimed to be the voices of a modern society. The music critics of the nineteenth century were torn apart by the cleavage in society, in mentality, in thought. They could no longer draw upon generally accepted ideas and principles; each stood alone and had to find his own way alone. Neither the romantic critics, who sided with the artist against the public, nor the others, who spoke for the public and against the artist, could claim that they represented the whole of society. The most talented became subjective: they put forth their private thoughts, impressions, and moods, enjoyed the glitter of their own ideas and style, setting off intellectual fireworks with no conviction that they shared a set of ideas common to the artist and society. Hanslick professed to command the unalterable laws of art; but despite his professions, he wrote malicious nonsense about some of the greatest composers of his time. He was a brilliant writer, but not a constructive one; and all his great talents did nothing to further the development of music. In the great European musi-

---

[1] The danger inherent in this separation of the lower middle class from the social body was overlooked, until Hitler transformed them into his barbarian army.

cal centers there were fascinating writers, full of ideas, imagination, learning, wit. But how few of them were among the leading men of their epoch! Ludwig Speidel, the most imposing of the Viennese dramatic critics between 1867 and 1900, used to say, "Criticism is the immortality of a day." That seems very little, when one considers that criticism is one of the greatest spiritual forces of the human mind. But how few critics can boast even of that amount of immortality!

The fact is that criticism — musical and otherwise — lost the ground under its feet in the nineteenth century. The most honest among the critics were skeptics, who were content to give forth their judgments as personal impressions. They do not disguise their personal moods and reactions under the name of general ideas, as Hanslick still tried to do, but honestly confess that what they have to say about art is only the fruit of chance personal impressions. When Jules Lemaître — certainly one of the most interesting dramatic critics of the nineteenth century — was attacked for using the word "I" in his criticisms, he answered:

A critic has a right to speak of himself as a critic and in connection with the subjects of his criticism. It is his duty to speak of himself whenever he keenly feels the relativeness and feebleness of his judgments, and especially whenever his confessions may help his readers to complete or to rectify their own judgments — in short, whenever he is not quite sure of himself and feels his weakness. . . . So doing, he demonstrates, not self-assurance and presumption, but modesty. There is far more pride in impersonal criticism, because it tries to hide its weakness. A critic is a human being, I assure you.

Lemaître's skepticism is very instructive. It demonstrates the feeling of loneliness and isolation of a fine modern critic, who is so gripped by doubt that he is not even sure of his fugitive impressions. What he says is very human and modest, but it is nothing more than the cheerful scepticism of Montaigne, who laughingly destroyed the medieval belief in dogma; moreover, it is a tired scepticism, weak, and knowing its own weakness. The same position that Lemaître, as a neurotic grandson of the forceful Sainte-Beuve, took in the paragraph we have quoted, Anatole France took as a neurotic grandson of Voltaire, when Hébrard, editor of the *Temps*, persuaded him to write literary criticism. He wrote:

Criticism is a sort of novel for the use of advanced and curious minds, and every novel is an autobiography. The good critic is he who relates the adventures of his soul, using his discussion of some masterpiece of art as an excuse. Objective criticism has no more existence than has objective art, and those who believe that they convey anything in their work except themselves suffer under a grievous delusion. The truth is that we can never escape from ourselves. This is one of our greatest wretchednesses. What would we not give to be able for one moment to look at heaven and earth with eyes whose facets were like the facets of a fly's eye, or if we could comprehend nature with the simple and primitive brain of an orangutan! But such things are not granted to men. We are shut up in our personalities as in a perpetual prison. The best thing for us to do is to recognize this terrible state of affairs and to confess that we are talking about ourselves, if we have not the strength to be silent. If a critic is honest, he must say: Gentlemen, I shall talk about myself, using Shakespeare as an excuse, using Racine as an excuse, using Pascal as an excuse, using Goethe as an excuse. It is a splendid opportunity to do so."

It is always interesting when a man of Anatole France's talent talks about himself, using some great poet "as an excuse"; and many such fine, intelligent, and poetic "talks" are to be read in France's *La Vie littéraire* ("*The Literary Life*"). But this is not criticism — or not pure criticism, in the usual sense of the word. It is poetry, or inspiration, or impressionism. Criticism is another thing: it is the use of human intelligence, vision, and application, to the end of discovering the lasting values in works of art. The talent for criticism is a special talent, dependent — like all other human talents — upon personality. But the critic's personality is not a solitary one, it is in communication with the ideas that are working and struggling to prepare the future, and with the society that must build the home of the future.

V. THE RISE OF THE DAILIES. THE MUSIC MARKET

The decay of European society in the nineteenth century, the disintegration and separation of classes, shook the whole ideological structure, and the many contradictions and contrasts of the disordered epoch deprived criticism of firmness. The breakup of criticism into more or less intelligent games, played by subjective minds at shaking tables, became the more lamentable, the more opportunities for critical work increased with the increasing circulation of the modern press.

The victory march of the modern press had started in England, where after 1830, political warfare, together with economic and technical development, had seized upon the press as a means of shaping public opinion. At the same time, similar factors had produced an increase in the number of the great dailies in France; and the liberal revolution, combined with the introduction of industrialism, had produced a similar result in Germany. Between 1815 and 1851 the circulation of the *London Times* rose from 5,000 to 40,000. In 1836, the Paris *Presse* sold 10,000 copies and *Le Siècle* 38,000. By 1846 the circulation of *La Presse* had risen to 20,000, that of *Le Siècle* had fallen to 31,000. (The *Journal des débats*, for which Berlioz wrote his criticisms, had a circulation of from 10,000 to 15,000.) But all this was only a modest beginning. In 1855 the London *Daily Telegraph* was founded, and thereafter from time to time achieved the largest circulation in the world. Journalism of wide circulation had begun in Paris in 1836. From gigantic machines poured endless streams of paper, carrying the news into every house in the civilized world. In 1880 there were 120 journals in Paris, in 1890 the number had become 160, in 1900, 240. Berlin in 1900 had 45 journals. The "halfpenny" papers started their career in France in 1863 with *Le Petit Journal* and culminated in the London *Daily Mail*, which was founded in 1896 and rose to a circulation of 2,000,000 readers.

Thus was musical criticism presented with a mighty platform from which to promulgate opinions, spread enlightenment, and assume leadership. Although criticism had lost much of its inner strength in the shaken world of the nineteenth century, here were new tasks and a new impulse. Together with these great advantages there were great difficulties too. One of them, we have already touched upon — the dependence of the dailies upon their readers. The music critic often found himself forced to repeat the witty remark of Alphonse Karr when he was reproached for not having taken the lead in a parliamentary fight: "What do you expect? I am their leader — I have to follow them." But there were other and equally dangerous disadvantages. Since the middle of the nineteenth century, musical life had become more and more a great business. The producer and the manager became the real rulers of the musical world. Artists had their fixed value in the musical market. Virtuosos, conductors, entire orchestras, even great composers, had their course in the quotations of the musical stock exchange. There were booms promoted by publicity; there were even swindles. Common business interests connected managers and newspapers — a coalition of economic powers which the spiritual power of the music critics could not always successfully oppose.

One of the mightiest tools of human progress and enlightenment had become a plaything of the intelligence. The intelligences were sometimes fascinating, sometimes mediocre. There were great writers among the music critics in all the countries of Europe, composing their *feuilletons* and articles and criticisms with learning, wit, and charm, and sending forth their voices over the gigantic loud-speakers of the modern daily. In no musical period had musical criticism displayed such virtuosity of style and such brilliancy of presentation, cast so much light on technical problems, or shown so much general intelligence as it did (and still does in our times) in the musical columns of the great dailies. But, as we have seen, all this splendid critical work had to be performed at a time when the ground was shaking with the thunder of a coming revolution, and when the life of society and the life of the spirit had lost their connection with each other. Composers, too, had to choose between living with

their ideas in isolation and coming to some agreement with the
modern business mentality. A great modern composer, Richard
Strauss, after a revolutionary beginning, made his compromise
with sensationalism and the cult of publicity, with the speculative tendency of business and the general currents of his time,
and, after doing some of the boldest work of his age, began pro-
gressively to lose his creative force, repeating his once shining
formulas like a virtuoso and selling them at bargain prices. As
in all epochs of descent, creative artistic ability was outweighed
by vastly increased production, bartered away by agents and
producers, and advertised by publicity. The development of
classical-romantic music had come to an end, and Schœnberg
burned its last remnants to ashes. Europe had arrived at the
close of an old age and was afraid to begin anew. No one could
fail to recognize the crisis in society, production, and art.

Among the music critics, there were some men who had a
thorough understanding of the nature of this crisis — notably
Paul Bekker, Adolf Weissmann, and Ernest Newman. None of
them analyzed the state of the times and of the music of the times
more perspicaciously than Weissmann did in his book, *Problems
of Modern Music* (English translation, 1925). The chapter entitled "The Music Market" in this book is the best account of
the difficult conditions under which composers were obliged to
work during the time of crisis, and the clearest estimate of the
social conditions of musical life.

The intelligent work done by music critics in the period of
crisis was a wonderful display of the art of letters and of the
critical faculty — a brilliant sunset at the close of an age of
music, which was ending — like all great epochs of art when
they reach exhaustion — in a lavish display of virtuosity. In
musical criticism as well as in the other arts, virtuosity means
intelligence and imagination severed from creative spiritual
forces, intelligence and imagination amusing themselves, without foundation or fixed ideas — the play of personal forces without any connection with society, extreme individualism, and
subjectivity. All periods of transition show these signs of a

brilliant intelligence which has lost its home and its basis. It was the same when the great epoch of Greek art drew to its close, the same when the glorious age of Renaissance and Baroque art ended. In these periods, there were the same intellectual fireworks, the same motley hues of virtuosity, the same blaze of technical accomplishment that are present in the musical criticism of our times — whether it is Bekker's, Weissmann's, Einstein's, Newman's, or Huneker's. Such men we enjoy, even while we admit that almost all of this criticism had ceased to be part of the progressive forces of the intellectual world. Critics had become either the mouthpieces of the reactionary mentality of the readers of the dailies, or the slavedrivers and the slaves of the publicity business, or journalistic entertainers, or solitary virtuosos, or literati amusing themselves with the iridescent soap bubbles of their ideas and imaginings.

Unchanged, immortal, and indestructible, the type of the so-called expert, the dry critical artisan, who uses old formulas as shoemakers use old lasts, survives all periods. It is of this type of music critic that Verdi was thinking when he wrote in one of his letters:

Criticism does what it is its duty to do. It judges, and must judge, according to existing rules and forms. The artist, however, must cope with the future, see new worlds in chaos; and when, far, far ahead on his new path, he perceives a little light, he must not be frightened by the darkness that still shrouds it. He must march forward; and if he often stumbles and falls, he must rise again and press on forward.

Undeterred by crises — indeed, hardly aware of them — the dried-up expert goes on through all the changes of history, measuring with his tapemeasure, eternal as genius itself.

Chapter Eighteen

MODERN MUSICAL CRITICISM

MODERN musical criticism developed in the great European countries and in the United States in response to the particular conditions of life, the economic structure, the social and spiritual atmosphere, which exist in any great country. The tasks of musical criticism were, in all countries whose soil and air nourished a musical and a literary life, the same; the music critics must contribute to the development of musical life in their respective countries. The means were different in each country. But above all the particular tasks, rose a still higher task, which has been best formulated by the great English critic Matthew Arnold: "The criticism, which alone can much help us for the future, the criticism which throughout Europe is at the present day meant, when so much stress is being laid on the importance of criticism and the critical spirit, is a criticism which regards Europe as being, for intellectual and spiritual purposes one great confederation, bound to joint action and working to a common result."

Add to this spiritual and intellectual confederation the Americas, and we have a background of the high ideal against which it is proper to consider the men who, in the great musical countries, have been the leaders of public taste in our time. The wealth of critical figures is astonishing. Composers, scholars, writers with a taste for the arts, journalists, have been and are working in every country on great dailies and magazines; and, in the gallery of present-day music critics, every kind of human greatness and littleness is represented, from enthralling virtuosos to banal journeymen.

I. GERMANY

Germany was the leading musical country of the nineteenth century, for there great composers had formed an uninterrupted musical tradition. From the baroque school to the classics, from the classics to the romantics, and from the romantics to the moderns, music flooded Germany like a mighty river whose majestic waters never cease to turn mills, to bear ships, and to transform their own energy into power and light.

Italy at the same time was a country of great operatic music, the tunes of which seemed to grow out of her soil and easily entered the life of her people, the noisy bustling of the *piazza*, and the chatter of the crowds in the coffee houses. I have heard arias of Donizetti's, Bellini's, and Verdi's sung by fishermen in the Bay of Naples under a silver moon, by beggars sitting at the doors of Roman churches, and by girls wrapped in black shawls and hurrying with clattering slippers over the marble bridges of Venice. This direct union between opera and common life in Italy did not require musical criticism. The response of the public in Italian opera houses to operatic music was an immediate one.

In Germany, instrumental music of all kinds — symphonies, chamber music, concertos — produced intellectual pleasure. They impressed their hearers not only with musical beauty but with moral and spiritual ideas. The German opera, except for the popular *Singspiel*, was a kind of annex to the symphonic forms. From Beethoven's *Fidelio* to Wagner and Richard Strauss, the symphonic orchestra dominates the singing voices. There was less sensuousness and more "spirituality" in German music — a situation which asks the aid of musical criticism. The relationship between the public and music in Germany was never simple and natural; it was complicated by an intellectual element, which produced strain.

France, the third great musical country of Europe, did not complete the development of her musical taste, after the glorious Romantic age, until the end of the nineteenth century, when she consciously returned to the lucidity and sensuality of Rameau. Claude Debussy proudly named himself "Claude of France." Around 1900 France was beginning the countermovement against the oppressive mass of Wagner's music dramas by conjuring up the old French tradition of the days of Voltaire, Watteau, and La Fontaine. Thus in France music was an intellectual force, not an elementally sensual force as it was in Italy, or a moral force as it was in Germany.

For the Germans music was always more than a sensuous delight in forms. The concept of music as an expression of intellectual and moral ideas had taken deep root in Germany since Luther made the chorales and church music the expression of the Protestant creed. In the Catholic parts of Germany, where the influence of Italian music was great and the Italian sun shone over the Alps, there was more of splendor and sensual brilliance than in Protestant Germany, and all the great composers of the post-Bach era, except the pessimistic Brahms, were Catholics and grew up amid the resplendent luxury of Catholic church services. Nevertheless they were, consciously (as in the case of Beethoven) or unconsciously (as in the cases of Haydn, Mozart, and Schubert), imbued with the humanistic ideas of German philosophy, which had transformed religious ideas into moral ideas. This union of music with ideas and with moral sentiments gave the musical life of Germany its seriousness and ponderousness. The German musical public did not have the happy naturalness of the Italian opera lovers or the intelligent taste of the French. It was serious, and not sensual, in the cathedral of music. This peculiar attitude of the German public to music imparted its solemnity and solidity to musical criticism. It was a long time before musical criticism in Germany lost the solemn pomposity that characterized all the German musical critics of the eighteenth century; indeed, under the guise of dry pedantry, it can still be found among minor German musical critics today. Not until Schumann had given it romantic charm and Hanslick the lucidity of the French *feuilleton* did German musical criticism lose its ponderousness. As late as the middle of the nineteenth century Wagner could still write his long winding sentences, which grope their way through a mist of cloudy ideas like a traveler through the thick fog of a winter night. The great dailies finally gave musical criticism more of a sense of actuality, the livelier tempo of modern affairs and commerce, the heightened breathing of the modern age. Provincial standards had to go. The world had become smaller in the age of the telegraph and the telephone, and first nights in Paris, London, and New York were reported in the columns of German newspapers and discussed over breakfast the next morning.

As we have had occasion to remark, there were 45 daily papers published in Berlin in 1900. Leipzig had 8, Munich 12, Hamburg 8, and Stuttgart 8. Some of the Berlin dailies were among the best informed and best written newspapers in the world. Even in the smaller towns there were papers that enjoyed a worldwide fame. In the great new house of German journalism, music critics had to don new, modern clothes.

Much, however, as the times were changing in Germany, music remained an integral part of public life there. Even when, after the Franco-German War of 1870, the spirit of speculative enterprise swept through Berlin, the new capital of a new empire, this basic conception of music did not essentially change. There were more than eighty opera houses in Germany, all well subsidized by courts or states or municipalities. Berlin alone had four great opera houses, each an artistic personality with clearly distinguishable characteristics. Towns such as Dresden, Munich, Frankfurt, Hamburg, Stuttgart, Düsseldorf were proud of their opera houses and their old operatic traditions. Famous concert orchestras played in Cologne, Munich, Frankfurt, Dresden, and other German cities; little Meinigen had a celebrated orchestra, among whose conductors were such men as Hans von Bülow, Max Reger, and Richard Strauss. The choral societies in the towns along the Rhine were particularly famous. Every capital city of the thirty-eight states that, until 1933, formed federal Germany was a cultural center, whether it was the seat of a court like Dresden or Weimar, or a free merchants' town like Hamburg or Frankfurt. The music critics in these musical centers were often imposing personages. The criticisms of men such as Paul Bekker in Frankfurt or Ferdinand Pfohl in Hamburg or Otto Neitzel in Cologne were regarded as authoritative all over Germany.

The German public demanded that the music critic should have not only learning, literary art, and experience, but also that moral concept of music which is a feature of the musical life of Germany. To be a critic of rank, one had to be serious and authoritative. It was for the reporter to be mobile and swift and superficial. The critic took his time, pondered his verdict thoroughly, and wrote his articles with the profundity of a professor, exhausting every aspect of his subject. Contrary to the practice in France, composers were seldom chosen to be the music critics of daily papers in Germany.

One exception was Engelbert Humperdinck (1854–1921), who wrote musical criticisms for the distinguished *Frankfurter Zeitung* from 1890 to 1895. At the time, he was already a noted composer. Richard Strauss, who as a young man conducted in Weimar between 1889 and 1894, had discovered Humperdinck's fairy-tale opera, *Hänsel and Gretel*. "A masterpiece of the first water," he wrote to the composer when he was preparing to conduct the opera for the first time at Christmas, 1893. "What refreshing humor, what delicious naïve melodies, what art and fineness in the handling of the orchestra, what perfection in the form of the whole work, what flowery invention, what splendid polyphony, and everything original, new, and truly German," runs Strauss's critical paean. "My dear friend, you are a great master, who has bestowed upon the dear Germans a work that they hardly deserve."

Humperdinck was a fine and modest man and a fine and modest music critic. He was a kindly critic, even toward composers. He was enthusiastic about Hugo Wolf (who regarded him as one does a kind uncle and called him "My dear, good Humpi"), and about Max von Schillings and Hans Pfitzner. There was no poison in his ink. Only slovenliness in performances of the great works of Wagner aroused his fury, a very gentle fury indeed, a fury that wore gloves. He was moved rather to mocking humor than to hatred when he encountered imperfection on the operatic stage or the concert platform. When Madame Nordica appeared in Frankfurt in *Traviata*, dressed in sensational gowns, Humperdinck wrote:

No little impression was produced by the wonderful color symphony of her costume, concerning the costliness of which Dame Fame had already spoken wonders, and compared with which even Verdi's orchestra perforce appeared dull and expressionless. To sing a fitting song of praise to the deep clarinet-green of her dress in the first act, the delicate oboe-rose shades in the second, the brilliant harp glissando of her lace dress in the third act and the dull flageolet-blue in the death scene, one would have to be either a poet or a dressmaker.

To composer-critics, the editors of German periodicals preferred musicians with an educational background — teachers of theory, or professors at conservatories, or musicologists. Heinrich Ehrlich (1822–99), who was the authoritative music critic in Berlin from 1886 to 1898, began his career as a piano virtuoso and later became professor of piano at Stern's Conservatory in Berlin. He was celebrated as an author of books on piano technique and of methods for the piano; his books on ornamentation in the piano music of Bach and Beethoven have been translated into French and English. Max Loewengard (1860–1915), music critic in Hamburg from 1904 on and widely known, had been a professor at the conservatory there and published scores of books on theory. Rudolf Louis (1870–1914), music critic in Munich from 1897 on, was the author of a widely used outline of harmony. Otto Neitzel (1852–1920), well-known music critic of Cologne, had been a professor at the conservatories in Strassburg, Moscow, and Cologne before he began writing musical criticism in 1887. Many German music critics had exchanged the conductor's stand for a desk in a newspaper office. Among them were Paul Bekker and Leopold Schmidt. Noted scholars in the history of music who were also music critics were Josef Sittard in Hamburg, Adolf Aber in Leipzig, Eugen Schmitz in

Dresden, and — first of them all — Alfred Einstein, who until 1933 was music critic for the *Berliner Tageblatt*.

German readers are more interested in depth of meaning than in beauty of form. Ease, clarity, precision and balance, regularity and simplicity, which are qualities inherent in the Romance languages, are not inherent in literary German. Literary German had not grown up at courts and had not been polished by an elegant society. It had less beauty than force and expressiveness. This is why, among the music critics for the daily papers in Germany, only a few could be called born writers. They were first of all experts, competent judges of the art, musical authorities. They seldom enjoyed writing as an art in itself, wielding their pens as a fencer does his sword. The German music critics' virtues were not the virtues of style. They were reliable, serious, cultured men, more scholars than journalists. Well as men like Paul Bekker, Ferdinand Pfohl, and Alfred Einstein wrote, perhaps only Adolf Weissmann in Berlin could bear comparison with the colorful imagination of James Huneker or the virtuosity of Ernest Newman or the fine grace of Camille Bellaigue.

The German dailies accommodated their critics with plenty of space in which to set forth their well-founded opinions. Certainly in no other country were musical questions treated so earnestly and so thoroughly as they were in Germany. The idea of music as entertainment was unfamiliar to the German mind. As a consequence, musical criticism in Germany had dignity and weight, and music critics were responsible for an important part of Germany's public and cultural life. The critics were almost a species of town councillor, members of the magistracy, public officials of municipal life. Indeed, they were often policemen, tracking down evil doers. Their importance was increased by an aura of officialdom, and on the heads of some of them one seems to see the beadle's cap with the threatening brass eagle which dominated life in Germany until 1933. In that year the same music critics pinned on the crooked cross and kowtowed to Goebbels.

II. AUSTRIA AND BOHEMIA

I write the name Vienna, and the six letters suffice to evoke another climate. Here the German fog has vanished. Here there is more sensuousness and less gravity. In the air sound the melodies of Schubert, the waltzes of Johann Strauss. People sit in the courtyards of little taverns on the outskirts of the city, under flowering apple trees and fragrant elders. Elegant and stylishly dressed ladies and gentlemen lean back in their carriages, which are carrying them to the racecourse under the chestnut trees in the Prater, or to some restaurant in the Vienna Woods where the women may laugh louder and with more of promise. Through the whole world Vienna was famous as the city of merriment, of joy in life, of beautiful women, of gaieties, and of music. I refer, of course, to Vienna before the first World War, which was to draw deep lines on that lovely face. Vienna, like Paris, was a feminine city, caressing visitors, smiling, offering her embraces. None of the German cities was feminine.

It is easy to understand that in this gay Vienna musical criticism was a different thing from musical criticism in Germany. Yet it was certainly no less serious than the "scientific" criticism of Germany. From the time — about 1866 — when Vienna began to change into a modern capital, through whose old streets rustled the paper wings of modern dailies, most Viennese music critics were experts, men of wide learning and culture. Hanslick, as we have seen, was Professor of Musical History and Esthetics at the University of Vienna. He knew the musical life of France, Italy, and England from personal experience. His authority was recognized internationally. Besides Hanslick, Ludwig Speidel, the old lion of Viennese dramatic critics, wrote musical criticism, displaying his mastery of language in this field also. A profound connoisseur of all the arts, he was a musician as well. When he wrote of Schubert, his heart opened. At a time when Bruckner was still being laughed at in Vienna, Speidel wrote poetic essays on the marvelous landscape in which Bruckner's music had grown up like a forest or an orchard. As an example of Speidel's writing I shall quote a paragraph from his essay on Mozart, written after the performance of a "Mozart cycle" at the Vienna Opera House:

Mozart, from whatever point of view he is regarded, is the unequaled master of opera. He carried the Italian opera to its highest point; he absorbed the legitimate elements of Gluck's reform; he laid the foundation of German opera and carried it to its classical culmination. His *Idomeneo* shows how he set himself against Gluck's opera, how he puts an end to its one-sidedness and — an incomparably greater musician than Gluck — finds the solution of dramatic problems in music itself. The *Elopement from the Seraglio* is the spring song of German opera. Here all the nightingales of poetry warble, here a new world of dramatic construction appears. Here not only is the dramatic situation musically alive, but the figures of the drama too, with their moral personalities and their national distinctions, are expressed in sound. Take the figure of Osmin — here an inexhaustible spring of musical characterization bursts into being, to flow on and on and turn the mills of Mozart's successors. Here Weber and Meyerbeer are Mozart's pupils. In the *Elopement from the Seraglio* Mozart took the German *Singspiel* and raised it to an undreamed-of height. In the *Marriage of Figaro*, the *Singspiel* has risen to comic opera, a piecemeal form has become a perfectly rounded work of art. This opera was a miracle in its time and, properly considered, it has never ceased to be a miracle. Look at Figaro, the Count, the Page, and then at the women, the Countess, Susanna, and so on down to the stupid little goose of a girl who lost the Count's needle — what a crowd of figures, not one of whom does not live and move and have being, musically. The wealth of invention is incredible; nothing could be more admirable than the clear sense of beauty that restrains and arranges all this exuberance. Never was there music more beautiful, more charming to the ear. The first finale, into which the full stream of the action pours and which allows the most contrasting feelings to sound harmoniously together and side by side, weaving orchestra and human voices together in an endless web — this finale of the *Marriage of Figaro* will stand for all time as an unequaled masterpiece. Mightier heavenly and earthly powers come on the stage in *Don Giovanni*. With them Mozart's genius grows. Although he was more at home than anyone else in the world of charm, of carefree pleasure, of playful, happy love, he well knew the deceitful exterior of this earth of ours, he was aware of the demonic powers that work below, and — for all his gaiety of spirit and his need for a happy existence — a living sense of the tragic was a part of his nature. It was this that enabled him to create *Don Giovanni*, the only musical tragedy we have.

With equal thoughtfulness the critic takes up *Così fan tutte*, *The Magic Flute*, and *The Clemency of Titus*. I quote only his sentences on *The Magic Flute*:

After all these works, for which he paid with his soul, he could still create *The Magic Flute*, the first German opera and perhaps the last. To be so popular and at the same time so profound, to set the priest beside the merry-andrew, and to combine playful quips with Dantesque greatness — in the musical-dramatic realm until now, only Mozart has been capable of such an achievement.

These lines, which exhaust all that can be said as a survey of Mozart's operas, I did not take from a book. They were written for a day, and with the day they disappeared. They are part of a *feuilleton* — a little leaf that fell from a tree on Vienna's Ringstrasse on January 30, 1880.

Ludwig Speidel was German, not Austrian, by birth. He had come to Vienna by the old traditional route, by which, even in the Middle Ages, men had traveled from Swabia to Austria: the Danube. Once each week a gaily painted wooden ship sailed from the mighty Gothic steeple of the Cathedral of Ulm to the mighty Gothic steeple of the Church of St. Stephen in Vienna. It was a gay sail: musicians played dance music from the Alps on board, and yodelers woke the echoes along the banks. The Viennese called the ship "the elm box." [1] Ludwig Speidel was one of the many Swabians who sailed from Ulm to Vienna in the "elm box." In Vienna he felt at home; he was captivated by the Viennese landscape, which he described like a poet in many of his *feuilletons*.[2] He soon became the most powerful dramatic critic in Vienna. In Speidel's case as in Hanslick's, the connec-

---

[1] *Ulme* — elm
[2] Four volumes of Speidel's articles were published in Berlin in 1910. The publication of further volumes was stopped by the outbreak of war in 1914.

tion between critic and public was close, although Speidel had none of Hanslick's grace — a lack for which he made up by his power, his imagination, and his seriousness. When he was angry, he could destroy a play with one thrust. Theatergoers and first-nighters in Vienna would wait several days for the appearance of Speidel's criticism, before they knew whether they liked a new play or not. There was perfect teamwork between critics like Speidel and Hanslick and newspaper readers in Vienna. Writers knew how to write, and readers knew how to read. Outside Vienna, a similar state of affairs was to be found only in Paris: a cultivated, elegant society whose taste was formed by great critics and journalists, and great critics and journalists, whose style and taste mirrored the taste and moods of the public.

Besides Hanslick and Speidel, who were the unchallenged leaders of criticism in the age of Brahms and Bruckner, there were other outstanding musical critics on the great Vienna dailies: Max Kalbeck, the biographer of Brahms; Richard Heuberger, the composer of the popular musical comedy *The Opera Ball*; Robert Hirschfeld, the first critic who dared to cross swords with Hanslick (in a pamphlet, *Eduard Hanslick's Critical Method*, 1885) and a musicologist who made his contribution to musical history with a study of the fourteenth-century theorist Johannes de Muris. These men were all solid musicians and brilliant writers. Like every refined society that has taste and a tradition, Viennese society between 1867 and 1914 was responsive to style, to the personal in writing, to grace and wit. Readers were inclined to lay less stress on accurate judgment than on stylistic graces. Unlike the Germans, the Viennese would not tolerate dry and pedantic learning such as had made Leopold Schmidt the leading Berlin music critic from 1897 on. They even preferred a quite unprincipled cynicism spiced with literary charm to the utmost learning without any literary grace. Wit and intelligence of the kind that shone and entertained at cafes and social gatherings were never absent from Vienna's newspapers. Nor were they lacking among Vienna's music critics. It was precisely this superficial Viennese wit that, being itself sterile, regularly turned against such great artists as Wagner, Bruckner, and Mahler. But Vienna loved to play; and even seriousness had to smile in order to impress.

In 1884 a small Viennese weekly began to publish musical criticisms by an unknown writer which disturbed the charming atmosphere of life in Vienna. The readers of that charming society were roused to fury by the criticisms of this musical fanatic who would not play the favorite Viennese game, "Don't take things seriously." The critic was Hugo Wolf (1860–1903), at that time a young man of twenty-four who had just arrived in Vienna from Salzburg, where he had been an insignificant assistant conductor in an insignificant theater, rehearsing dull musical comedies. No one knew that the young musician who burst into the reactionary musical world of the resplendent capital, furiously attacking what Viennese society applauded, was a great composer, the greatest song writer after Schubert and Schumann — for his first songs were not to be published until four years later.

The weekly for which Wolf began to write criticism with all the rapture of a young Wagnerian was published to cater to the vanity of a rich society. It was named the *Wiener Salonblatt* ("*Drawing-room Sheet*"). On the cover of each issue was a photograph of a male or female aristocrat, published according to a fixed tariff. The pages were filled with news of the court and the aristocracy — accounts of the parties, the engagements, the marriages, the hunts, the dances of the eighty families who, according to Napoleon, ruled Austria. Stock-exchange quotations were published as another alluring bait. Hugo Wolf's criticism was about as much at home in this journal as a pure and pious youth would be in a brothel. The proprietor may have been getting some private fun out of the naïve young writer, whom he turned loose for two years — 1884 and 1885 — as a joke for his elegant readers.

Wolf wrote for the society which sat in the Opera House boxes at performances of Meyerbeer's operas and Italian operas and particularly at ballets. To this elegant, superficial, refined society he preached the gospel of Wagner, Liszt, and Berlioz with the religious fanaticism of the young musician who had kissed Wagner's hand in the Imperial Hotel in Vienna. It was this society that he attacked; it was at their tastes and their preferences that he tilted with his critical lance, like a young Don Quixote tilting at windmills. Here is a sample of his tone in a criticism of one of the Philharmonic concerts, which at that time were conducted by Hans Richter:

Gade, Dvořák, Molique, and, out of charity (what a gigantic exertion!), a symphony of Mozart's. Bravo, Herr Conductor! You show taste, good will, industry, devotion, earnestness, perseverance, and a goodly portion of ambition! What will it lead to? Surely, you cannot intend to rise to the dizzy height of performing Haydn's baby symphonies? Beware of the difficulties of such an undertaking, the sleepless nights, the drops of bloody sweat! . . . No, Herr Conductor, you must spare yourself, pamper yourself, you need to rest. Continue to favor us with Dvořák's rhapsodies, with Gade's overtures, with Molique's violoncello concertos. Why a Mozart symphony as the closing number — and particularly the wonderful one in E flat? It is a much too complicated piece . . . you are ruining yourself with rehearsals; and the hope of hearing you conduct Czerny's *School of Velocity* (the orchestration of which Herr B.[1] was kind enough to undertake) at the Philharmonic concerts will again be lost to us forever.

With the same fury with which he attacked the easy programs and the lack of rehearsals which were customary with the Philharmonic, Wolf rages at the cuts made in *Tristan and Isolde*:

Only cut quickly and confidently — everything else follows of itself. Among the Indians he is most respected who can show the largest number of scalps. Just so among his colleagues, that conductor enjoys the highest esteem who most nearly flays a score, who can boast that his red pencil has cut off not merely the scalp but the whole head and tail of the plot together. The Indians content themselves with the scalp and are savages. Conductors tear their victims limb from limb and are, generally speaking, civilized — in fact they would like to be considered artists. Artists!

[1] Wolf means Brahms.

Wolf was always ready to attack, to stir up smoldering controversies, to insult public and artists. He felt himself the representative of a new generation. When Berlioz's *Symphonie fantastique* was performed at the conservative Philharmonic concerts, he addressed the members of the orchestra:

Let the members of the Philharmonic not disdain the applause of the young, who from standing room and galleries joyfully greeted their most excellent performance no less than the magnificent work itself. Where greatness was at stake, the young have always been pioneers. Let us not be deceived by the venom and the dishonorable proceedings of our critical opponents. We have the shield of truth to protect us, we bear the sword of enthusiasm to strike our enemies with, and "War to the Philistines! War to the critics!" be our watchword henceforth.

The Philistines of Vienna had an uneasy time as long as Wolf continued to write.

In the same article Wolf advises that, instead of Berlioz, the Philharmonic play

Diabelli's pieces for children or Brahms's symphonies. . . . If Master Brahms caresses the happy heart or Master Diabelli discommodes the abdomen, of what consequence is it? But what will that thorn Hector Berlioz do to the fine feelings of a distinguished Viennese concert audience? You fools! Do you suppose that those sublime spiritual forms that forever dance around the inspired artist, revealing to his eyes, which thirst for clarity and miracle, things never yet heard or seen or dreamed or divined, in the ineffable light and with the thunder-voice of the Godhead — do you suppose that they wear your misshapen forms, speak with your squeaking voices, and carry your tiny clockwork in their breasts?

These words might have been written by Hoffmann or Berlioz himself; they have the same passionate romanticism, the same plenitude, as the exorcisms of those two masters.

During his two years as a critic Wolf never wearied of waving the red flag of Wagner, Berlioz, and Liszt, never hesitated to plant it on top of a barricade. As a young Wagnerian in the age of Hanslick, he opposed Brahms. When Brahms's piano concerto in B flat was performed at a Philharmonic concert, Wolf signed his criticism with a skull and crossbones. On another occasion he jibed at people who "despite their fat bellies, fasten themselves to a much-talked-of man, and hold on like noughts after a figure one — if it is impossible to do it with Wagner, Brahms will serve."

So Hugo Wolf the music critic did not advance Hugo Wolf the composer; and, when his first songs appeared some years later, he was far from being able to count on the sympathy of the critics. His family was horrified when they read one of the first criticisms on his songs and wrote to him wishing to console him. But Wolf answered their well-meant letter as follows:

I am surprised at you for being annoyed by the stupid criticism in the *German Times*. Yet you know that it is silly twaddle, and that it was written by a man who understands absolutely nothing. Absurd newspaper chit-chat! It would be too bad if I were dependent on the critics' judgments, or if you were to gage my achievements by such twaddle. Thank God, I compose well enough to be able utterly to despise the judgment of the critics.

Unfavorable criticisms were not the worst thing that could happen to a composer like Wolf. He could always meet unfavorable criticisms with the self-assurance of a creative mind. It was worse when Hanslick put Hugo Wolf under the great ban and Wolf's name disappeared from the columns of Hanslick's paper. As time went on, Wolf became famous, and even Hanslick had to recognize the greatness of the man whom he had excommunicated from his church of conservatism.

The criticism of Hugo Wolf was a stormy episode in Viennese musical life. There were comic episodes too. As, for instance, when Heinrich Reinhardt, a composer of frothy operettas, wrote criticisms in which he tried to prove that Mahler did not know how to compose and, in fact, was not a musician at all. However, the majority of Viennese music critics were serious people, many of them musicologists. Among them were Elsa Bienenfeld, who did well-known research work on the seventeenth-century *Quodlibet*; Egon Wellesz, the great specialist on Byzantine music; Max Springer, the authority on Gregorian chant and the writer of several books on the subject. Julius Korngold continued the tradition created by Hanslick, and Paul Stefan was internationally known as an enthusiastic admirer of modern music. Richard Specht composed articles and books replete with impressionistic color.

An active intellectual and artistic life existed in the Alpine provinces of Austria too. Among the provincial towns, Graz could boast of her long musical history. In the seventeenth century the beautiful city, whose houses surround the castle hill with its old belfry, was one of the chief centers of Italian music north of the Alps. The Archdukes of Styria had Italian composers, organists, and singers in their service. The young aristocrats who studied at the university of Graz in the seventeenth century performed Italian operas. In the same century Johann Joseph Fux, composer at the court of the Emperor Charles VI, although better known as the author of a celebrated treatise on counterpoint, was born in Styria. Such men as Busoni, Felix Weingartner, and Joseph Marx studied music in Graz and wrote their first compositions under the influence of its beautiful Alpine landscape. In this musical city there was a high standard of musical criticism. In 1899 Ernst Decsey began writing musical criticism for the Graz *Tagespost*; his books on Bruckner, Hugo Wolf, and Johann Strauss form a colorful trilogy of Austrian life and art. The post of music critic on the other Graz daily was occupied by Wilhelm Kienzl, who held it for twelve years. When he began to write criticism in Graz, he was already a celebrated composer. His opera *Der Evangelimann* was performed for the first time in 1895 in Berlin, whence it traveled to more than three hundred operatic stages all over the world. While this popular opera was being translated into thirteen languages, the composer, a romantic enthusiast for Wagner, wrote his musical criticisms in a little town in the Alps. Both Decsey, who became a music critic in Vienna after the first World War, and Kienzl, who had also moved to Vienna, died there during the Nazi occupation.

One of the most interesting musical centers in old Austria was Prague. In Prague, with its great castle and its Gothic cathedral overlooking the broad stream of the Vltava, with the huge Baroque palaces on the slopes of its hills, and the green domes of its churches, Austrians and Czechs lived, worked, and strove with one another. Two forms of musical culture developed side by side. The musical life of the Austrians of Prague was the older. In the old opera house on the Fruit Market, which had been built by Prague's aristocrats, Mozart had conducted the first performance of *Don Giovanni* and Weber had swung his energetic baton. In the nearby Teinkirche Gluck had sung as a choirboy. One of the palaces of the Mala Strana, with a balcony held up by four stone Moors, had belonged to an early patron of Haydn's, Count Morzin. In the nineteenth century the German opera house in Prague was one of the leading opera houses in the world. Anton Seidl, Gustav Mahler, Karl Muck, Otto Klemperer, Artur Bodanzky, Alexander von Zemlinsky, Georg Szell, were conductors there.

After the beginning of the nineteenth century, when the Romantic movement wakened nationalistic forces everywhere in Europe, the Czechs became conscious of their national creativity, particularly in the art of music. Modern musical activities among the Czechs began with the collecting of folk songs from the peasants. The first collections were made early in the century; the Czech poet Jaromir Erben published eight hundred such songs in his *Kytice*. The idiom of these songs was recognized as peculiar to the nation and began to be imitated. It is in connection with these songs written in the style of Czech folk songs that we first meet the name of Hanslick, who composed a few of them while he was a student in Prague. In 1826 the national music entered the opera house with the first Czech opera, *Dratenik*, by Franz Škroup, who was also the composer of the Czech national anthem. The idiom of Czech folk dances and folk songs was heard more and more, and music of Czech life, Czech history, and Czech landscape permeated the art music of great composers like Bedřich Smetana and Antonin Dvořàk. In

Smetana's operas and symphonic poems the Vltava rushes, the forests of Bohemia rustle, peasants dance, the old kings march to their castle high above the river accompanied by mail-clad knights, water nymphs float like the fogs of moonlit evenings, Hussites sing their chorales. In Dvořák's music peasants dance around the maypole and old crones tell old tales. The national life and the national dreams of the Czech people were transformed by music; and musical institutions, led by the Czech National Theater in Prague, which opened on June 11, 1881, with Smetana's *Libussa*, became armories in the Czech nation's struggle for political independence.

The Czech music critics in Prague had a double duty to perform: they had on the one hand to assist in the awakening and the development of the national forces of their people, on the other to connect the new musical life of their country with the current of European ideas. Among the men who performed this double duty with energy and greatness of soul, the most famous was the composer of the opera *The Bartered Bride*, Bedřich Smetana (1824–84). He returned to Prague from a stay in Weimar and Göteborg in 1862. After he had crossed the border of Bohemia on his outward journey, he had written the moving sentences: "Shall I see these dearly loved mountains again, and when and with what feelings? When I leave them I am always filled with longing. Farewell, my dearly loved country, my beautiful, great, unique country! May I rest in your soil. Your earth is sacred to me." Thus the national feeling that was to animate his operas and symphonic poems was awakened abroad, as he longed for the forests and mountains, the peasant huts and the ancient castles, of his country. In Weimar he met Liszt, who admired his music, which was luxuriant and vibrant with all the colors of the modern orchestra. On his return to Prague he was imbued equally with the modern spirit of the epoch of Wagner and Liszt and with an ardent desire to celebrate his country and his people in his music. He was attacked as a Wagnerian by narrow-minded critics, but was soon recognized by his countrymen as the artist whose music expressed the beauty of their

dreams. His melodies became the modern folk songs of Czechoslovakia.

In 1864 Smetana became the musical critic of the newly established Czech daily *Národny Listy* in Prague. He had already
written some articles criticizing the musical life of Prague for
the monthly *Slavoj*. "The public musical life and activities of
our capital," he had said, "are nothing compared to those of
great cities abroad." Czech musical life in Prague was, at the
time, provincial at best; the national rise was but just beginning.
So little was the Czech language esteemed, that Smetana wrote
his criticisms in German.

Modest but obstinate, Smetana worked hard to raise the
standard of Czech musical life. In reviewing performances of
operas at the Provisional Theater, he campaigned to make it the
birthplace of a Czech national opera. Half of the Provisional
Theater's repertory consisted of Italian operas. More or less
sensational guest stars were imported to attract the public.
Smetana vigorously demanded that Czech operas should be performed. He fought against the system of guest stars and advo-
cated the formation and education of an ensemble. His artistic
credo was: "Performances by guest stars have no value for us;
what we need is a regular repertory, artistically directed. That
is what forms and purifies understanding and taste." He fought
against "cuts" in classical operas. He fought for performances
of Mozart, Beethoven, and Wagner.

He was in turn attacked by one of the most narrow-minded of
the genus music critic, F. Pivoda, singing teacher and critic for
the Prague *Národni Pokrok*. Pivoda scented the Wagnerian in
Smetana and tried to throw suspicion on him, accusing him of
being a man without national feeling. Smetana's opera *Dalibor*,
in which the romantic line of the Czech kings was evoked, was
to Pivoda, "foreign music, incapable of life." Even the *Bartered
Bride*, with its popular tunes and national dances, did not escape
Pivoda's criticism. "With its ballet," he wrote, it "sighs for
Paris, and with the following aria (for orchestra with soprano
accompaniment) for the heaven of Germany." Smetana pub-

lished a strong answer: "By way of farewell to Mr. Pivoda, music critic of the *Pokrok*: . . . Thus have we deciphered the reason why you, wise Sir, rage so furiously against me. It is pure personal hatred. Hence all this malevolence, all this meanness, all these lies! I am grateful to you for having opened my eyes; I can answer you only with utter contempt."

In the quarrel between Smetana and Pivoda, two young writers sided with the great composer. One of them was Ludevit Procházka, the other Ottokar Hostinsky, later a noted professor of esthetics at the Czech university in Prague. One of Hostinsky's pupils was Zdeněk Nejedlý, professor of the history of music at the University of Prague, who wrote with equal erudition on the history of music in Bohemia, on Smetana, and on Richard Strauss.[1] Among the best of the Czech music critics was Joseph Bohuslav Förster, who was the first to interpret Mahler's music to the Czech public. He wrote musical criticism in Hamburg and in Vienna as well, and was a sensitive and poetic writer. For many years the musical criticisms of Emanuel Chvala furnished food for thought to the readers of the Czech dailies *Politik* and *Národni Politik*. Chvala's work was objective and authoritative.

Among the Prague music critics who wrote in German, Richard Batka, a prolific author of books on musical subjects, was well known even beyond the borders of Bohemia. But when Czechoslovakia won independence in 1918, the Czech language came into its own; Czech musical life became more and more active; and Smetana's dream became a reality. The old domes and steeples of Prague, and the medieval royal castle, and the palaces and gardens of the castle hill looked down upon the modern capital of a new state, in which Smetana's music had become the triumphant music of an independent nation. In the castle of the Czech kings a wise old philosopher — Masaryk — sat at his desk, but every peasant's house was Smetana's home.

On the palette of old Austria the motley national colors of

---

[1] After the Nazis occupied Prague, Professor Nejedlý fled to Russia, whence he returned to the liberated city as minister of culture and education in May, 1945.

Polish and Hungarian music and musical criticism were not lacking. The music of these and many other races met in Vienna. And the music critics of Vienna were the intermediaries through whom the art of the peoples of the Danube valley was brought to western Europe. It was the Viennese critics who discovered such works as Smetana's *Bartered Bride* and Janáček's *Jenufa* and many works of Hungarian composers, and brought them to the attention of the world. Again, it was they who brought many French and Italian composers (Massenet, Puccini) to the attention of the east. Austrian, German, Slavic, Romanian, and Hungarian culture mingled in Vienna until 1918, and the Viennese music critics remained men of wide views and cosmopolitan mentality until the first World War unfettered the forces of nationalism that destroyed the old Austria.

III. FRANCE

France had been the motherland of criticism, and from the middle of the eighteenth century on, critical intelligence here developed every variety of finesse and every shade of analytical sagacity. Here the spirit of criticism joined forces with the virtuosity of the conversation in the salons. It was the spirit of criticism that sharpened its tools in the articles and comments of newspapers, and in the witty satires of malicious revues performed in small theaters and making game of all the happenings of political, artistic, and social life. It was the spirit of criticism that shot its poisoned darts in the little *chansons* that poets recited in the crowded cabarets of Montmartre and Montparnasse. Paris, with her old tradition of wittily commenting on the events of the day, was the capital of critical thought in Europe. There was also an old tradition of writing in Paris, carefully fostered and guarded by the French Academy. The art of clear, keen, and witty writing had been developed by a long line of great masters in criticism. No other country in Europe could equal France in the combination of critical perception with perfection of form. All the masters of musical criticism, from Hanslick to Huneker, Gilman, and Newman, had learned from French writers. Historical development and contemporary life in France had created a literary culture that influenced any Frenchman who took up a pen. It was this old literary culture, this firm literary tradition, that gave the essays of musicians such as Gounod and Saint-Saëns their classical clarity, charm, and ease.

Among the modern French music critics, Camille Bellaigue (1858–1930) represents the French academic style at its best. His clarity, nobility, and dignity are in the line of the best French literary tradition. A man of thorough culture, from 1884 and 1885 on (in the former year he became music critic of the *Correspondant*, in the latter of the *Temps* and the *Revue des deux Mondes*), he impressed his readers with his polite elegance and with the calm superiority of a scholar whose mind had been nourished by the great French classical writers. In similar fashion the French literary tradition was maintained by other Parisian music critics — most of them also musicologists — who published their criticisms in various dailies and magazines. Among them were Arthur Pougin, Paul Scudo, Louis Laloy, Paul Landormy, Henri Lavois, Jean Chantavoine, Henri Curzon, Adolphe Boschot, Hugues Imbert, Adolphe Jullien, and Henry Prunières. In contrast to the dignified scholarship of such men as these, there was the fresh wit of Henri Gauthier-Villars, who joked about music in the style of a Paris *gamin*. For Paris was not only a city of learned academicians but a city of mockers and jesters too. Ever since the Renaissance the crowds had gathered around the singers and poets who sang their ironical chansons at the foot of the statue of Henri IV on the Pont Neuf.

From the days when Berlioz had tossed his mane of red hair over his writing, it had been a tradition of the musical world of Paris that composers should write criticisms. Such well-known composers as Ernest Reyer, Gustav Samazeuilh, Pierre Lalo, and Florent Schmitt have been among the ranks of Parisian music critics. The composer of *Carmen*, Bizet (1838–75), came very near to becoming a music critic. In fact though it is not generally known, he was a music critic for one day. An article by him signed with the pseudonym "Gaston de Betzi," appeared in the *Revue nationale et étrangère* on August 3, 1867. Others were to have followed; but as the editor refused to allow the critic to attack Rossini's biographer, Azevedo, in his second article, Bizet gave up his new profession and preferred to make his living simply as a composer.

In this interesting article Bizet defends composers as critics: "That, upon some pretext of honesty and comradeship, a creative worker, who is continually occupied with the highest and most characteristic questions of art, should not be allowed to judge the works of his colleagues, seems to me absolutely illogical and in the highest degree unjust." He excuses himself for not being able to write so well as a number of other critics whom he mentions by name (including Reyer) but he claims to have at least two of their qualifications:

1. A profound study of music and of everything that pertains to it.
2. Honest convictions, which neither my friendships nor my enmities will influence. I shall tell the truth, nothing but the truth, and as far as possible the whole truth. I belong to no sect, I have no colleagues; I have only friends, and they will no longer be my friends if they do not respect my free judgment and my complete independence. Respect for all — that is my motto! Neither flattery nor slander — that is the line I intend to take. . . . I have a horror of pedantry and false culture. Certain critics of the third and fourth rank use and misuse a would-be technical gibberish, which they understand as little as the public does. I shall carefully guard against this ridiculous perversity. There will be no information here about octaves, fifths, tritones, parallel fifths, dissonances, consonances, resolutions, ligatures, anticipations, inversions, delayed cadences, crab-canons, and other such pretty matters.

Bizet attacks sterile polemics:

Real composers have become scarce, but parties and sects are increasing phenomenally; art grows miserably poor, technology grows superfluously rich. Judge for yourself: we have French, German, and Italian, as well as Russian, Hungarian, and Polish music, not counting Arabic, Japanese, and Tunisian, all three of which have come into great favor since the opening of the International Exposition. . . . Then too we have the Music of the Future, of the Present, and of the Past, as well as philosophical and political music, those discoveries of recent years. And we have melodic, harmonic, and learned music (the last the most dangerous of all). What folly! For me there are only two kinds of music: good and bad. Béranger defined art as follows: "Art is art and that's all."

He makes an impassioned attack upon national prejudices in music:

Does not genius belong to all countries and to all ages? An artist has no name, no nationality; he is inspired or he is not, he has genius, talent, or he has not; if he has it, he should be accepted, loved, praised; if he has it not, let him be at least respected, pitied, and forgotten. . . . Let us therefore be sincere and true; let us not demand of a great artist the qualities that he does not possess, let us benefit by those he has. When a passionate, yes brutal, temperament like Verdi's endows the art with a strong and living work kneaded out of gold, dirt, gall, and blood, we dare not coolly say to him, "But, Sir, that is not tasteful, that is not genteel!" Are Michelangelo, Homer, Dante, Shakespeare, Beethoven, Cervantes, and Rabelais by any chance genteel?

He closes:

Verily I say unto you, composers are the pariahs, the martyrs, of modern society. Like the ancient gladiators, they fall with the cry, "*Salve, popule, morituri te salutant!*" Ah, music! What a beautiful art! But what a wretched profession! Well, Patience! And above all, Let us hope!

Reading this noble-minded program, one regrets that Bizet could not continue his critical work.

The series of French composer-critics closes with Claude Debussy (1862–1918). The great musician contributed articles to various periodicals from 1901 to 1918. From April to December, 1901, he wrote for the *Revue Blanche*, the leading literary review of the new generation of French artists. From January until July, 1903, he published a daily article in *Gil Blas*; in October, 1902, and May, 1903, he published in *Musica*. In January, 1903, he contributed to the *Mercure de France*, in 1904 and 1906 to the *Revue Bleue*, and in 1908 and 1909 to *Figaro*. He also wrote

occasionally for *Comoedia* and the *Journal* (1908, 1910).   During
the musical seasons of 1912–13 and 1913–14 he reviewed concerts
for the *Bulletin* of the French Section of the International Society
for Music.   After his death, which took place in 1918, a book
containing selections from his articles and which he had prepared himself, was published.

As early as 1901, when he was writing for the *Revue Blanche*,
Debussy had invented the lay figure of Monsieur Croche ("Mr.
Eighth-note") as a mouthpiece.   Monsieur Croche, "a bitter
and sarcastic Debussy," is a descendant of Hoffmann's romantic
Kapellmeister Kreisler and, like his ancestor, a poetic character.
Debussy introduces him to his readers like a novelist:

> It was a lovely evening. I had decided to idle. I mean, of course,
> I was dreaming. I do not want to imply that anything of great emo-
> tional value was happening, or that I was laying the foundations of the
> future. I was simply enjoying that occasional carefree mood that brings
> peace with all the world. The door bell rings. Enters M. Croche.
> A spare, wizened man, and his gestures were obviously suited to con-
> ducting metaphysical discussions. His features can best be pictured by
> recalling those of Tom Lane, the jockey, or those of M. Thiers. He
> spoke almost in a whisper and never laughed, occasionally enforcing
> his remarks with a quiet smile which, beginning at his nose, wrinkled
> his whole face, like a pebble thrown into still water, and lasted for an
> intolerably long time.

The ferocious words that Debussy puts into the mouth of this
strange man are those of an *enfant terrible* who dares to say out
loud what his well-bred father has contented himself with mur-
muring in secret.   It is Debussy, when M. Croche says:

> I am much more interested in sincere and honestly felt impressions
> than in criticism, which often enough resembles brilliant variations on
> the theme, "As you don't agree with me, you are mistaken," or "You
> have talent; I have none. It is useless to go any further." In all com-
> positions I try to fathom the diverse impulses that inspire them and
> their inner life. Is not this more interesting than the game of pulling
> them to pieces like curious watches? People forget that, as children,
> they were forbidden to pull their jumping-jacks to pieces — even

then, such behavior was treason against the mysteries — and they continue to poke their esthetic noses where they have no business to. Though they no longer rip open dolls, they explain, pull apart, and cold-bloodedly slay the mysteries; it is comparatively easy; besides, it makes conversation. Well! An obvious lack of understanding excuses some of them; but others act with greater ferocity and more premeditation, for they are under the necessity of protecting their little talents. These have a loyal following.

It is Debussy, when M. Croche utters tirades against counterpoint as "parasitical complexities that make music as ingenious as the lock of a strongbox." It is Debussy who advises musicians not "to listen to music written by cunning hands, but to that which is written in Nature's script. . . . To see a sunrise is more profitable than to listen to the Pastoral Symphony." It is Debussy who says, "in spite of so many attempted transformations, the symphony belongs to the past by virtue of its studied elegance, its formal elaboration, and the philosophical and artificial attitude of its audience." And finally, who does not recognize that it is the voice of Debussy when M. Croche says: "Do you know anything more splendid than by chance to discover a genius who has been unrecognized through the ages? But to have been such a genius oneself — can any glory equal that?"

This dreamy genius, whose nerves trembled like aspen leaves, had the sharpest wit. Sarcasms glitter from every essay. In one on the Paris opera house he mocks:

Everyone knows our national opera house, at least by repute. I can assure you, by painful experience, that it has not changed. A stranger would take it for a railway station, and, once inside, would suppose it was a Turkish bath. They continue to produce curious noises, which the people who pay call music, but there is no need to believe them so implicitly. By virtue of special permission and a state subsidy, this theater may produce anything — it little matters what, as elaborately luxurious "loges à salons" have been installed in it, so called because they are most convenient places for not hearing anything of the music. They are the last salons, where conversation still takes place. . . . There will never be any change, short of a revolution, though revolu-

tionaries do not always consider such institutions. We might hope for
a fire, were fire not too undiscriminating in its effects on undoubtedly
innocent persons.

The wit of Paris glitters in Debussy's essays.

Few other writers have Debussy's gift of characterizing a musician in a few lines. He is a master of witty caricature. He
describes the elegant conductor Felix Weingartner, and in two
sentences produces a living picture: "Weingartner's personal
appearance suggests at first glance a new knife. His gestures
have a kind of angular grace." Or he describes Richard Strauss:
"Richard Strauss has no wild mop of hair, no epileptic gestures.
He is tall, and has the free and determined bearing of those great
explorers who travel among savage tribes with a smile on their
lips." Characterization cannot be more artful and more striking.
What humor when Debussy writes of Grieg and pictures him
mockingly: "From in front, he looks like a genial photographer;
from behind, his way of wearing his hair makes him look like
the plants called sunflowers, dear to parrots and to the gardens
that decorate little country railway stations." Anyone who
has seen the great Wagner conductor Hans Richter on the platform will verify the justness of Debussy's remark: "If Richter
looks like a prophet, when he conducts the orchestra he is God
Almighty; and you may be sure the God himself would have
asked Richter for some hints before embarking on such an adventure."

But Debussy was not only sarcastic and witty; he could give
praise too. Some lines of his on Mussorgsky will serve to show
him in this vein:

He will leave an indelible impression on the minds of those who love
him or who will love him in time to come. No one has given utterance
to the best within us in tones more gentle and profound; he is unique
and will remain so because his art is spontaneous and free from arid
formulas. Never has a more refined sensibility been conveyed by such
simple means; it is like the art of an inquiring savage, discovering
music step by step through his emotions.

Or some lines on Richard Strauss's *A Hero's Life*:

After a minute or two one is captured first by the tremendous versatility of his orchestration, then by the frenzied energy which carries one with him as long as he chooses. . . . It is a book of pictures or even a cinematograph. But one must admit that the man who composed such a work at so continuously high a pressure is very nearly a genius.

Debussy's criticism is impressionistic, like his music. He formulated his idea of criticism in the sentence, "To render one's impressions is better than to criticize, and all technical analysis is doomed to futility." His nervous, dreamy, capricious, and witty personality was the only standard for his judgments on music. With him, musical criticism is the art of rendering his moods, his inclinations, and his preferences. It loses its backbone, and gets "nerves." It is musical criticism dissolving in a sparkling and fascinating display of brilliant inspirations.

It is impossible to take leave of the once so joyous and witty country where critical intelligence was polished by so many great artists from Boileau and Voltaire to Anatole France, without making a bow to Romain Rolland (1866–1944), equally important as novelist, dramatist, poet, essayist, and musicologist. From 1898 on Romain Rolland [1] published a number of articles on Berlioz, Richard Strauss, Debussy, D'Indy, and others, in the *Revue de Paris*. These articles, which are all masterpieces of thoroughgoing critical analysis, like the sketches of elder musicians in his *Musiciens d'autrefois* and his books on Beethoven and Handel, were republished, under the title *Musiciens d' aujourdhui*, in 1908. In all these works his imagination is vivid, his style clear, fluent, and easy, and his analytical power brilliant. It is always a bright and beautiful day in Rolland's musical landscape, and one enjoys walking there beside one of the masters of French.

IV. ENGLAND

Contemporaneously a similar development was taking place in England.

[1] I had the honor of introducing Rolland to Germany, translating his book *Paris as a Musical City* as long ago as 1905.

England was a great musical country in the Elizabethan period, and the greatest European market for music in the eighteenth century. After a long period of stagnation, by the end of the nineteenth century national musical forces had gathered strength again, and, with Edward Elgar, there appeared an English composer whose imposing personality was recognized in every center of music. The modern musical movement inspired younger English composers — Gustav Holst, Cyril Scott, Goossens, Vaughan-Williams, Delius, Bliss, Bax, and others — who contributed handsomely to modern musical technique and ideas.

In the nineteenth century musical criticism in England was in the hands of weighty, solid, generally conservative experts. From 1830 to 1868 Henry Chorley (1808–72) was the musical oracle of the London *Athenaeum*; like the bigwigs in all countries, he was one-sided and reactionary. His *Thirty Years' Musical Recollections* (1862) and his *Autobiography* (1873) show his strong but narrow personality. Two English music critics of German descent — Friedrich Niecks (1845–1924; professor of music at Edinburgh University and music critic of the *Monthly Musical Record* and the *Musical Times*) and Francis Hueffer (1843–89; music critic of the London *Times* from 1878 to the time of his death in 1889) represented the type of the learned expert with dignity and solemnity. From 1846 to 1879 the music critic of the *Times* was James Davison (1813–85). Like Chorley, he wrote his memoirs, which were published after his death under the title *From Mendelssohn to Wagner*. It was not until the turn of the century that, with Edward Dent (1876–), modern musical tenets found their way into the musical criticisms of the old *Athenaeum*, the stronghold of English musical conservatism.

The most interesting music critic in England is Ernest Newman (1868–). He was the first in that country to represent the type of the literary music critic and to supersede the dry solidity of the experts by imagination, brilliance, and virtuosity of style. His writing is colorful and combines scholarly solidity with liveliness; he has wit, ideas, ease, and a happy mixture of common sense and extravagance. He began his career as a music critic on the Manchester *Guardian* in 1905, continued it on the Birmingham *Daily Post* from 1906 to 1919 and on the London *Observer* from 1919 to 1920. In March, 1920, he joined the staff of the *Sunday Times*. Newman displayed his sparkling talents in the United States, as guest-critic for the New York *Evening Post* during the season of 1924–25.

Newman has expressed his conception of musical criticism in the following words:

Musical criticism is apt to become too much of a mere matter of wine-tasting, a bare statement of a preference for this vintage or a de-cided taste for that. We need to study musicians as a whole, as com-plete organisms, hanging together by virtue of certain peculiarities of structure. . . . In the long run human folly and human failure are just as interesting to the student of humanity as its wisdom and its tri-umphs; and the critic should always aim at being an impartial student of Humanity, not a mere wine-taster or a magistrate.

Newman has contributed greatly to the understanding of Hugo Wolf, and some of his finest analysis has been bestowed on Richard Strauss:

Not a Wagner manqué, nor an illegitimate son of Liszt, but the cre-ator of a new world order of things in music, the founder of a new type of art. The only test of literature being alive is, as Dr. Georg Brandes says, whether it gives rise to new problems, new questionings. Judged by this test, the art of Strauss is the one sign of a new and independent life in music since Wagner.

Strauss's symphonic works were still being hissed in London when Newman wrote of *Don Quixote*, "If this is not surpassingly great music, there is no music in the world, worthy of this name. . . . This kind of music adds to our knowledge of man and the world as much as does a play of Ibsen or a novel of Tolstoi."

Newman possesses the gift of short and striking characteriza-tion. For example, he speaks of the "cosmic magnificence of *Also sprach Zarathustra*, the graphic humor of *Till Eulenspiegel*, and the supreme humanity of [Strauss's] greatest work, *Don*

Quixote.'' In a few words he hit the nail on the head when he called Strauss "the first complete realist in music." Of the three chief essays on Strauss by modern music critics (Adolph Weissmann, Huneker, and Newman) Newman's is the profoundest and the subtlest.

With Newman musical criticism in England became a department of literature. Besides being a musical expert, he is an effective writer, a virtuoso of style, who plays on words as Sarasate and Paderewski used to play on their instruments. His seriousness is impressive, his grace captivates, his wit amuses, his irony enchants. With Newman's contemporary, Bernard Shaw (1856–   ), English musical criticism took another direction — that of intense subjectivity. As it had with Debussy, criticism lost all its dogmatic stiffness when Shaw set off the sparkling fireworks of his wit, his malice, and his guttersnipe insolence. Surrounded by solemn experts who sat at concerts with knitted brows and long faces, Shaw consciously played the clown, cracking jokes, turning somersaults, and hiding his keen mind under the mask of a jester.

"I cannot deny [Shaw has written] that Bassetto [1] was occasionally vulgar; but that does not matter, if he makes you laugh. Vulgarity is a necessary part of a complete author's equipment; and the clown is sometimes the best part of the circus. . . . I purposely vulgarized musical criticism, which was then refined and academic to the point of being unreadable and often nonsensical."

Consciously again, he set his clowning against the magisterial attitude of conventional musical criticism. "I am only a critic and therefore do not profess to speak authoritatively," he joked; and when one of his readers reproached him with having been unjust in a criticism, Shaw answered cheerfully: "No doubt I have; who am I, that I should be just? . . . The fact is, justice is not the critic's business; and there is no more dishonest and insufferable affectation in criticism than the impersonal, abstract, judicially authoritative air, which . . . is so easy to assume and so well adapted to rapid phrase stringing."

[1] Shaw signed his articles "Corno di Bassetto."

Shaw's criticism, therefore, was extremely personal, as befitted a "combatant anarchist in music." He uses his dynamite to demolish the prejudice that demands such a thing as objectivity from a critic:

People have pointed out evidences of personal feeling in my notices, as if they were accusing me of a misdemeanor, not knowing that a criticism written without personal feeling is not worth reading. It is the capacity of making good and bad art a personal matter, that makes a man a critic. The artist who accounts for my disparagement by alleging personal animosity on my part is quite right; when people do less than their best . . . I hate them, loathe them, detest them, long to tear them limb from limb and strew them in gobbets about the stage or platform.

Shaw mocks at the "inoffensive, considerate, say-nothing-to-nobody sort of criticism" and at the "gentlemen, who keep only one quality of margarine, which they spread impartially over all composers of established reputation."

His strong and capricious personality is always kept in the foreground. In one of his articles, he describes his case of influenza in detail, in another a toothache: "After a moment's hesitation I went to my dentist's. There is nothing that soothes me more after a long and maddening course of pianoforte recitals than to sit and have my teeth drilled by a finely skilled hand." When he gets an uncomfortable seat in a concert hall or the hall is badly ventilated or he has to pay a shilling for a program, he rages: "I paid a shilling for my programme. The editor informs me with the law of libel in its present unsatisfactory condition, I must not call this a fraud, a cheat, a swindle, an imposition, an exorbitance, or even an overcharge." Shaw's amused readers are not even spared from learning of his dislike for the violoncello: "Ordinarily I had as soon hear a bee buzzing in a stone jug."

The English oratorios, which, according to an old tradition, the English public regards as sacred, regularly provoke a fit of rage. According to Shaw, oratorios are either "dull imitations of Handel" or "unstaged operettas on scriptural themes, written in a style in which solemnity and triviality are blended in the right proportion for boring an atheist out of his senses." Elsewhere he speaks of the "well-known inadequacy of my constitution to just such penitential exercises," and calls the British chorus "the most terrific of human institutions." Handel festivals are nothing but a "multitudinous dullness."

Certainly there was never a more amusing, witty, and entertaining musical critic than Shaw. He was forever throwing the keenest jibes into the face of the solemn English public, with all the joy that a boy has in throwing stones. He writes: "I felt more than ever what a privilege it was to live in a convenient art-centre like London, where the nearest opera is in Bayreuth." And again: "The primary function of Italian opera is to provide a means of passing the evening for a clique of deadheads in evening dress." When the great violinist Ysaye was forced to play encores at the end of a concert, Shaw reported the fact thus: "He threw a bunch of thistles to the donkeys at the end of the recital." At Vieuxtemps he gibes: "Vieuxtemps's real name now is Vieuxjeu." On occasion he can be rude. When Sir Charles Stanford's _Irish Symphony_ was performed in London, Shaw wrote: "When Professor Stanford is a genteel, cultured, classic, pious Mixolydian, he is dull beyond belief." He calls the directors of the London Philharmonic an "impossible body of hardened malversators of our English funds of musical skill." Shaw's irony does not even spare himself. He struck at his own vanity (which was perhaps the source of his subjectivist criticism) when, after receiving some flattering letters from readers, he wrote:

Some of them mean nothing more than to nobble me with a little flattery; and they are the wise ones; for I need not say, that I delight in flattery. Even when there is no mistaking it for sincere admiration, I am pleased to find that anybody attaches sufficient importance to my opinion, to spend a postage stamp on an attempt to humbug me. Flatter by all means! And remember that you cannot lay it on too thick. The net pleases the bird no less than the bait.

Shaw's jokes and laughter, his mockery and derision, his

playing with irony as one tosses tennis balls, his funmaking and his sharp thrusts must be taken as a kind of window dressing for a shop in which substantial goods are for sale. Shaw inherited a decided musical talent from his mother, who had a beautiful voice and sang in concert and opera. As a young man, he worked hard at music. He played the classical symphonies, and *Lohengrin*, and Bach. When he speaks of Bach or Gluck, his mocking voice becomes strangely serious: "Bach belongs not to the past, but to the future — perhaps the near future." Gluck is "a great master, one whom we are hardly to recognize yet." Despite the remark we have quoted on the "primary function" of Italian opera, Shaw analyzes Italian operas with love and understanding; nothing more striking has ever been written about the hackneyed *Trovatore* than Shaw's sentences:

Il Trovatore is in fact unique, even among the works of its own composer and its own country. It has tragic power, poignant melancholy and a sweet and intense pathos that never loses its dignity. It is swift in action and perfectly homogeneous in atmosphere and feeling. It is absolutely void of intellectual interest; the appeal is to the instincts and to the senses all through.

Equally masterful is his characterization of Verdi's *Falstaff*: "*Falstaff* . . . is lighted and warmed only by the afterglow of the fierce noonday sun of *Ernani*; but the gain in beauty conceals the loss in heat." Shaw analyzes singers with complete knowledge. He is a real expert in all matters of the technique of singing. But the greatest musical passion of his life was Wagner, and on the hill at Bayreuth one could meet the tall, lean Irishman with the white beard of an old sorcerer at any Wagner festival. And on them he wrote with deepest insight.

Bernard Shaw began writing musical criticism in London in 1889 for the *Star*. The editor of this weekly, T. P. O'Connor, had engaged the young Socialist to write on politics. Shaw's political articles, however, proved to be powder kegs; O'Connor decided that he must put him in a less dangerous corner, whereupon Shaw proposed that he should write musical criticism, "because [Shaw's account of the incident runs] I believed I could make musical criticisms readable even by the deaf." In 1890, having started London laughing, he moved to the *World*, for which he wrote until 1894. His musical criticisms have been published in four volumes.

V.　RUSSIA

A glass of spirits in your hand,
Your head chained to the Pole,
Your feet to Caucasus —
So, Holy Russia, you lie
In deep and moveless sleep.

These celebrated lines in which Neshdanov described his country ceased to be true when the Romantic movement swept over the wide plains and the high mountains of Russia in the first half of the nineteenth century. The colossus awoke and stretched his limbs. Famous poets and novelists — like Pushkin and Turgenev and the giant pair, Tolstoi and Dostoevsky — and great musicians grew out of the soil of the vast country, inspired by its people and its landscape, and mysteriously linked with the soul of Russia.

Musical criticism was a part of the spiritual labor performed by Russian musicians after the hour of awakening. In Russia musical criticism was not scientific research as in Germany, or a brilliant display of wit as in France, but a struggle with the problems of modern Russia, a battle, a striving after the future. Music critics were comrades in arms of the composers and stand-ard-bearers of new ideas. When Balakirev — sitting at the piano improvising or playing scores with his admiring pupils Mussorgsky, Rimsky-Korsakoff, Cui, and Borodin — became the leader of the "mighty handful," the first great Russian music critics became members of the group too. Cui became the literary spokesman of the national school, together with Vladimir Stassov, the ardent critic whose name was to appear on almost every page of the history of Russian music for nearly half a century. Alexander Serov, the first Russian music critic worthy of the name, fought for Wagner, Liszt and Berlioz opposing the modern European program to the national program of Balakirev's group. "My position? To be the opposition," said Stassov to a foreign visitor who asked him what position he held in Russian musical life.

The battle between artists who wanted to connect Russia's creative genius with European currents, and artists who wanted to remain close to the Russian soil, to the muzhik, to the mysticism of the Byzantine church, is and will perhaps remain an eternal conflict in Russian life, for one third of Russia belongs to Europe, the other two thirds to the East. This struggle between opposing forces in Russia was represented for the first time in modern history by the first great Russian musical critics.

Alexander Serov (1820–71) created a sensation when he published his first articles, on "Music and Virtuosi," on "Spontini and his Music," and on "*Don Giovanni*," in the *Contemporary* and the *Pantheon*. In 1856 he was made musical editor of a newly established weekly, the *Musical and Theatrical Herald*. In addition to his articles in Russian, he wrote in French for the *Journal de St. Petersbourg* and in German for the *Neue Zeitschrift für Musik*; carrying on in the latter a polemical war with Oulibichev, the biographer of Mozart.

When Liszt came to St. Petersburg in 1842, Serov experienced "the highest revelation that has yet been vouchsafed to me." Liszt played him his *Don Juan* fantasy, and Serov confessed: "In a few moments I lived through years of an undreamed-of concentration of existence." The impression made upon him was even deeper when he heard Wagner's *Tannhäuser* in Dresden in 1858; he called it "the highest work of art yet produced by the human intellect." A fighting Wagnerian from that time forth, Serov sent home a proclamation that Anti-Wagnerians were *ipso facto* "idiots." The leader of the conservatives in Russia at the time was the celebrated pianist Anton Rubinstein — all-powerful, as he was backed by the court and by St. Petersburg officialdom. The Conservatory, which Rubinstein founded in 1862, and the Russian Musical Society were the staff headquar-

ters of the Anti-Wagnerians in Russia. Balakirev's pupils were
Wagner haters too. When *Lohengrin* had its first performance in
St. Petersburg in 1868, Balakirev, Dargomyzhsky, Cui, Mussorgsky, and Rimsky-Korsakov sat in a box and made deroga-
tory remarks about the new opera. Serov sharpened his critical
pen and wrote an enthusiastic article, both on the work and the
performance, for the *Journal de St. Petersbourg*.

He had visited Wagner in Zurich in 1858. Wagner called him
"a curious, intelligent man," and, later, went to see him in
Vienna. In 1868, Serov went to Munich, where he heard *Tristan*
and the *Meistersinger*, and to Triebschen, where Wagner was living with Cosima — writing the score of *Siegfried*, and walking
with Cosima and Nietzsche and his big black dog on the shores
of the green lake. "His tender soul, his pure feelings, his lively
and cultured mind made his friendship one of the most precious
possessions of my life," wrote Wagner of his Russian admirer.

Serov was a bitter enemy of Balakirev and his group. He re-
nounced his friendship with Stassov, because the latter held that
Glinka's *Ruslan and Ludmilla* was the height of operatic art,
whereas Serov claimed that distinction for *Tannhäuser*. He was
an interesting man, who wore the same hat for twenty years and
lived on his enthusiasm for Wagner, Liszt, and Berlioz, a hot-
tempered critic, fearlessly candid and loving a fight. There is
something overheated in Serov, who was admired by such men
as Tchaikovsky and the young Rimsky-Korsakov, and roused
hatred in others; perhaps his untempered romanticism was due
to the drop of restless Jewish blood that he inherited from his
mother.

The cause of Russian national music was upheld with equal
energy by Vladimir Stassov and César Cui.

Stassov (1824–1906) was the opposite of Serov. Serov idol-
ized Wagner. Stassov was intolerant of every German composer
except Beethoven. Serov nicknamed Balakirev's group "the
Russian invalids." Stassov supported them. Serov attacked
every new work by Balakirev or one of his followers. Stassov's
idol was the young Balakirev. The battle between Serov and

Stassov filled the columns of the newspapers. Serov sneered at the "Russianists," Stassov at the "music of the future." Swords clashed. Blood flowed. It is part of the Russian character to fight passionately for ideas.

Stassov was an inspiring and a fascinating personality. He supplied Balakirev, Mussorgsky, Borodin, Tchaikovsky, and Rimsky-Korsakov with ideas for symphonic poems and opera librettos. It was he who gave Borodin the idea for *Prince Igor*. He suggested the idea of *Khovantchina* to Mussorgsky and helped him to construct the libretto of *Boris Godunov*. To him Tchaikovsky dedicated his symphonic poem *The Tempest*, and Mussorgsky his *Khovantchina* — the latter in the words: "To Vladimir Vassilievich Stassov, my labor (according to my ability) inspired by his love." In a wonderful letter, Mussorgsky told Stassov what he meant to him: "You are necessary to me, not because you are dear to me, but because you expect much of me. But I demand still more — and so, draw me on as a magnet would. Without you I should soon be done for. No one has seen my inner self more easily and consequently more deeply than you; no one has pointed out my path more clearly."

Stassov's enthusiasm for Russian musicians did not cool as he grew older. He praised Liadov, called Glazounov "our young Samson" when the seventeen-year-old composer's First Symphony was performed in St. Petersburg, and recognized the talents of Scriabin. After Mussorgsky's death Stassov wrote the memorial biography of him. And when Stassov died in 1906 in St. Petersburg, Glazounov composed the *Prelude in Memory of Stassov* — the first (and so far the only) composition mourning the death of a music critic.

At the same time as Stassov, César Cui (1835–1918) was another spokesman and champion of Balakirev's group, setting forth the ideas of the national school in books and articles. The son of a French officer and a Lithuanian lady, Cui came to St. Petersburg in 1851, where he met Balakirev and studied with him. The "musical eagle," as Balakirev named his pupil, became his master's weapon-carrier and shield-bearer when he began to write musical criticism for the important St. Petersburg daily *Vedomosti*, in 1864. He hurled violent denunciations against the Italian opera, which had dominated the social life of the aristocracy in St. Petersburg since the end of the eighteenth century, when Paisiello was opera director at the court of the Empress Catherine. He attacked Rubinstein, who had accused the young Russian composers of having "barbaric tendencies." He opposed Wagner. But he never tired of fighting for the ideals of the young Russian composers, who were his friends and comrades, and with whom he exchanged ideas and criticism. A composer of operas himself (*The Prisoner of the Caucasus* and *William Ratcliffe*, performed at St. Petersburg in 1859 and 1869 respectively) he finished Mussorgsky's *Fair at Sorochinsk*.

His articles and his book *La Musique en Russie* ("*Music in Russia*"), which Cui wrote in French and published in Paris in 1880, set forth the ideals of the national Russian school. Cui describes the members of the group as reformers of opera who excel in "pregnant intelligence and in specific characterization, not only of each character, but also of the period and the atmosphere of the drama." Cui strongly opposed Wagner's innovations and criticized Mussorgsky severely for using leitmotivs — "a cheap device," in Cui's estimation. He regarded Tchaikovsky's and Rubinstein's music as "lamentable," because it was not Russian enough in character. Cui, who was not a Russian by descent, but half French and half Lithuanian, was the most fanatical of the Russian nationalists. This was at once his greatness and his shortcoming.

A bitter antagonist of the Russian national school was Hermann Laroche (1845–1904), a Russian of German extraction, who became Tchaikovsky's intimate and lifelong friend. Rimsky-Korsakov called him "a Russian copy of Eduard Hanslick"; and it is true that it was he who made the Russian translation of Hanslick's book, *On the Beautiful in Music*, and wrote a preface for it. Laroche functioned as a critic in St. Petersburg and in Moscow, since he lived in both cities in turn, lecturing at the two conservatories on the history of music. His critical articles were collected and published in one volume in 1894.

Among the ranks of the composer-critics, we find, from 1871 to 1876, no less a figure than Tchaikovsky (1840–93). In 1871, when Laroche left Moscow for St. Petersburg, his friend Tchaikovsky began to write more or less regularly for the Moscow *Gazette*. He wrote for other publications too, notably on the occasion of his journey in company with Laroche, Nicholas Rubinstein, and Cui, to attend the first performances of Wagner's *Ring of the Nibelungs*. Tchaikovsky's reviews of that great event appeared in the *Russian Gazette* and will not increase his fame. His comments were harsh and narrow-minded, without any of that nobility which is an honor to critics and artists alike. Tchaikovsky was himself extremely sensitive about bad criticisms on his own compositions: he never forgot Hanslick's devastating opinion of his violin concerto and used to quote it in conversation to the day of his death. His criticisms on the *Ring* are, however, far ruder and more violent than anything Hanslick ever wrote. The music of the *Rheingold* is "incredible nonsense." In the *Ring* there are "beautiful passages, but as a whole it is a deadly bore. The ballet *Sylvia* [1] is a thousand times finer." After the last chord of *The Twilight of the Gods*, "I felt," writes Tchaikovsky, "as if I had been let out of prison. . . . Bayreuth left me with a disagreeable memory." The melancholy passion of Tchaikovsky's symphonies will endure. His musical criticism will be forgotten, like other impudent criticisms by lesser men.

The Russian musical critics of the order of Stassov, Serov, and Cui have a special quality. They remind one of characters in a Russian novel. They brood heavily over the problems of music, and are capable of fanatical enthusiams and of no less fanatical hatreds. The music critics of no other country took their task so earnestly. The future of Russian music seemed to weigh on their minds like a heavy burden. They knew no more serious questions than the questions a new symphony or a new concerto placed before them. Their controversies, their passion, their battles over music remind one of the fanaticism with which re-

[1] By Delibes.

ligious men argue over dogmas. For such critics music was
1 either a handicraft nor art for art's sake. It was a part of the
spiritual life of Russia. Music critics and composers worked for
the same goal with the same zeal — a brotherhood of Russian
men of soul.

It would seem that the tendency to heated controversy has
been preserved among the music critics of Soviet Russia. The
critical outcry over Shostakovitch's opera *Lady Macbeth of
Mzensk* in that country is sufficient evidence of the fact. When
the conditions of criticism in Soviet Russia become better known
it will be possible to discuss these questions with more data and
more objectivity. The high wall that has surrounded Russia for
the last thirty years, concealing its musical life, is still an ob-
stacle to accurate knowledge. We do know that in Soviet Russia
music has been largely and systematically fostered by the state.
There have been important composers in Soviet Russia, great
opera houses, concerts of all kinds, a careful musical education.
The social position of composers, singers, virtuosos, and actors
has been high. Such progress is unthinkable without active
musical criticism. But we must wait until we are able to learn
in what manner the Soviet Russian music critic has performed
his task of spreading musical culture and advancing musical
progress, and what degree of spiritual freedom has been permitted to the leaders of artistic taste.

VI. THE UNITED STATES

Music, which for a time was mere entertainment, part of the
show business, or at best a bit of colorful decoration on the
fringes of American life, has become an integral part of the spiritual forces of the country. The intense musical life of the
United States now surpasses all European countries in the
wealth of means at its disposal, in the extent of its territory, and
in the number of its musicians. Musical education in colleges
and universities, in public libraries and forums, in music-school
settlements, museums, and public parks, and through the player-
piano, the phonograph, and finally the radio, has formed a new

generation of music lovers and laid a broad foundation on which American musical life may develop to still greater heights of understanding and love. The direction of this development is already gratifyingly apparent: it is away from a commercialized musical life and toward musical activity by the public itself.

The American music critics have accompanied this development as chroniclers of the events of the day, as interpreters of the public taste, and as bringers of musical enlightenment. The great music critics of Boston and New York rank (as our survey will show) among the finest writers in the world. This fact is the more noteworthy, since American newspapers generally regard music critics not as literary personalities but as specialized reporters. The practice of hastily writing criticisms immediately after the performance in order that they may appear in the following morning's paper is generally rejected abroad because it is conducive neither to thorough consideration nor to the graces of style.[1] With the American dailies it is customary. The music critic is often a kind of Lone Ranger, who gallops into the concert hall, strikes down the criminal — composer or virtuoso — and disappears like lightning. And a judicious observer of American musical life, Eric Clarke, writes in his *Music in Everyday Life*, that, in some instances, "newspapers may be pardoned for thinking that musical events might be covered by the baseball reporter . . . or by the society editor with insipid sentiment and unabashed adjectives." In spite, however, of such handicaps, men like Henderson or Huneker or Gilman or Philip Hale managed to meet the most exacting standards of literary art. More important still — in spite of all the bellowing of publicity, of all the evil influences of trade, big money and the other lubricants of the machinery of newspapers and the musical market, they succeeded in maintaining an idealistic conception of art and utter personal integrity. Their high standards were not equaled everywhere and by every member of their profession. Here, as

---

[1] Sir Charles Villiers Stanford, in an article on "Some Aspects of Musical Criticism in England," calls this hasty, night-written musical criticism "a hardship to the writer, an injury to the producer, and a mischief to the public."

in other countries, there may be swamps beside mountains. But the mountains are high, and they are landmarks that indicate the road.

Musical criticism worthy of the name began in the United States in Boston.

Old musical and artistic traditions were strongly rooted in Boston, which amidst the thunder of American life preserved the quiet dignity of a town of patricians. Poets, philosophers, and artists lived there, and the proximity of an old and famous university produced an intellectual atmosphere that hovered over the activities of businessmen, merchants, and shipowners. Puritanism kept a sense of ethical values alive. There was an old tradition of musical activity in Boston, which can be traced at least as far back as to the end of the eighteenth century. In 1808 the Pierian Sodality was founded and began to scatter the seeds of musical enlightenment. In 1815 the Handel and Haydn Society took its place in Boston's musical life; in 1818 it was able to give a complete performance of the *Messiah*. 1837 saw the beginning of choral singing in the city's public schools. In 1862 Harvard's Department of Music was inaugurated, and John Knowles Paine began to lecture there on the history and theory of music. Boston's musical evolution culminated in 1880 with the formation of the Boston Symphony Orchestra, which from Henschel to Koussevitzky has maintained its position as one of the world's greatest orchestras.

No man did more for Boston's musical progress than John Sullivan Dwight (1813–93), who may be called the father of serious musical criticism in the United States. He was the leading spirit of the Harvard Musical Association, which from its foundation in 1837 helped the cause of music, especially at Harvard, and which in 1851 built the Boston Music Hall. He was Major H. L. Higginson's constant adviser in the work of founding the Boston Symphony Orchestra. During the last summer of his life he was busy with the plans for Symphony Hall, which was to be the home of serious music in Boston.

In 1851 Dwight conceived the idea of publishing a journal

which should be "the organ of the musical movement in our country." "It needs a faithful, severe, friendly voice," he wrote in the first issue of *Dwight's Journal of Music*, which appeared the following year, "to point out steadfastly the models of the True, the ever Beautiful, the Divine." This ethical approach to musical criticism was the legacy he left to the Boston music critics who succeeded him. For more than thirty years he fought for what he conceived to be the beautiful in music. He was the first music critic in this country who succeeded in interesting musically untrained and even indifferent readers. A conservative, equally opposed to Wagner and Brahms, he displayed the courageous idealism of a man imbued with the spirit of the Brook Farm colony and Emerson's ethical conception of art.

As in most cities with old traditions, artistic taste in Boston was conservative. Writing on Brahms's First Symphony long after his first hearing of it, William Apthorp confessed that nothing in music "sounded more positively terrific than the slow introduction to the first movement did to us then," and that "some twenty or thirty years before, Schumann's B-flat major variations had seemed about the *ne plus ultra* of 'cat's music.'" Dwight showed himself a true Bostonian when he found Brahms's First Symphony "depressing and unedifying" and "a work coldly elaborated, artificial; earnest, to be sure, in some sense great." Wagner represented to him "the denial of music." Elsewhere he writes, "Wagner, while in our view wrong in his musical theory and right in many of his special criticisms on existing operas, must yet be a man of extraordinary talent, nay creative talent, perhaps a genius." Dwight was at his best when he was analyzing Beethoven or Mozart's *Don Giovanni*. He was a man of limited views, but serious and honest, and the first American music critic to have a high ethical standard. He wrote, "Music must have some most intimate connection with the social destiny of Man; . . . if we but knew it, it concerns us all."

When Dwight died in 1893, Apthorp wrote an account of his

character and virtues for the Boston *Evening Transcript*. He calls *Dwight's Journal of Music* "certainly the highest-toned musical periodical of its day, all the world over." He continues: "[Dwight] was a born critic in the highest sense . . . a man of the keenest perception of beauty and grandeur, who could make you see the beauty he saw and make you feel with him the grandeur he felt." His style was "brilliant, solid, impeccable. Better prose than his was hard to find anywhere; for facility and neatness, for elegance and unforced grace, it approached that of the best French masters." Apthorp gives an attractive picture of Dwight's "dreamy, sybaritic, intellectually luxurious nature. . . . Whether it was a fine day, a fair landscape, a poem, a Beethoven symphony, or a lobster salad with champagne, his enjoyment of it was something wonderful to contemplate."

The torch that fell from Dwight's hand was taken up by William Foster Apthorp and Philip Hale.

Apthorp (1848–1913) wrote for the *Evening Transcript*. If Matthew Arnold's dictum, that the necessary qualities of good prose are "regularity, uniformity, precision, balance," is correct, Apthorp was certainly one of the best of American musical writers. His sentences flow quietly, like a broad stream. The ideas are conveyed without effort, the clauses are nicely balanced in the manner of the classical English essayists. In spite of his seriousness Apthorp is always alive, he makes his point, he is even witty. Nothing could be better as characterization than his sentences on the coronation scene in Meyerbeer's *Prophet*: "The ceremonial music in this scene is certainly as gorgeous as could be wished; it is a fitting musical expression of the glittering pomp of a gala church ceremony. One is tempted to call it the most splendid ceremonial music money can buy."

Apthorp did not believe in the type of dogmatic musical criticism that Dwight had practiced. He wrote:

The critic's true position is that of an interpreter between the composer, or performer, and the public, and to a certain extent also the guardian of popular taste, but it is not for him to try to play schoolmaster to the artists. . . . Sitting in judgment on music like an aesthetic

Rhadamanthus and deciding ex cathedra that this is good and that is bad — this seems to me about as preposterous a position as a fallible mortal can well assume; and in this, as in most serious matters, it is hard to be preposterous without doing more harm than good. . . . Authority perhaps! but it is the question in my mind, whether a critic should properly have any authority at all. Dogmatic and authoritative criticism would be all very well if the critic were possessed of one thing — omniscience! . . . To my mind, criticism should be nothing but an expression of enlightened opinion, — as enlightened as possible but never dogmatic.

Apthorp therefore likes

the French style of so-called personal criticism; where the critic writes over his own signature, gives his own opinions for what they are worth and fights for his own ideas. He stands admittedly as a representative of nothing but his own ideas; and he is enabled to place these in the strongest light. What he writes will be truly alive and suggestive; it will set people thinking; and this is perhaps the very best thing that any criticism can do.

Apthorp helped to form the public taste not only by his critical articles but, from 1892 to 1901, through his program notes for the Boston Symphony concerts. Good as Apthorp's notes were, they were surpassed by those of Philip Hale (1854–1934), who wrote the program notes for the Boston Symphony for thirty-two years (1901–33). To read Hale's program notes is to read the best book on music old and new, written by a man of the highest culture, of extensive learning, and one gifted with a fascinating literary style. He quotes Juvenal, Samuel Johnson, and Sir Charles Napier to illustrate Saint-Saëns, William Blake and Walt Whitman to illustrate Schubert, and Richardson to illustrate Richard Strauss, with perfect ease. He handles facts as a good golfer handles his club. If experience, wisdom, loftiness, nobility, and literary virtuosity make a master, the extraordinary man who looked down upon the landscape of music from the balcony of Boston's Symphony Hall as from a high mountain must be called one of the greatest masters of musical criticism.

Philip Hale studied in Berlin, in Munich, and in Paris. He loved France and kept his admiration for French intelligence and grace all his life. It was he who brought Vincent d'Indy to this country and suggested that the house of Schirmer publish Debussy's *Pelléas and Mélisande*. The influence of French models on his style was apparent from the beginning of his career as a music critic. At first he wrote for the Boston *Home Journal* (1889–91), then for the Boston *Journal* (1891–1903), and finally for the Boston *Herald* (1903–33).

Lawrence Gilman characterized Hale's manner as follows: "The writer never spoke as a major prophet, but as one who might be discussing a favorite subject over a demitasse. Anyone is privileged to disagree and those insisting upon their eternal verities are referred to any one of the hundred books where the musical monuments are enshrined in ringing platitudes of praise." That is the French manner in criticism — strolling on the boulevards and conversing as a man of intelligence with men who appreciate intelligence. "He did not scruple to amuse," I quote Gilman again. "He was almost indecently readable. He never hesitated to lighten musical instruction with diversion and with wit."

Hale wrote about new and old music with equal impartiality. He did not use the classical masters to beat down living composers who were the masters of his time. There is profound insight in his characterization of Handel: "This giant of a man could express his tenderness known only to him and Mozart; for Schubert with all his melodic wealth and sensitiveness, could fall at times into sentimentalism and Schumann's intimate confessions were sometimes whispered. Handel in his tenderness was always manly." Of Haydn he says, with equal wisdom: "Haydn's music is not all beer, skittles and dancing. There are even gloomy pages in some of his quartets; tragic pages in his *Seven Last Words*; and the prelude to the *Creation*, depicting chaos, is singularly contemporaneous." Of Mozart he writes: "His music, whether it vitalizes stage characters or is absolute, as in the three famous symphonies and in the chamber works, is as the music on Prospero's isle: 'Sounds and sweet airs that give delight and hurt not.'" No one has written more judiciously than Hale on the subject of Schumann's oft-reviled orchestration: "It has been urged against Schumann that his symphonies were thought for the pianoforte and then orchestrated crudely, as by an amateur. This, however, is not a fatal objection. He has his own orchestral speech. Good, bad, or indifferent, it was his own. He could not have otherwise expressed himself through the orchestral instruments."

With fine sensitivity, Hale wrote about Brahms and (a rare exception anywhere outside of Germany and Austria) about Bruckner. Brahms's Fourth Symphony he calls "a structure in granite." Although he refers to Bruckner's "irregular, uncontrolled genius," he speaks of him as one who "had apocalyptic visions and spoke musically with the tongues of angels," and praises his Seventh Symphony, saying, "There are pages that come closer to Beethoven at his greatest than we find in the symphonies of other composers." And again: "There are grand thoughts expressed in a masterly manner in Franck's Symphony and in the Symphony in B flat by Vincent d'Indy; the introduction to the finale of Brahms' First Symphony has elemental grandeur and spiritual intensity; but Bruckner's spirit in the Adagio and in the main body of the Scherzo of the Seventh Symphony is nearer akin to that of Beethoven." His comment on Bruckner's Eighth Symphony is beautifully expressed: "There are pages that remind one of the visions seen by John on the isle of Patmos. . . . It is a stately temple in which mortals forget the paltry cares and tribulations of earth and gods appear calm and benignant."

Hale's appreciations of Richard Strauss show complete understanding: *Don Juan* is "a daring brilliant composition; one that paints the hero as might a master's brush on canvas." *Till Eulenspiegel*: "The story is medieval and Rabelaisian, and the music is quite as broad as the tale." *Don Quixote* is "incomparably beautiful"; and "the opening of *Thus Spake Zarathustra* is colossal in its elemental grandeur."

But Hale's great love is Debussy. I quote from his poetical criticism of the *Afternoon of a Faun*: "A masterpiece of imaginative poetry in tones; it is a thing of flawless beauty. . . . There is the suggestion of sunlight and warmth, forest and meadow dear to fauns and nymphs. There is the gentle melancholy that is associated with a perfect afternoon. There is the exquisite melodic line, and there is harmonic suggestion with inimitable coloring, that is still more exquisite." Equally sensitive is his response to *Ibéria*: "There is the suggestion of street life and wild strains, heard on bleak plains or savage mountains; of the music of the people; of summer nights, warm and odorous; of the awakening of life with the break of day; of endless jotas, tangos, seguidillas, fandangos, of gypsies with their spells brought from the East; of women with Moorish blood."

The influence of Bostonian musical criticism extended to New York and became one of the most important of the spiritual forces that shaped musical criticism in the latter city. Two of the great New York music critics, Finck and Aldrich, had been pupils at Harvard of John Knowles Paine, the first professor of music appointed by an American university, who had made Harvard the leading school of American composers. Thus in their formative years Finck and Aldrich were influenced by the idealism of Boston's musical leaders. It was from Philip Hale that Gilman later learned the art of writing program notes.

The classical age of New York musical criticism began about 1880, when the "Great Five," Finck, Krehbiel, Henderson, Huneker, and Aldrich, called up the rain, the sun, and the clouds over the fields of music. The age of industrial expansion had transformed New York from the "provincial town of two-story houses, where pigs ran through Broadway and ate the refuse," described by Theodore Thomas in his autobiography, into the capital of a new empire of bankers, merchants, shipowners, speculators, and industrial magnates. The new society of the wealthy installed itself in the Metropolitan Opera House, which opened its gilded splendors, to the melodies of *Faust*, in 1883. The activities of such men as Leopold Damrosch, Franz Kneisel,

Theodore Thomas, and Anton Seidl began to educate the public toward an appreciation of serious music, and started New York on its way to becoming one of the world's great musical centers and its greatest musical market.

Musical life in New York — as everywhere else — was stirred to its depths by the work of Richard Wagner. His merits were argued in every household. Music and musical esthetics had ceased to be things that mattered only to experts, and even the hardest and most uncultivated money-getter would take sides on the Wagner question over his brandy and cigar. The newspapers gave more space to music; and the music critics, although they were poorly paid and regarded as loafers compared with the busy reporters who ran through the city sniffing out news, assumed a position as leaders of public taste. The "Great Five" were imposing figures; their voices sounded above the tumult of the city, speaking words of learning, experience, and intellectual energy.

Henry Theophilus Finck (1854–1926), who from 1881 on wrote for the New York *Evening Post*, was a kindly writer, who discussed music vividly and enthusiastically. Here is a short self-portrait:

> When I became a music critic in 1881 at the green age of twenty years, I undertook as most young critics do, to lay down the law for artists who knew a hundred times as much as I did. I soon got over that silly attitude, having become convinced that the only important function of criticism is to discover and boom genius or superior merit. . . . The "noble art of praising" is the chief delight of my life.

These are noble words, which do honor to the man who wrote them. Finck was firmly opposed to the kind of rudeness that transforms that fine instrument the pen into a bludgeon: Rude attacks are

> no more excusable in a civilized community than it would have been for the reviewer, on meeting the author on the sidewalk, to slap his face or kick him into the gutter. . . . The musical critics of leading newspapers are still allowed to act like wolves, hyenas, and harpies,

sparing neither the dead nor the living. It is a curious phenomenon, which makes one doubt whether music really has charms to soothe the savage breast.

Most of his enthusiasm, Finck reserved for Wagner, Grieg, and Massenet. In many cases his exaggerated praise does more honor to his amiability than to his critical acumen. That "Massenet's creations will outlive by decades the majority of Brahms'" or that the operas of Richard Strauss "are already moribund, whereas Massenet's are more popular than ever" is certainly naïve exaggeration rather than critical insight. But one enjoys meeting such a kindly soul, who believes that critical blame is "a mental disease, a species of phylloxera threatening the best works of genius."

Finck called the New York critics "the most unmerciful in the world." This reproach does not apply to William James Henderson (1855–1937), the cultivated, fine, warm, considerate critic of the *Times* from 1887 to 1902 and of the *Sun* from 1902 to 1937. Few critics took up the cause of Wagner with more understanding than Henderson. His book on Wagner still interests by its ideas and its style. One of his gifts was a peculiar aptitude for characterizing pianists: Moriz Rosenthal is "the pianistic whirlwind." Bülow is "the highest living embodiment of musical intelligence. . . . We may be astonished," Henderson continues, "electrified, paralyzed by the others; we are convinced by the doctor. The others compel us to acknowledge their own greatness; the doctor forces us to bow before the greatness of music." Franz Rummel is "in the language of athletes, the best allround pianist before the public." Joseffy is "deficient in elevation of sentiment" but great "by crystalline purity and clearness, coupled with a delicacy and neatness which transformed everything he touched into a sort of Queen Mab scherzo."

In an article written for the *Musical Quarterly*, Henderson set forth his idea of musical criticism: For him musical criticism is the foremost agent in bringing to the public a perception of the nature of musical art and the ends sought by composers. . . . The true desideratum, after all, is not the infallibility of criticism, the acquisition of a ready made opinion is sought only by the intellectually incapable or indolent. A real man prefers to think for himself; and the best criticism is that which compels him to do so. Therefore what we should value most in critical commentary is its point of view, its endeavor to attain an altitude, from which the whole breadth of the subject may be surveyed.

Henderson was a born journalist. He reported yacht races just as expertly as he wrote on music. In addition to his books on musical subjects, he wrote a textbook of navigation which was used by the American Navy.

Henry Edward Krehbiel (1854-1923), too, was a scholar as well as a journalist, and equally great in both professions. His books on musical subjects fill several shelves. Among them are the English version, completed by Krehbiel, of Thayer's biography of Beethoven; a book on Negro music, which he championed as material for serious works by American composers; and books on the Metropolitan Opera, the New York Philharmonic Society, the Oratorio Society of New York, on piano music, and on Wagner, whom he admired. But he was first and foremost a newspaperman, who had reported baseball games and murder cases for the Cincinnati *Gazette*, and who, when he came to New York and joined the *Tribune* [1] in 1880 as music critic wrote also on yacht races and shipwrecks. At night he sat at the night city editor's desk, or interviewed politicians, or wrote editorials. Where he found time to acquire his vast erudition was his secret.

Krehbiel had [so writes Richard Aldrich] a place in America that corresponded to that of the great critics of the nineteenth century in

---

[1] Krehbiel came to the *Tribune* as successor to R. G. Hassard, who had become music critic of that paper in 1866. Hassard too wrote articles and editorials in addition to his criticisms. Gilman praises him as "a man of exceptionally rich and liberal culture" and says that the articles he wrote on the *première* of Wagner's *Ring of the Nibelungs* in Bayreuth in 1876 were "the most enlightened and far and away the ablest, that were sent to any American newspaper."

Europe; a place of commanding influence and authority. He had put the profession of musical criticism upon a higher plane of knowledge and competence in all that makes for a true basis of judgment, than it had ever occupied in America before his day.

Krehbiel was a conservative critic, one of those pontiffs who conceive that they know the eternal laws of musical beauty. Nevertheless, he had deep insight into much new music (Brahms, Tchaikovsky, and other Russian composers), feeling its appeal because it did not move beyond his fixed boundaries. For half a century Krehbiel sat on his throne with dignity, blessing right-thinking composers and banishing the sinners against what he believed to be the unchangeable laws of music. Like all stern and dogmatic critics, he made a great impression on his readers, whom he wished to lead into the paths of musical righteousness and whom he educated through his books, his daily criticisms, and his program notes for the New York Philharmonic Society's concerts.

Compared with the severe Krehbiel, Richard Aldrich (1863–1937), who had been Krehbiel's assistant on the *Tribune* from 1891 to 1901 and was musical editor of the *Times* from 1902 to 1924, appears worldly. He enjoyed his prestige as a born member of the rich society of New York. His clear, fluent treatment of musical subjects charmed his readers. His effort to be impartial won him friends, and his learning, expressed in an attractive style, contributed to the general development of taste and knowledge. Aldrich hated "pontification" He was always a member of high society, talking easily and gracefully about serious music.

The most fascinating personality among New York's "great Five," a colorful writer, and a virtuoso of style, a man who has already become a legend, was James Gibbons Huneker (1860–1921). He wrote first for the New York *Recorder* and *Morning Advertiser*, from 1900 to 1912 for the *Sun*, from 1912 to 1919 for the *Times*, and from 1919 until the time of his death for the *Sun* again. A novelist, a critic of painting, and a musician, he was at home in all the arts. He is a man of glittering adjectives and decorative similes. The fumes that rose from a glass of beer shaped themselves in his thought into figures and ideas. His curious mind was eagerly interested in all the currents of European artistic life. In a single essay he quotes from or mentions Rémy de Gourmont, Walter Pater, Jean Marnold, Flaubert, Gerhart Hauptmann, Saint-Saëns, Browning, Walt Whitman, Claude Monet, Ibsen, Tolstoi, Dostoevsky, Nietzsche, D'Annunzio, Rodin, Böcklin, Stuck, Hugo, Tintoretto, Yeats, and Goethe. Perhaps only Georg Brandes could equal him in his feeling for the tidal waves of modern European art.

Huneker's sketches of musicians are always dazzling; they shine like an impressionistic painting, startling with their motley colors. At a time when Richard Strauss's value was still being questioned, Huneker wrote with absolute certainty:

He is the only living issue in music today; no other master has his stride, his stature. . . . As the great narrator in modern prose is Gustave Flaubert, so Richard Strauss is the greatest musical narrator. . . . In his gallery of psychological portraiture Strauss becomes a sort of musical Dostoevsky. He divines Maeterlinck-like the secret tragedy of existence and paints with delicacy, with great barbaric masses, in colors that glow, poetic and legendary figures.

Here is Huneker's description of *Zarathustra*:

This is the vastest and most difficult score he ever penned. It is a cathedral in tone, sublime and fantastic, with its grotesque gargoyles, hideous flying abutments, exquisite traceries, prodigious arches, half Gothic, half infernal, huge and resounding spaces, gorgeous façades and heaven-splitting spires — a mighty musical structure.

No other music critic in New York had anything like Huneker's gift for brief, striking, and often surprising characterization. I quote at random:

Handel's music is like a blow from a muscular fist. . . . Mozart, the sweetly lyric, the mellifluous and ever gay Mozart, made sonatas as God carves the cosmos. . . . Mendelssohn's music was Bach's watered for general consumption. . . . Wagner, a brilliant, disputatious, magnetic man, waged a personal propaganda; Brahms . . . lived quietly and thought highly. . . . Grieg built his nest overlooking Norwegian fjords and built it of bright colored bits of Schumann and Chopin. He is the bird with the one sweet, albeit monotonous note. . . . To play Chopin, one must have acute sensibility, a versatility of mood, a perfect mechanism, the heart of a woman and the brain of a man. . . . What a master miniaturist is Brahms in his little piano pieces! There he catches the tender sigh of childhood or the faint intimate flutterings of hearts stirred by desire. Feminine he is as is no woman; virile, as few men.

Every sentence is personal, hitting the mark — a capricious "brain wave," yet a profound judgment.

In a few sentences, Huneker contributed more to the modern conception of Wagner than others have done in big books. He describes "Richard of the footlights" rightly as "the last of the great romantics; he closed a period, did not begin one." He is

revolutionist, genius by the grace of God, and a marvelous moulder of other men's ideas. . . . He had genius and his music is genuine, but it is music for the theatre, for the glow of the footlights; rhetorical music it is and it ever strives for effect. There can not be music to touch the tall stars of Bach and Beethoven, we know; yet why compare the two methods when they strive for such other and various things? Wagner arrogated everything for his music drama.

Huneker was conscious of the spiritual bond between Wagner and the French Romantics:

Wagner was the Celt, with a dash of the Orient in his blood, and he bubbled and foamed over with primal power, but it was not the reticent, grave power of the Teuton. . . . Whether it was Wagner's early residence in Paris, or perhaps some determining pre-natal influence, he surely had a vivacity, an esprit, imagination, and a grace denied to most of his countrymen, Heine excepted.

This is all original, masterfully expressed, personal, and interesting.

In one essay Huneker sketched the whole history of the modernist movement of the nineteenth century in a single short paragraph, the equal of which for clarity and concentration it would be hard to find anywhere. He pictures the Romantic movement:

> Victor Hugo flamed across the historical canvas like a painted scarlet meteor; Berlioz's mad talent, expressed by the symbolical coloring of his orchestration — color carried to insanity pitch — was a lesser musical Hugo. Delacroix, with his brush dipped in the burning sun, painted vertigoes of color and audacity of conception. All was turbulent exaggeration, all was keyed above the normal pitch of life, and in the midst the still small voice of Chopin could be heard. [Followed the epoch of Naturalism, in which] the Cerberus of realism barked its first hoarse bark. [Then came the period of Puvis de Chavannes, Monet, Rodin, Verlaine, Anatole France. The poets became] musicians in words. They followed Wagner; all are the descendants of Edgar Allan Poe. . . . Symbolism, a soft green star, is but a pin-prick in the inverted bowl of the night, but it sings like a flame in thin glass. Its song was beautiful, as the twilights of Chopin's garden or as the waving of the trees in Wagner's luminous forest.

I wonder whether in all the books on the art of the nineteenth century that have been published in America since Huneker's day, there are passages as well expressed?

In the chorus of the younger New York critics who formed themselves by the great old generation the lyrical voice of Lawrence Gilman (1878–1939) reminds one of the deeper tones of Huneker. Like Huneker, and like all the young writers who admired the flamboyant language of Flaubert and Wilde, and the poetry of Yeats, Baudelaire, and Verlaine, he loves precious adjectives. He had wanted to be a painter before he began his career as a music critic on *Harper's Weekly* in 1901. Perhaps this explains why — like Huneker, the art critic — he had such a colorful imagination, dipping his pen as it were into a painter's palette. He too was fond of citing modern poets and painters. In the fifteen hundred words of his essay on "The Music of To-morrow," he quotes or refers to: Maeterlinck (twice), Vernon Blackburn, George Russell, Keats, Shelley, Rossetti, Monet, and Yeats. He was sensitive to modern music, especially when it played on the nerves. His analysis of Debussy is subtle and penetrating:

There is marvellous music in his *Pelléas and Mélisande* — undoubtedly, thus far his masterpiece — music of twilight beauty and glamour, music that persuades and insinuates, that persistently enslaves the mind. [The *Nocturnes* are] conceived half in the spirit of landscape, half in the mood of reverie. [The *Afternoon of a Faun* is] music of the most inveterate subtlety, of the most aerial refinement; yet it grips and abides. . . . His music is colored, not with the hue and quality of moods, which are the result of vague or specific emotional stimulus, but as it were their astral images. . . . There is passion in his music, but it is the passion of the desire, less of life than of the shadow of life.

No less penetrating is Gilman's appreciation of Richard Strauss — "a typical example of the art in its most characteristic present phase." His *Don Quixote* is

indisputably one of the great things of music — a work charged to the brim with humanity, with eloquence, with commanding beauty; there is nothing quite like it in the entire literature of the art. It marked the summit of Strauss' achievements.

But Gilman, even in his admiration for Strauss, is always the critic, and he hit the mark when he wrote:

Strauss never touched, has never attempted to touch that region of experience which lies over the borderland of pure spiritual consciousness; and it is toward that region that all the . . . finer elements in our modern art and thought are surely swerving. . . . Strauss represents a declining impulse toward the incessant exploitation of the dynamic element in life. There is another and more enduring impulse . . . that for the vibration of the spirit beneath.

Gilman was the author of the New York Philharmonic Society's program notes from 1921, and music critic of the *Herald-Tribune* from 1923, until the time of his death in 1939, his rich and sensitive personality contributing importantly to the musical development of New York.

Philip Hale, Huneker, and Gilman represent the highest standard of musical criticism, and furnish a model for the further development of the profession in the United States. The more musical activities in this country increase, the more important the contribution of critics such as these will be seen to have been. Part of the business of criticism — the education of music lovers, the diffusion of a knowledge of music — will be taken over by radio commentators, who constitute the popular annex to musical criticism, a sort of musical university for the common man. But there is no more effective tool with which to build a new musical world than the written words of the masters of musical criticism.

EPILOGUE: THE FUTURE OF
MUSICAL CRITICISM

WE HAVE reached our goal, perhaps embarrassed by the abundance of material and somewhat exhausted, but richer by the experience of two hundred years of musical criticism. We have seen great men and little men, writers with splendid minds, authors of the first rank, virtuosos and simple artisans, men with ideas and men with prejudices, noble figures and mean ones. Now the time has come to draw our conclusions and to see if we can throw a light into the future.

The best thing that the history we have reviewed can teach us is an awareness of the close connection between the development of musical criticism and the general development of ideas. The individual man today who believes that he is influencing the course of musical development with his criticisms is not so free as he thinks himself. He is shaped by the spiritual trends of his times. He shares their greatness and their littleness, their values and their faults. He is dependent upon the contemporary social structure, upon its development as well as upon its guiding ideas. Doing his work in the period between the death of an old culture and the birth of a new one, he is at the mercy of all the troubles of the time in which he lives and writes. These are reasons enough for a critic to be modest, unassuming, free from pride and vanity.

The history of musical criticism demonstrates that every great epoch produces its own type of music critic. The critic of the Age of Reason differed from the Romantic critic, and the Romantic critic differed from the critic of the modern technical and industrial age. There can be no doubt that the coming epoch will shape its own type of critic, who will, of necessity, be different from the contemporary variety. The modern critic is subjective; he writes down his impressions; like a fascinating virtu-oso, he permits his intelligence to shine for a moment on the subject of a musical performance; he is the hasty, brilliant critic of the daily papers, who gives a performance like an actor on the stage.

Critical types, to be sure, do not entirely disappear. The dog-matic critic created by the seventeenth century has survived as a fossil in many places. The romantic critic, feeding on his own raptures and enthusiastic outbursts, is not yet completely ex-tinct. But the latest phase of the European critical spirit has been subjective, and it has been — in its best representatives — a fascinating and brilliant phenomenon. Such a critic is perhaps comparable to the virtuoso of the modern piano or violin, or to that prima donna of the modern concert stage, the star conduc-tor. The critical subjectivism of Europe grew out of the shat-tered soil of modern society; it appeared when the unity of musical society was destroyed and its parts fell asunder. It is the dazzling product of a decaying society in which the individ-ual mind has broken loose from the general social mind.

Conditions in America have been somewhat different from conditions in Europe. The democratic form of life has made the critic the leader of a public discussion. Thus the opinions of the professional critic are kept in check by public criticism, and the errors and exaggerations characteristic of a free-for-all discussion are counterbalanced by the possibility that a rude block may be hit with a wedge of the same kind. When Bernard Shaw, with his usual frankness, says, "Musical criticisms, like sermons, are of low average quality simply because they are never discussed or contradicted," his statement does not entirely correspond with the facts of American life. Another condition, in addition to the spirit of democracy, has prevented the outgrowth of hy-pertrophic subjective criticism in America, and that is the feeling of the great critics that they are responsible for the de-velopment of musical culture and public taste in a country that is making its first strides towards leadership in music.

Things were different in Europe. Germany, the leading

European musical country, had kept her feudal structure under superficially modern forms. Critics, consequently, were not leaders of free, public discussions, but magistrates, authorities, superiors. They had their fixed place on the social ladder. In musical life there was no higher authority than theirs. Readers, both lay and professional, accepted their verdicts with the usual obedience of Germans. At the utmost they shook their clenched fists behind the critic's back, or made sarcastic remarks at parties. The critical faculties of society at large, however, were not sufficiently well developed to function vigorously. The democratic spirit was still weak; it had no firm roots. Thus it could come about that when the great crisis developed at the beginning of the twentieth century and the political, social and economic struggle became ever more violent, the life of the spirit lost its foundation and was divorced from the struggle going on about it.

At the same time, France, the glorious motherland of modern criticism, had become over-refined, tired, exhausted, Bergson's philosophy plumbed the darkest depths of mysticism. Painting shook off the bonds of reality. Music became dreamlike and its contours dissolved. Musical criticism grew tired, too. It lost its connection with the spirit of society, and fled to the lonely island of personal feelings and isolated impressions.

The European spirit had lost its stability, its power to base itself on the ideas of society. Nietzsche's philosophy had already denied all standards of morality and had abused democracy, employing the intoxicating power of words to destroy the strongest pillars of European society. This dazzling philosophy became the first great artistic expression of the crisis which was to shake European spirituality to its roots. Criticism was drawn into the struggle, displaying its most brilliant colors and gleaming like rotting wood. The first World War revealed the European social, moral, and political crisis and set the world on fire. Fascism and Hitlerism followed, and the world was drenched in blood.

An old chapter of European history is ending in crime, bloodshed, and annihilation; a new chapter is beginning in terrible labor pains. Perhaps after the spirit of peace succeeds the agony of war, there will be a new epoch, and a new social structure with a new art and a new relationship between art and society. Yet no living man can foretell the future.

But everyone is permitted to dream and to hope, and we hope for the formation of a more homogeneous, a juster, and more peaceful society in devastated Europe — a society which will secure a broader basis for the life of the spirit. If such dreams come true, music may become an integral part of the life of the masses, and the task of the critics as leaders of public taste and promoters of musical culture may become more and more important. Musical criticism may lose some of the glamour and virtuosity that are inherent in subjective criticism, and the subjective critic may perhaps become as out-of-date as the dogmatic critic was in the nineteenth century. But the loss will be more than balanced by the growth of a feeling of responsibility for general culture. There will be, perhaps, more simplicity, and more unadorned objectivity in criticism, and the critics may well assume the attitude of teachers who are responsible for the enlightenment of society. Thus the rift which began to separate artist and public in the nineteenth century may once again disappear, and the critic may take his destined place as the interpreter of musical creation to society. He may once again diffuse knowledge and enlightenment. Society and the artist may once again join forces, united by the great ideas of their time.

It would be childish to believe that the developments we hope for will end all the errors, all the weaknesses that are inherent in criticism produced by human beings. The words of Fontenelle, "Wherever there are human beings, there are follies, and forever the same follies," will be as true in the future as they were in the past. But the morality of criticism will be higher, and the relation among the creative, critical, and receptive parts of musical society will be more just, and in better balance.

In the eighteenth century, when musical criticism set out on its journey, it wished to infuse life, society, and art with more reason, more light, more humanity. Now, when criticism is about to enter a new historical period, its work may be the new and difficult task of helping to make life and art the common property of all. No greater task has ever been entrusted to musical criticism; no nobler work has ever been laid upon noble men.

Index

NORTON PAPERBACKS ON MUSIC

PARRISH, CARL, *editor* A Treasury of Early Music

PINCHERLE, MARC Corelli: His Life, His Work N441

PINCHERLE, MARC Vivaldi N168

SACHS, CURT World History of the Dance N209

SCHOENBERG, ARNOLD Structural Functions of Harmony *Revised* N478

SCHRADE, LEO Monteverdi N490

SCHUMANN, ROBERT On Music and Musicians N482

STEVENS, DENIS Tudor Church Music *Revised* N344

STRAVINSKY, IGOR An Autobiography N161

STRUNK, OLIVER, *editor* Source Readings in Music History: I, Antiquity and the Middle Ages; II, The Renaissance; III, The Baroque Era; IV, The Classic Era; V, The Romantic Era

WALTER, BRUNO Of Music and Music-Making N242

WEISSTEIN, ULRICH, *editor* The Essence of Opera N498

WESTRUP, J. A. *and* F. Ll. HARRISON The New College Encyclopedia of Music N273

WIORA, WALTER The Four Ages of Music N427